Mr. In-Between

What's changed most in your lifetime? The switch from land lines to cell phones? From snail mail to email? How about the transition from Bugs Bunny to Buzz Lightyear? Those Bugs and Daffy cartoons you loved as a kid look nothing like the PIXAR classics *Toy Story* or *The Incredibles*.

Mr. In-Between: My Life in the Middle of the Animation Revolution is the fascinating and hilarious saga of one of animation's computer graphics pioneers, Bill Kroyer, making his way to Hollywood to end up as a key figure in the technical revolution of animation's "Second Golden Age". He provides an artist's explanation of the fundamental principles of animation, from the basic mechanics of motion to the immersive, artful experience of visualizing and realizing the performance of an imaginary character.

Rather than a scholarly listing of films and filmmakers, this book is instead a captivating first-person journey through what may be the most important transition in the history of the arts—the transformation and renaissance of the animated film in the digital age. An important work for scholars, and an eye-opening and page-turning adventure for any film or cartoon fan, *Mr. In-Between* is a book that has the ultimate writing credit.

Bill Kroyer *was there.*

Key Features:

- Explains the step-by-step evolution of the digital tools of computer animation, from the most basic primitive "scripted" motion to the current application of artificial intelligence.
- Describes some of the most remarkable, eccentric, and colorful geniuses who populated the quirky now-vanished subculture of "hand-drawn animation".
- Takes the reader on a worldwide tour of animation studios on four continents, explaining the vast cultural differences, but common artistic devotion, of animators in places as diverse as communist China, Europe, India, and the Philippines.
- Recounts fascinating and surprising interactions with world-famous celebrities who worked with the animation industry, including legendary musicians, Oscar-winning actors, and the King of England.

Mr. In-Between
My Life in the Middle of
the Animation Revolution

Bill Kroyer

CRC Press
Taylor & Francis Group
Boca Raton London New York

CRC Press is an imprint of the
Taylor & Francis Group, an **informa** business

Designed cover image: Bill Kroyer

First edition published 2025
by CRC Press
2385 NW Executive Center Drive, Suite 320, Boca Raton FL 33431

and by CRC Press
4 Park Square, Milton Park, Abingdon, Oxon, OX14 4RN

CRC Press is an imprint of Taylor & Francis Group, LLC

© 2025 Bill Kroyer

ISBN: 9781032904733 (hbk)
ISBN: 9781032904726 (pbk)
ISBN: 9781003558231 (ebk)

DOI: 10.1201/9781003558231

Typeset in Minion
by codeMantra

For Sue,
Because you're still the one
And
Ralph
Ya shoulda been here

Contents

Preface

My good friend Tom Sito, author and animation's Grand Raconteur, liked to quote Winston Churchill: "History will be kind to me, for I intend to write it".

In writing this book, it was not my intention to elevate my place in animation history. One difference I believe between animated films and live action films, or animated characters and live actors, is that it is relatively easy to tell good from bad, competent from downright incompetent. A live actor's performance could be subjectively judged, but if an animated character's arms flew off, or their head bulged as they turned, or their face froze while their jaw flapped up and down with no relation to the words being spoken, even the novice critic could say: "That's bad animation".

It's not humility, but simple objective observation, that makes it apparent that as an animator I was never on the level of the great animators of my generation. Witness the work of Glenn Keane on Ariel or Kathy Zielinski doing Ursula in *The Little Mermaid*; of James Baxter's ballroom scene in *Beauty and the Beast*; of Eric Goldberg's hilarious and brilliant Genie in *Aladdin*.

And it was more circumstance than success that has me often mentioned with my close friends and roommates who became some of animation's greatest directors: Brad Bird (*The Incredibles, Ratatouille*), Join Musker (*The Little Mermaid, Moana*), or Henry Selick (*The Nightmare before Christmas, Coraline*).

It's not like I didn't do anything. I have done quite a bit, and some of it, I'm happy to say, is considered pretty good. But as far as this book is concerned, the major credit that I bring to this story of animation's big transformation, and the people who lived through it, is that *I was there*.

I've had two truly magical moments in my life. The first happened when I was meditating under an oak tree on a backpacking trip when I came to the realization that my life as a single guy was over. I was going to "pop the question" and become the devoted husband of one woman for the rest of my life. I did that, and Sue and I have been together for forty-five happy years.

The second was watching a *Super-8* film of the very first animation I ever did. As I watched the character I had drawn move on the screen, I had the jolting realization that it seemed alive. I had given it life. It was in that crystalized, magical moment that I knew I had found my vocation. I am the most blessed of men. I have never spent one second of my life wondering if I married the right person or chose the right profession.

Perhaps "chose" is the wrong word, because I never considered it a choice to choose animation as my profession. I could not resist. I was totally addicted to the idea of creating life in cartoons. After I saw that first scene, nothing else ever occurred to me. As luck would have it, I was entering the profession at its low point. That resulted in two things. First, I was able to work, and learn, without a lot of competition because the industry was so moribund. Second, I rode the wave of growth and success as the industry grew to heights never imagined.

Unlike live action, the animated film is the only type of film where the imagery is 100% created by artists. There's a saying that "there are no cigarette butts in animation", meaning no one accidentally leaves something around the set that shows up on film. If it's in the frame of an animated film, someone intentionally designed it and put it there. Because the imagery is 100% created, no medium was more impacted by the digital age. Animation, remember, encompasses and utilizes all the great artforms: drawing, painting, sculpture, architecture, acting, dancing, music, photography, and writing, to name a few. To this day, animation leads the way in technical innovations. That transition, from "pencils to pixels", was a Renaissance-level transformation.

My book doesn't pretend to cover the full scope of animation history, but by luck, it was exactly that period of change, the digital age, that I experienced personally. I hope that by reading this book, you'll get a grasp of not just what happened, but how it felt to be there, and why the people who made the movies you love did what they did.

Chuck Jones, the legendary creator of Bugs Bunny, once said: "If you can turn the picture off and understand the story, it's radio. If you can turn the sound off and understand the story, that's animation".

There aren't many pictures here—and no sound (unless you read out loud). But I hope my book helps you understand the story.

- **Bill Kroyer**

Acknowledgments

The person most responsible for me writing this book is, not surprisingly, my wife Sue. In addition to being my loving wife for over four decades, and the not-so-secret weapon of my professional success, she retains that knack of knowing what I should be doing to make myself useful. When we actively retired from the business and moved back to Wisconsin, she knew I needed something constructive to do in those housebound winter months. "Write your memoir", she said, "because as the years go by you might forget things".

As usual, she was correct. After I had written the manuscript, I knew I needed a fresh eye to read it. Fortunately, I had a local friend who was a renowned film historian and author whom I felt would give me an unbiased appraisal. That friend was Patrick McGilligan, and if you look him up, you will see his glorious creative credentials. Patrick took my manuscript and said nothing for weeks, making me a bit worried. But when he did respond, he felt I had written something worthwhile. Following Patrick's suggestions, I did a few more revisions and submitted it to publishers.

I thank Sean Connelly and Danielle Zarfati at Taylor & Francis for being so enthused about the book and shepherding it through the publication process. I thank my good friend, and greatest illustrator I know, Steve Pilcher, for doing the cover illustration, Rich Moore for the character design, and the super-talented Leslie Hinton for doing the layout and design of the book jacket. I thank the world's greatest caricaturist, John Musker, for providing my cartoon image.

The contents of the book, and the pathway of my life, would not have been possible without the many wonderful, talented people I have had the privilege to have known and worked with. Foremost of these are my "fellow Rats", John Musker, Henry Selick, Brad Bird, and Jerry Rees. Those brief years I spent as their roommate at Disney were the most formative of my creative life, and it has been a true blessing to have been able to remain friends as all of their careers soared to heights that we humble interns could not have imagined.

My professional credibility was bolstered by the good luck to have my projects animated by the likes of Kathy Zielinski, Darlie Brewster, Wendy Perdue, Tony Fucile, and Doug Frankel and designed by the peerless Ralph Eggleston, Rich Moore, Mike Giaimo, Vicky Jensen, and Steve Pilcher.

I don't know how I could have made it in animation if not for the miraculous coincidence of being hired for my first job by Frank Terry. I was just one of the hundreds of young animators he so lovingly and brilliantly trained. We all miss him. I owe a lot to John Hughes, Pauline Tso, and Keith Goldfarb, owners of Rhythm & Hues Studios, and my supervisors Lee Berger and Richard Hollander, for not only providing me with the most nurturing work environment in the history of Hollywood but also the chance to be immersed in that pioneering technological creativity. I thank Bob Bassett and Janell Shearer for giving me my academic home at Chapman University and allowing me to try to pass along some of my knowledge and experience to the next generation.

I'm indebted to the friends who shared their stories with me, including Dave Spafford's story of the Pago Pago sign and Mike Gabriel's "Easter Egg" for Roy Disney, stories that were "oral history" for a lot of us animators but I felt should be preserved.

As I reflected on these memories, it occurred to me that nothing in this book would have happened if it hadn't been for that unexpected and undeserved encounter with Chuck Jones in his hotel room in Chicago so many years ago. As one of the greatest legends of animation, Chuck certainly doesn't need a nod from me to enhance his legacy, but I cannot imagine what my life would have been if he had not taken the time to view my crude attempt at animation. I like to think that it was his director's eye that allowed him to recognize some glimmer of potential in me, but the fact that someone of his stature would suggest that I might have a chance to be part his beloved profession set my life course. My words about Chuck Jones might not mean much, but his words to me meant everything.

If this book sparked your interest in animation and the people who make it, I humbly recommend you check out the two-volume set of interviews that Tom Sito and I wrote a few years ago titled *On Animation: The Director's Perspective*. Those books were the brainchild of producer Ron Diamond, who recognized the importance, and timely opportunity, of getting personal time with those brilliant artists.

About the Author

Bill Kroyer is an Oscar®-nominated director of animation and computer graphics commercials, short films, movie titles, and theatrical films.

He was born in Chicago and graduated from the Medill School of Journalism at Northwestern University before departing for Hollywood to pursue a career in animation.

Trained in classic hand-drawn animation at the Disney Studio, he was one of the first animators to make the leap to computer animation as Computer Image Choreographer on Disney's ground-breaking 1982 feature *TRON*. He pioneered the technique of combining hand-drawn animation with computer animation on projects such as his theatrical animated feature film *FernGully: The Last Rainforest* and his short film *Technological Threat*.

As Senior Animation Director at Rhythm & Hues Studios, he directed animation on scores of commercials and many feature films, including *Cats and Dogs*, *Garfield*, and *Scooby Doo*.

Bill served as co-chair of the Science and Technology Council of the Academy of Motion Picture Arts & Sciences and was a three-term Governor of the Academy's Short Films and Feature Animation Branch. In 2017, Bill and his wife Sue received the prestigious JUNE FORAY AWARD from the International Animation Society (ASIFA) for significant contributions to the art and industry of animation.

He was Director of Digital Arts at the Dodge College of Film and Media Arts at Chapman University in Orange, California, from 2009 to 2020, and currently, he serves as Professor Emeritus.

He is the co-author with Tom Sito of the two-volume set of interviews with the great animation directors titled *On Animation: The Director's Perspective*.

He and Sue have been married for forty-five years and currently live in Wisconsin.

Snow White Rollin' on the River!

It's March 29, 1989, and I'm sitting in the Shrine Auditorium in Los Angeles at the 61st Academy Awards because *I'm nominated for an Oscar!* Even at that early stage of my Hollywood career, that situation qualified as a long, strange trip from my, shall we say, modest beginnings on the West side of Chicago.

Looking back, the night was full of symbolism. Although I was in a fog of nervous panic, a few things made it through my mental haze. There was 26-year-old heart-throb Rob Lowe cavorting on stage with a rather lame Snow White impersonator. How fitting. The animation industry was at its commercial and artistic low point, with the "Second Golden Age" not even suspected, and Hollywood, as it is wont to do, was rubbing that in. Snow White, the fairest of them all, being offered up to critical ridicule by mouthing Tina Turner's "Rolling Down the River"? This would not be the last time that the Oscars would treat my beloved animation medium with questionable frivolity—and I'd be in the middle of that.

But this night, I was in the middle of another symbolic situation. I was seated in-between my two fellow nominees for Best Achievement in Animated Short Film. To my left was John Lasseter, creator of *Tin Toy*, and to my right, Cordell Barker, nominated for *The Cat Came Back*. Cordell's film was created using the very same hand-animated, hand-painted techniques used to make animated

DOI: 10.1201/9781003558231-1

films since 1915. John's film, on the other hand, was created using something radically new—computer animation.

Cordell made his film all by himself in his apartment in Winnipeg, Canada. John made his film at a facility in the Bay Area called PIXAR. After this night, Cordell would go back home and continue life doing what many of us consider to be the life of the quintessential animator. He'd labor quietly, privately over his animation desk and draw, draw, draw. John Lasseter, however, would go on to create the most successful animation studio in history. As Walt Disney had created the medium of the theatrical animated feature film, John Lasseter would create the medium of the CG-animated feature film.

My life would be somewhere in-between these two careers. I'd continue to animate, and I too would have a studio. Nothing as great as PIXAR, but I'd work on some films you would have heard of. Even the film I was nominated for this night, a short called *Technological Threat*, was right in the middle of this historic industry transition, because my film *combined* hand-drawn cartoons with CG-animated characters. That was a first.

When I was nominated for the Oscar, I was completely taken aback. The Academy was nowhere on my radar. I had been a Disney-trained animator, drawing cartoons on paper—as it had always been done. But when I finished my gig as one of the world's first "computer animators" on Disney's classic film *Tron,* I really got the bug about what computers could do. That's when I got the idea to start my own studio and combine the two techniques. When *Tech Threat* got nominated, I had no idea what to do.

My wife Sue knew. "We have to take the whole family to the Oscars!" The immediate barrier to that wonderful idea was that the Academy only gives each nominee one guest ticket. When my wife told that to her mother, the fearsome Jeannie Daugherty Nelson of Racine, Wisconsin (think Irish mafia without the restraint), Jeannie's response was: "That's the most rotten thing I've ever heard of. Get the tickets!"

And strangely, we did. Seventeen tickets! We hit up every friend we had in the Academy to surrender their seats. In those days, a member could surrender both their tickets to a guest. Since the 1989 Oscars were in the massive Shrine Auditorium, there were lots of seats. My parents, Sue's parents, our siblings, and our tiny animation crew all went and sat in the nosebleed seats on the upper balcony.

My Mom sat next to a lady of her own age. When she told her that her son was nominated, the lady replied, "My son too. Tom Hanks". (He was nominated for *Big*) "How exciting!" my Mom replied. "Not really", said Mrs. Hanks. "He never wins".

The moment arrived for our award. The presenters were Carrie Fisher and Martin Short. Get it? Martin Short presenting the Oscar for Best Short. Clever. Martin read the nominees, open the envelope, and said, "The Oscar goes to T..." I swear I saw his lips form the "T". *Technological Threat*!!?

"*Tin Toy*", said Martin Short. John Lasseter leapt to his feet and crawled over me. All I can remember about his speech was that he wore black and white sneakers with his tux. John has always been cool. He accepted the gold statue, went back North, and proceeded to assemble the studio that would usher in the new age of animation.

If there was one moment that marked the transition from the old world to the new—from the analog to the digital age—this was it. I later learned that my film, *Technological Threat*, had been particularly popular in France, where the critics made much of the fact that it was the perfect visual allegory for that transitional moment.

Because I had worked in Hollywood for the past 14 years, I started my career in the "old world" of animation. I was lucky enough to meet most of the geniuses who had invented the industry. Neither they nor any of us had a clue about how much our world was about to change.

The world of hand-drawn animation was a very small but worldwide community of people who, it could be argued, shared one of the most unique skills on the planet. In 1950, the world had thousands of physicists, brain surgeons, and concert violinists, but less than 200 A-list character animators. They were the people that had that rare ability to draw with incredible, dimensional precision and to do so on hundreds of sequential drawings to create the illusion of a performance. When you saw the seven dwarves, or Dumbo, or Cinderella, or Bugs Bunny, you were watching characters that you *believed* and *cared about*. It never occurred to you that you were watching a stack of drawings.

As you might imagine, sharing that unique talent and passion for the artform created an equally unique culture. These were men (and a few women) who had a Peter-Pan resistance to growing up. They loved cartoons; they were silly, irreverent, hilarious, and constantly rebellious to the rules they often labored under. In the struggle with authority, they did have one trump card. You could not create animation without them.

The computer would change that. When the computer could build the character as a 3D model, and all that needed to be done was manipulate the model, many people could do that quite well. That difference would make the animated film the most financially profitable medium in Hollywood. It would radically transform the workforce, bringing in thousands of new workers, destroying some careers, creating others—then destroying them. It would even change the way live-action movies were made. With the latest intrusion of artificial intelligence, it is a transformation that continues to this day.

The transition from the pencil to the keyboard had many of the same phases of other industrial revolutions. First, there was doubt, denial, and dismissive thoughts that it would or should happen. Then, there were the incremental, amazing advancements that whittled away at those reservations. There were landmark achievements and, finally, the wholesale adoption of the new technology.

By chance, I had made a film representing that change, and now, I was about to be right in the middle of it, not just as an observer, but as a fateful participant. How did a Midwestern public school kid who had never met a single person who made their living as an artist end up in the middle of this artistic revolution?

2

It All Started with a Wink

You may have heard Walt's Disney's famous answer when asked how he felt running an entertainment empire. "I think we should remember that it all started with a mouse!" he said with his wry grin. My own career in animation didn't start with a mouse. It started with a snake.

I was a journalism major at the Medill School of Journalism at Northwestern University in Evanston, Illinois. Why journalism? My working class Dad did not think a person could make a living drawing pictures (he certainly never knew one who did), so he refused to sign me into the art classes in high school. But writing was sort of creative, so I went to work writing for the school paper. Although I actually spent most of my time drawing cartoons, as luck would have it my articles made me the winner of the *Chicago Tribune's* McCormick Award, which came with a big college scholarship. So off I went to The Medill School of Journalism at Northwestern University.

I had to make a thirty-second commercial for an advertising class, and since I was still drawing a lot of cartoons for the *Daily Northwestern*, I thought I'd make a cartoon film. I bought a book from the bookstore titled *Animated Films* by Preston Blair. As it turns out, almost every animator of my generation started with that book.

4 DOI: 10.1201/9781003558231-2

That's when I first learned the most basic thing about animation. *It is frame-by-frame filmmaking.* While live action filmmakers just press the trigger on the camera and capture twenty-four images per second as the film whirls through the gate, animators have to draw each one of the twenty-four images individually and then record them individually! Click click click. The magic of how individual images transform into moving images is due to the principle of "persistence of vision" in your eye. When an image hits your retina, it doesn't vanish instantly. It slowly fades. So if you slap another image on there before the previous one fades, they blend together in a way that makes it seem like smooth action.

I remember my Mom taking me to see Disney's *Sleeping Beauty* in 1959 when I was nine years old. I distinctly remember having the realization that what I was watching was drawn and painted images. But how could they move? I figured that there would have to be so many individual pictures going by so fast I could not see them change. After a moment of calculating how many that would be, I dismissed the number as incomprehensible. I went back to enjoying the movie and never thought about it again until I picked up the Preston Blair book years later.

I discovered that you didn't have to draw a picture for *every* frame. You could shoot each drawing twice (two frames each) and there would still be enough changing to fool the eye. And since I was shooting on *Super*-8 film, there were only sixteen frames per second! Easy? Eight drawings still seemed like a lot of work for one lousy second of screen time. That meant I had to draw 240 drawings for a thirty-second film.

I decided to animate a snake because I didn't want to do all the work of animating arms and legs. I did give the guy a hat. I can't remember what the message of this commercial was supposed to be, but I had him rise up from the bottom of the frame with his back to us, turn to camera, and wink. Then he smiled and slunk away.

I photographed my pile of drawings and took the tiny spool of film to the drug store for development. Two days later it came back. I threaded up the Super-8 projector, turned off the lights, and ran the film. My little snake rose up, turned, and winked at me.

And my life changed forever.

I presume, and I have decades of experience to support this theory, that the feeling I had at that moment is the singular reason why most animators become animators. It is the reason they become completely devoted and addicted to this art, and once in it, cannot imagine life without it.

Because, at that moment, when the little snake winked at me, *I had created life!*

I often say that animation is the most God-like profession. Doctors may save lives, actors my imitate lives using their own bodies, but the animator creates a living being out of nothing. Although it is a being that you, the audience, know cannot possibly be real, for some reason, the movement of that character creates the illusion of life. Think about it. The most famous, popular, world-famous stars are fabrications of the animator. Mickey Mouse, Bugs Bunny, Shrek, Buzz Lightyear—ageless and totally believable international celebrities.

And I now I had made a snake come to life! I was hooked. Up to that time I had had countless odd jobs, from paperboy to waiter to factory worker, but from the moment I saw that wink I became so obsessed with animation that I have never earned a dollar doing anything but animation.

But how to do that in Chicago? There were commercial studios in New York, and of course, the famous animation studios in L.A., but I was in-between those cities in the animation desert of the Midwest. Then—another fateful coincidence.

3

Annie's Sugar-Coated Nightmare

After my transcendent experience of creating the snake, I dove into animation as a true addict would. I made a hand-drawn short film about a rebellious water drop (imagine that story pitch!) that won the college film festival.

At the time, I was volunteering for a food co-op called Cornucopia. It was founded by my good friends Bruce and Claudia Meyer, and its goal was to bring cheaper fresh food to poor inner-city neighborhoods in Chicago. The warehouse was on west Lake Street, a rough neighborhood, because it was the only warehouse cheap enough to make the venture possible. Our hippie crew worked hard to help the neighborhood.

One night Claudia was closing up late and three teenagers came through the door and robbed her—at gun point—of the day's proceeds. A day later that money was mysteriously returned. Apparently word had gotten around the neighborhood that these weird hippie kids had their hearts in the right places. Despite the crime that was rampant in that part of town, neither the co-op or any of the workers were ever bothered again.

Our organizers would go to a church or community centers and give their speech about how a food co-op worked, the basic idea of pooling your money to buy food at better prices in larger lots. It got pretty monotonous to give this talk

DOI: 10.1201/9781003558231-3

five times a day, so I came up with the idea of making an animated film about how a co-op worked. I did that, and our crew now took a Super-8 projector to the meetings and showed my film. It not only made their job easier—it was very successful in explaining the idea and forming new buying clubs.

I was about to graduate from Northwestern, wondering how I could make a living at animation, when a phone call came from Loop College. Somebody from the school had seen my co-op film at a church meeting. Would I be willing to make a 16mm version for the college's inner-city aid program?

And just like that, I was a professional animator!

I now had a budget to make a film. Real money! It was time to up my game, so I built my own animation stand. If you have never seen one, an animation stand is the essential tool for photographing hand-drawn animation. It is basically a tabletop with a column rising above it. The camera is mounted on the column, and travels up and down to be closer or farther from the table, thus zooming in or zooming out from the artwork.

The tabletop has pegs to hold the artwork in place. That's another fundamental feature of hand-drawn animation. The artist works on paper that has holes that, when fitted over corresponding pegs, holds each successive drawing in precise registration.

(When Walt Disney hired Salvador Dali to develop a sequence for *Fantasia*, he handed Dali a stack of punched animation paper. Dali looked at the holes, handed it back, and said he could not work on such paper. "Why not?" Walt asked. "Because it already has a design!!" Dali screamed.)

The pegs on the tabletop hold the paper in place, and a piece of glass, called a "platen", presses down on the paper to keep it flat. The tabletop rests on a set of tracks that allow the table to slide back and forth and left and right, to allow for panning the artwork past the camera.

The most famous, technically advanced, and finely-machined animation stands were made by the Oxberry Corporation. They cost thousands of dollars. My stand, made of 2–4's and basic hardware, cost about 100 bucks. But it worked.

I made the co-op film and titled it *Co-Op Story*. The movie *Love Story* was a big hit at the time so I thought that title was clever. Luckily for me, Loop College loved it and commissioned a second project. This film would be about nutrition. It would address the very serious problem of inner-city kids eating too much junk food. We called it *Annie's Sugar-Coated Nightmare*.

Working with the college's nutritionists, I wrote the script, then did a basic storyboard. A storyboard is like a comic book. It is a series of still drawings that visualize what the film will look like. The art of storyboarding is complex and critical to the animation process, and I will talk more about it later. The work I did at this time, completely untrained and amateurish, does not deserve examination.

I was a one-man studio, so I did all the designs of the characters, drew all the animation, created the backgrounds, inked the drawings on to acetate cels, and painted them. Nothing innovative—that's the way animation had been done since 1915.

This was long before the internet, so although I did do a cursory search to see if there was anyone in Chicago doing animation, I couldn't find anyone. I was completely on my own, learning while doing. In retrospect I might have found a few more books to help me out, but I just blasted ahead. It took me a year to make the ten-minute film. When you realize that ten minutes of screen time is 14,400 frames, you can see why it took so long.

While I was working on the project, Northwestern University had its yearly film festival. Since I had won that festival two years earlier with my animated water-drop film I pitched the idea of doing a seminar on animation. After all, I was the big (and only) animation expert in the Chicagoland area! I did the seminar and gave a talk on the basics as I had learned them. Remarkably—and I did not find this out until years later—there were two people in that audience that would profoundly impact my life.

One was Karen Johnson. She had just started her own little animation studio in Racine, Wisconsin. She would get her sister Sue involved in animation, and six years later Sue and I would meet—and marry—at the Disney Studios. The other was John Musker. Although he took over my job as cartoonist on the Daily Northwestern, we would not meet until that same fateful week that I started at the Disney Studio. He not only became my Best Man and close friend, but the legendary co-director of *The Little Mermaid*, *Alladin*, *Moana*, and other Disney classics.

Just as I finished *Annie's Nightmare*, the big Chicago International Film Festival announced that one of its judges would be the world's most famous animator Chuck Jones. Chuck was one of the legendary Warner Bros. directors. He was a three-time Oscar-winner, but more than that, his cartoons were some of the greatest (a.k.a.funniest) cartoons ever made. Two of them, *What's Opera Doc* and *Duck Amuck* would soon be placed in the National Registry. This was my chance to meet a fellow animator!

I must insert here that I use that term "fellow animator" completely tongue-in-cheek. True, technically Chuck and I were both animators, but in the same way that U.S.S. Missouri and a rowboat are both floating vessels.

I still find it hard to believe I did this, but after meeting him briefly at a reception and finding out where he was staying, I actually carried a projector and my new film to Chuck's hotel room. He answered the door and I said, "Mr. Jones. We just met, but I'm an animator and I'd like to show you my film." You probably will never find greater evidence as to how charitable and generous Chuck Jones was than the fact that he invited me in to do that.

I will say this. In the age of hand-drawn animation, that particular skill was so rare, and the people who were drawn to it were so alike in their unabashed love of the art, that the community of artists did have a strange brotherhood. I like to think that Chuck extended that membership to me by sensing my sincere enthusiasm.

I plugged in the projector, hit the lights, and showed Chuck Jones my film. Looking back now, it is a very, very basic exercise in animation. But ever the gentleman, ever the teacher, ever the supportive artist, Chuck watched the whole reel. When it was over he turned to me.

"Did you say you have no training? That you did this all on your own? Self-taught?"

I reluctantly confirmed that was the case. Chuck thought for a moment.

"I think you have talent. I think you could make it in Hollywood."

Chuck Jones, the greatest animator on the planet, said that to me. And based on that sentence, I decided I really had no choice but to uproot my life and do exactly what he said. I was going to Hollywood.

4

Westward Ho

In 1975, the Hollywood animated film industry had lost its mojo.

Long gone were the days of the "First Golden Age", when Disney had that string of classic feature films from *Snow White* to *Sleeping Beauty*. The Shorts Departments of Warner Bros. and MGM that produced an endless stream of timeless cartoons (Bugs, Daffy, Roadrunner, Tom & Jerry) had shut down.

Most of the employment came from TV series, and the two big shops were Filmation and Hanna-Barbera (H&B). H&B was founded by Bill Hanna and Joe Barbera, ex-Oscar winners who had figured out a process called "limited animation" and made it big with series like *The Flintstones* and *Yogi Bear*.

It was called "limited animation" because not only did they not create a drawing for every frame, or a drawing for every-other frame, as they did in "full animation"; they didn't even draw the entire character! H&B pioneered ideas like splitting the characters into levels and "holding" the parts that didn't move. When Fred Flintstone talked, his entire body and head might be in a single drawing, and only his moving mouth was animated. There were many tricks, but you get the idea. By 1975 H&B was doing spin-offs of its previous series. It employed hundreds of artists who worked in *windowless rooms* in a building on Cahuenga Boulevard.

DOI: 10.1201/9781003558231-4

Filmation was founded by Lou Scheimer. This was the studio that did *Masters of the Universe*, and no one was more ruthlessly efficient (read: tightwad) than Lou. He developed the idea of "re-use", that is, constantly saving and re-using artwork that had already been created rather than drawing new artwork. The animators had "cheat sheet thumbnail pictures" on the walls above their desks that showed previous backgrounds, layouts and animated shots, and they were pushed to re-use these as much as possible. You were a hero if you could create an entire sequence without drawing a new picture.

Animated series had to have theme songs, and one thing animation shared with live action was the rigid monitoring by ASCAP (The American Society of Composer, Authors and Publishers). Every time a theme song was played on TV, the writers got a royalty. As you might guess, with thousands of hours of kids' shows, this added up to a lot of money. The story around town was that Lou Scheimer had a system. If you were lucky enough to be hired to write the music for a Filmation TV show, you had to accept a co-writer: Lou's daughter! So Lou raked in 50% of that ASCAP money! I heard this from his artists. Maybe they embellished the rumor because he was always squeezing them!

In 1975 Los Angeles had a dozen or so small studios doing animation for TV commercials. But when it came to high-quality feature work, there was still only one game in town: The Walt Disney Studios. Since the Fleischer Brothers had failed to compete with Disney back in the 1940s, the rest of the Hollywood studios had ceded that medium to the Mouse House. In 1975 the only non-Disney feature to make a dent in the American box office was Ralph Bakshi's risque *Coonskin*, and it was not a big dent.

I really did not know any of this when I rolled into town in March 1975 in my Ford Falcon van. After Chuck Jones' dictum, I had packed up and left Chicago right after New Year's. Not having seen the West, I decided to camp my way to California, so I did my own "great Western trip" and arrived three months later.

Since Chuck Jones was literally the only person I knew in Hollywood, I went right to his office on Sunset Boulevard. His secretary led me into his room. "Hello Mr. Jones", I chortled. "Remember me? Bill Kroyer from Chicago? You told me to come to Hollywood!"

Chuck looked up from his drawing board. "Oh yes, " he said. "Good Luck!"

I was taken aback. *Good Luck?*

"I thought you might hire me..." I stammered. I was never good at beating around the bush.

Oh I'm not hiring right now", Chuck said dryly. "Between pictures". After a few moments of polite chatting, he scribbled a name on a piece of paper. He told me to call the guy. He might be hiring.

And so, the hunt began.

5

How Cheap Will You Work?

The name on the piece of paper was Willie Ito. Willie was a Japanese-American who as a kid had endured the WWII internment camps, gone to art school, and had a great career at Disney, Warner Bros., and Hanna-Barbera. As you might imagine, he eventually attained something like legendary status in our animation community, but at this moment in 1975, he had just left H&B and was freelancing. In other words, he wasn't hiring. He gave me a few more names to call.

Thus began my odyssey of visiting every existing animation studio in Los Angeles. The good news was that I met almost everybody in charge of what then was a rather small business community. The bad news was that I was being rejected everywhere.

And why not? I had no professional experience, which was obvious, and my art samples were extremely odd. While every other prospective artist came to an interview with a portfolio full of drawings, I had a big manila envelope with a pile of samples of my "commercial art". It included the assorted greeting cards, concert posters, and brochures I had illustrated in Chicago to support my animation endeavors. How could I have been so clueless?

DOI: 10.1201/9781003558231-5

In the middle of this crusade, it occurred to me that since I was interviewing with everyone else, I might as well go for the top of the mountain. I called the Disney Studio and was quite shocked when they gave me a meeting time.

I wore my best clothes (corduroy pants and a long-sleeve collared shirt), tried to minimize the look of my shoulder-length hair by tying it into a tight ponytail, and headed to Burbank. I can hardly express the thrill of driving my beaten-up Ford van through that main gate on Buena Vista Street. I could not believe I was about to enter the hallowed halls of Disney Animation.

I was directed to the office of the head of recruitment. A very distinguished gray-haired gentleman showed me the brand new recruiting brochure the company was beginning to distribute to art schools. It was a very official and impressive, and seemed serious - until you got to that last phrase: "If you are interested, contact Donald Duckwall". DONALD DUCKwall!?

But Don was real person, and here he sat, starting the process that Disney had been avoiding for forty years - recruiting young talent to replace the veteran animators. The word "veteran" doesn't really do justice to these men. The group included the legendary "Nine Old Men", the nine animators that Walt had considered the foundation upon which he built his empire (the nickname came from FDR's reference to the Supreme Court).

These men started with the company before *Snow White*, and had animated on every feature film since then. They were geniuses, and had done what was unquestionably some of the greatest work the animated medium would produce. They had remained at their drawing boards for decades because Disney was still the only place that gave an artist the time and resources it took to do the very best work. Besides, who could you find to do it better than they could?

Over the years, production requirements did require the studio to hire some newcomers, but the rumor was that the Old Men were rough on them. Perhaps they didn't want to train their own replacements.

I would eventually have the privilege of becoming close to some of the nine, but on this day, they were unapproachable icons behind closed doors.

Remarkably, Don Duckwall took me on a personal walking tour of the animation department. That shows you how few people they were interviewing! It was mostly hallways with framed artwork, but we did visit the suite of Mel Shaw, Disney's preeminent development artist. A development artist does the first visual exploration on a film. They are free to paint and draw any imagery that they think might work for the story. Mel was drawing small pastel color pictures for a fantasy film that was still years away from production. It was tentatively titled *The Black Cauldron*.

We ended the tour in the office of Ed Hansen, the Animation Department Manager. Ed handed my "portfolio" (manilla envelope) to his assistant, Joanne, for her to look at. If the idea of a clerical worker, sweet as she might be, acting as the review committee for the world's greatest animation department seems odd to you, you are not alone. Years later, John Musker, the great Director and supreme caricaturist, would memorialize this process by picturing Joanne critically dissecting the portfolio of a bearded, robed Leonardo Da Vinci ("These drawings are just so darn cute...but they're not what we're looking for...").

Walt had died eight years earlier, and the problem with the department was that they did not want to deviate from his legacy. They were terrified of changing anything. That made for an interesting visit because I was seeing the department exactly as it was when Walt was around. But it did not bode well for future innovation.

Ed showed me some layouts for the film currently in production, *The Rescuers*. A "layout" is a pencil drawing of the environment. It is the image the animators use to animate over, and it will eventually be turned into a color painting for final photography. This particular layout showed an alley with laundry strung from clotheslines. It was here that I made the comment that sealed my doom.

This looks a lot like the alley in the spaghetti scene in *"Lady and the Tramp,"* I said.

In fact, it was probably the very same layout, or a slightly modified copy.

Ed gave me a rather icy look. "We do what we do best," he replied. In other words, we will continue to do exactly what Walt pre-approved.

Ed handed me my manila envelope. I did not have the necessary artwork for the committee to review. The portfolio must have "life drawings" (sketches of live models) and "quick action sketches' of people and animals in action, to indicate that I understood anatomy applied to motion. He told me to come back when I had those. And with that, Disney joined my list of rejections.

Never having attended art school, or even taken an art class, I was concerned about my ability to assemble the portfolio they were expecting. Besides, it would take time to do that, and I was running out of money. I had run through the list of studios to apply to. Maybe it was time to get back in the van and forget Hollywood.

The next morning I got a phone call from an animation producer named Ray Thursby. "You were in here the other day looking for work. I may have something. Are you interested?"

"Absolutely!" I said.

"Just one question," said Ray. "How cheap will you work?"

I thought for about one second. "I'll work for anything," I said.

"Great," Ray said. "Come to Spungbuggy tomorrow morning at nine. We'll pay you four bucks an hour to do in-betweens."

"GREAT! See you then!" I hung up the phone, elated. "What's an in-between?" I wondered.

6

What Is a Spungbuggy?

Spungbuggy was one of those small commercial studios I mentioned earlier. It was located on the corner of La Cienega and Sunset, right in the middle of the area that became famous as "The Sunset Strip". In fact, it was just two doors down from the most famous location on the street, Dino's Lodge at 77 Sunset Strip, made famous by the TV show of the same name. The restaurant was on its last legs when I arrived, long past the time when Ed "Kookie" Burns was parking cars. But the building was still there.

Spungbuggy had been founded by Herb Stott, a talented art director who decided he had the talent to direct commercials. He told me years later that his real motivation was to date beautiful models. Whatever his reasons, the studio did well. It produced primarily live action commercials, but because animation could be profitable, Herb opened an animation department.

I arrived at the address of 8506 Sunset (that nearby 77 Sunset Strip number was a catchy alliterative made-up address) and climbed the stairs to the main office. It was pretty hip; the waiting room had vintage furniture; there was a conference room with a table made from a Victorian pool table, and all the offices had spectacular views of L.A. Impressive.

DOI: 10.1201/9781003558231-6

I was ushered into Ray Thursby's office. Ray was a true industry old-timer, already in his 70s at this time but a rare gentleman in Hollywood who had forgotten more about animation production than most people knew. He was a master at writing the technical "exposure sheets" that told the camera operator how to photograph the artwork. Ray did this job to stay active. He didn't need the money.

Ray loved telling the story of driving back to L.A. after his service in WWII and stopping in a sleepy little town called Las Vegas. On a whim, he bought five acres of land for a hundred bucks. Twenty years later, a developer wanted to build homes in Red Rock Canyon - and Ray owned the entrance to the canyon! He made a ton of money. He would chuckle and say "That was about the best deal I ever made."

I could sense a bit of wry resignation in Ray's attitude as he described my deal. Day-to-day, no contract, cash payments, $4/hour. That's how Spungbuggy made animation profitable!

I accepted. Ray told me to follow him. He led me down the hall, through the beautiful lobby, and back down the stairs to the street! A few yards down, we entered another door at street level. In this windowless, drab, dry-walled room were jammed eight artists at their desks. Welcome to the somewhat less glamorous world of animation!

I was greeted by my boss, the Animation Director Frank Terry. Frank had a compact build, tossled blond hair, and a perpetually squinty expression. If discovering animation through my snake film was a miracle, and getting hired in Hollywood with no portfolio was fortuitous, then falling in with Frank Terry as my director would prove to be nothing short of a Godsend.

Frank was a brilliant animator, a thoroughly decent man, and would prove to be one of the great animation educators of all time. Years later he would be the head of the most famous animation school in the world, Cal Arts. But on this day, he was Herb Stott's junior partner in the studio and in charge of all animation production.

Frank shook my hand and plunked me down at the only empty animation desk in the room. "You're working with Bob," he said. With that, he went back to his office upstairs.

"Bob" was Bob Zamboni, a distant relative of the man who invented the famous ice-rink machine, but a veteran Hollywood commercial animator. Because he was an obsessive back-packer, the other artists referred to him as "Ranger Bob". Bob was tall, very gruff, with a full beard and mountain-man type jeans and a flannel shirt. He gave me a stack of drawings. "Just follow the charts," he said.

This is where I hit the pause button. As I mentioned, I had never done an "in-between." As you might guess, an "in-between" is a drawing that comes in between other drawings. In typical "full animation", the animator does the main drawings, called "keys", and the assistant animator does the rest.

Because I was self-taught, learning animation in an isolated bubble, I had never learned this method. I instinctively had used a system that I would learn had a name: "straight-ahead animation". In this style, the artist simply starts with the first drawing of a scene and works forward, drawing each incremental action as it comes. This was used in very early films, but was rarely used now because it had become obvious over the years that the "key frame" method was superior. With key frames, you could more clearly and carefully plot out the entire action.

As I looked at the stack of drawings Bob had given me, I could tell the order by the numbers on the lower right of each page. There were gaps in the numbers. I had drawings 1, 9, 14, 18, 25 etc. I also noticed little diagrams on the drawings. These were the "charts" that Bob had mentioned. The diagrams visually described the distance of each in-between drawing from the previous drawing. For example, a drawing that would be exactly half-way from one key drawing to the next key drawing would be "a straight in-between". Often that gap would get smaller and smaller as it approached the key, causing the action to "ease-out" and slow down.

I stuck the #1 drawing on the pegs (at least I knew what pegs were), stuck a blank sheet of paper on top, then placed the next key (drawing #9) on top of that. I knew I had to now make a drawing (#5) that was halfway between these two. I was considering how to best approach this when I glanced over and saw Bob staring at me. "Don't you know how to flip?" he asked. I just froze. I had been exposed as an idiot.

Bob nudged me out of my chair. He sat down, calmly removed Key #9 and the blank sheet, then placed Key #9 directly on top of Key #1, He put the blank sheet *on the top*. He slid the top two drawings between his fingers and started to flip them. By flipping back and forth between the two keys, he could see the difference in their shapes. Now he started to draw on the blank sheet. The clever thing, and the thing that took just a bit of practice to master, was by quickly flipping the order of the new drawing with the two keys one could see and create the image that belonged between them. The in-between!

Without ridicule or disdain, Bob simply looked up and asked, "Got it?" I shook my head "yes" and sat down again. I started my first day as an in-betweener. I had not just learned a new skill. I had learned that most animators are, unlike a lot of Hollywood, incredibly, genuinely nice people.

I was animating a falling hat. It was falling to the ground because the creature that had been wearing the hat, a bug, had just been blown to oblivion by a shot of RAID insect spray. I was to learn that Bob Zamboni was the sole animator in Hollywood that the RAID clients would trust to draw their famous, iconic "Raid Bugs". You have probably seen these characters, the rather scruffy insects with the bobbing antennae. Only Bob seemed to be able to capture their rough, sketchy look.

I labored intensely on that stupid little hat, making sure it was spaced correctly, making sure that as it rotated during its fall, its shape seemed solid and dimensionally believable. That aspect of animation - the ability to visualize dimensionality - was a prerequisite of "full animation". That was a natural talent I was blessed to possess. It made my career possible.

At the end of the day I handed my stack of drawings to Bob. He took the stack in his hands and did the classic motion that all animators master. He squeezed the top of the stack and using his thumb and forefinger on the bottom of the stack, fanned the drawings past his eyes like a flipbook. Bob flipped the stack a few times, then said, "I'll send these off to camera." He went upstairs.

A few minutes later Ray Thursby called me on the phone in the animation room. "You can come back tomorrow," he said.

I had survived my first day at Spungbuggy! I was about to start a two-year gig that would be the most explosive learning experience of my career. And in all that time, and to this day, I never learned why Herb Stott named the place SPUNGBUGGY.

7

Putting Pants on the Elves

Woody Allen once said: "Eighty-five per cent of success is just showing up." I had not heard that at the time, but I would have been a good case study. I came into Spungbuggy the next day and just kept showing up. They didn't officially hire me. They didn't even ask me to come back. I would come in every morning and go to that empty desk, and, lucky for me, the animators were busy, and there were always in-betweens to be done.

My second commercial was for the cleaning solution Mr. Clean, that muscular bald guy in the tight white T-shirt and pants with the gold earring. In my first shot, Mr. Clean, arms folded in his ready-pose, rose up from a shiny linoleum floor and smiled at camera. This was tougher than drawing a hat. Mr. Clean had anatomy, and every drawing was a slightly different perspective. I focused very hard and made sure I followed every detail of the key drawings the animator had provided.

In these days of hand-drawn animation, you could flip the pages of your scene to get a sense of how it was moving but you really did not know how the shot looked until you "sent it to camera" and had it photographed. This involved packaging all the drawings in a binder with an "X-Sheet" (a.k.a. exposure sheet) that listed exactly how each drawing was to shot. The cameraman shot the drawings

DOI: 10.1201/9781003558231-7

on an Oxberry animation stand. Since we drew on the day shift, cameramen shot our stuff on the night shift. When they were done, they dropped the film at a lab and a production assistant picked it up in the morning.

There were many labs in Hollywood in those days, including Deluxe, Foto-Kem, and the famous Technicolor lab. To be economical, Spungbuggy used CFI, which stood for Consolidated Film Industries, although the artists, based on customer satisfaction, jokingly said CFI really stood for "Can't Find it" or "C IF I care".

It was a big moment each morning when we animators came out of our downstairs hovel and climbed the stairs to the editorial department to watch our film on the movieola. A device few film students would recognize today, the moviola was like a mini-theater. It had reels, gears, a speaker, and a small screen to show the image. Frank Terry sat at the controls and each animator looked over his shoulder at the small screen as the footage played.

When my shot came up, Frank and the animator studied it carefully. Frank said a few comments which I could not hear. I followed the animator back downstairs. He flopped the stack of drawings on my desk and handed me an eraser.

"You need to erase all the lines around his crotch. He's got too big a bulge in his pants!" Even though I had followed the keys, apparently the lines I drew were too emphatic. That was my first big "revision" in animation: decreasing Mr. Clean's package.

Those wacky requests were not unusual. Mark Robman, another assistant animator, was a wanna-be actor who supported himself in animation. He told me he did a huge Keebler Elves commercial once, but when the client had the shocking realization that the elves were wearing tunics, and nothing else, he made Mark go back and add trousers to all of them. "If I ever write my bio about life in animation I'm going to call it 'Putting Pants on the Elves.'"

Every day I learned something new. I have always had a good work ethic, and me sticking my nose to that desk and cranking out good work each day finally got me a bit of job security. Ray Thursby raised my salary to $5 an hour!

It was right about this time that my best friend and college roommate, Gary Stromberg, rolled into town. Gary had majored in TV reporting at Northwestern and wanted to test the market for a job in L.A. He was crashing on the floor of my studio apartment in West Hollywood. He got a kick out of the fact I was supporting myself doing in-betweens.

"Mr. In-Between. That's who you are, Willie," he said. Then, channeling the old Bing Crosby tune "Accentuate the Positive, eliminate the Negative," he chortled, " and don't mess with Mr. In-Between!"

Gary didn't stay in L.A. but had a great career as the lead on-air feature reporter at FOX TV-Cleveland for over two decades.

But his jokey nickname for me stuck. Fifty years later he still calls me that.

It was not a joke that there was no better way to learn animation than to in-between the drawings of real animators. As my skills increased, I was given more responsibility. At Spungbuggy, they were happy to let you move up - as long as you didn't ask for more money. Within six months I had advanced from in-betweener to assistant animator to full animator. True, I was getting the easiest shots, but it was money in the bank to have commercial animation shots completed at the rate of $5 an hour.

In the world of hand-drawn animation, the most frightening, challenging, and exhilarating thing was that you started with a blank sheet of paper. As the animator, you not only had to draw the character well enough it make it look correctly like the character - you had to draw it correctly over and over again, in many, many poses, from every angle. It had to fit into the environment. As the character moved, you had to "preserve volume". No matter how the character turned or twisted, you had to preserve the illusion that the character was solid. It must not shrink or bulge or otherwise distort in a way that might distract the audience.

That was a key requirement of the skill: preserving the illusion of life. If you did not have that supreme technical drawing skill, the audience would not "suspend their disbelief" and watch a character. They would just be watching drawings.

The monumental difference between the great artist and the great animator was that the animator's drawings had to *move*. It wasn't enough to master all those drawing skills. You had to be a performer! You had to act! That's why the number of people in the human race who can animate by drawing is miniscule. How weirdly, weirdly blessed was I that I not only had some talent in this rare skill - I had discovered how to make a living doing it.

Because the animator has the freedom to literally *draw anything* on that blank page, it was fitting that the word "animation" had come to have the definition as "the art of movement." Rather than just attempt to technically move things, the animator can create movement that is designed and caricatured beyond what would happen in real life, beyond real-world physics. Not only that, the individual drawings are often distorted or exaggerated in ways that would look odd if you saw them as individual drawings but blend invisibly into motion.

This was the miraculous world of creation that was now opening to me. Terms like weight, volume, balance, squash and stretch, ease-in, ease-out, arcs, patterns of movement, anticipation and follow-through - these were just some of the seemingly endless tools of the trade that I was learning about.

One day I was handed a scene from a commercial for Hallmark Greeting Cards. In the shot, a cute little girl in a bonnet and a fluffy skirt is watering flowers with a watering can. The layout had her watering one plant, then turning to notice another plant behind her, then turning to water that plant.

The shot had those challenges of preserving volume and shape of not just the girl but her clothing, hat, and watering can as they all rotated 180 degrees. But I had been learning another principle about movement called "overlapping action." It is that simple truth that organic things, especially bodies, never move at the same rate or the same time. So, I had the girl's head turn first, followed by her shoulders, then hips, then legs, and the arm that held the watering can. I even had the fabric of her skirt drag a bit, then wave and settle after she had turned.

Although she was a caricatured character with cartoony proportions, her movement looked *believable*.

At dailies the next morning, Frank Terry ran my shot through the moviola. He paused, ran it back, then looked at again. And again. And Again. He turned to me with that squinty look and said, "Nice." After that, I started to get "A-list" commercials. I was a Spungbuggy animator!

8

The Tidepool off the River

In large studios, animators are often "cast", or assigned, to shots that are deemed best suited to their personal strengths or styles. Some animators are good at fast action, some better at comedy, some able to draw very complex or difficult characters. At Spungbuggy, there were none of those distinctions. Whatever job came through door landed on the desk of whoever was available. We're running a business here - with deadlines!

That variety, with those challenges, were ideal for learning. Frank Terry was a wonderful mentor. We'd discuss the shots first and review the layout so I thoroughly understood what it was he expected me to do. Then it was nose-to-the-grindstone work for me, knocking out the first "rough pass". This first version had relatively rough drawings that had just enough detail to clearly convey the direction the scene was headed. You could see all the actions, even though it looked "scratchy". This first test would be sent to camera.

To me, every dailies session was like Christmas morning. I could not wait to see my drawings come to life. Frank would precisely describe every tweak I had to make to fix the scene. Because we were a commercial house, I rarely got more than one revision pass. On my second pass, I'd fix all the motion and "tie down" the drawings by making them much cleaner, with all the necessary detail for the

DOI: 10.1201/9781003558231-8

inkers to follow. After this final pencil test was approved, the drawings went to the Ink & Paint Department.

In 1975, transforming my pencil drawings into a final color film was done by a method that had barely changed since the beginning of the artform in 1915. Ladies (they were, and had always been, primarily females doing this work) would place my drawing on pegs and lay a sheet of clear acetate - a "cel" - over the drawing. They would trace the drawing with ink. Depending on the design of the character, this could be black ink, or any combination of colors. The precision of this work was critical. After all, no matter how good the animator was, it was not his character you were seeing on TV or film. It was the inker's!

After inking, the cel was turned over and paint was applied to the back. By painting the back, the paint pooled in a perfectly flat, smooth way against the surface of the cel. When you see a painted cel (like in ALL the early Disney films) you see perfect color from frame to frame. If you looked at the back of the cels, you would have seen that the paint was rough and textured as it dried, because it was very thick paint.

Our I&P Department was headed by Aurel Pebley, a veteran former Disney inker who looked like a character from a David Lynch film. She had long fake eye-lashes, a massive red beehive hairdo, and incredibly long, perfectly mani-cured nails. It was a wonder she could hold a brush. But she was a genius. Her ink & paint girls were Spungbuggy's insurance that the characters on film would look great, even if the drawings they were given by novice animators like me were not the greatest.

I found myself animating every character imaginable. I'd do a wizard for a pizza ad, a panther for a fertilizer ad, a teenager for a shoe ad, and, of course, talk-ing car parts. I knew I was getting better when Frank trusted me with the iconic character Charlie Tuna. Charlie was the beret-wearing beatnik tuna that felt he was good enough to be canned, only to be constantly rejected. "Sorry Charlie - only the best tuna go into Starkist Tuna".

Because Charlie was such a famous character I went to great pains to draw him perfectly. It took me ten working days to complete the twenty seconds of screen time. That means I was working twice as fast as a Disney feature animator would typically work. But clearly, my work was not Disney perfection! Nevertheless, I was paid $5 an hour for those eighty hours, making my fee for creating the visual of Charlie Tuna a grand total of $400 - before taxes.

Because my commercial ran for months on national TV, Herschel Bernardi, the actor who recorded the voice for my animation, would reap over $40,000 in royalties! Does that seem fair? Welcome to animation.

After months of being a "full animator", doing entire commercials all by myself, I did feel it I was justified to ask for a raise from my $5 an hour. To do that, I was told I had to approach Herb Stott himself. I worked up the courage, went to Herb's office, and said, "Herb, I want my salary doubled, and I want two weeks of paid vacation." Without pausing for two seconds, Herb smiled and said "OK!"

He shook my hand and quickly showed me out. I realized immediately that I had vastly underbid myself. But hey – I loved animating!

It wasn't just that I found every day to be a miraculous creative experience, or that I was getting a better education than I could have paid for at a school. I was beginning to get to know the Hollywood animation community. All the guys at Spungbuggy were funny, self-deprecating, devoted artists - typical animation people. My wife Sue always said that if Hollywood was a rushing river of ambition and conflict, animation was the calm tide pool off to the side. My two-cent explanation of this is simple. The film business was fraught with hustlers. In animation, success was much simpler and more honest, because everyone could tell if you could animate or not. There were no fakers.

When I came to Hollywood, I knew absolutely nothing about Los Angeles or its neighborhoods. I could not have told you the difference between the names Compton vs. Culver City. By chance, because Spungbuggy was on Sunset, I rented a tiny studio apartment as near as I could get, which happened to be right in the middle of West Hollywood. That neighborhood was just beginning to develop as the center of the LGBTQ lifestyle of L.A., but as a straight guy who was making so little money I rarely even went to a local restaurant, I barely noticed the trend. I knew there were a lot of gay guys around, but I just figured that was a West Coast thing. My downstairs neighbor had a pink AMC Pacer with the license plate: IM RU2.

My focus was the animation community. I started to go to lectures at the Screen Cartoonists Union, even though I was not a union member. I tried to attend any animation event I could find. I heard the Union was having its yearly "T-Shirt Dance" at a Hollywood club and found out that only requirement was a jokey T-Shirt and a $5 entry fee. I got a T-Shirt (I can't recall what it was) and went to the dance.

It wasn't really "a dance", because the animation world in those days was about 85% guys - and very geeky guys at that. These were opposite of swingers. Their kind of party was just to drink small amounts of beer and talk about - what else - animation! What a pleasure! But the most amazing aspect of the event, and it is even more amazing in retrospect, was the amount of older, veteran, *famous* animation people who attended.

When I walked in the door, the first person I noticed was a celebrity that was so iconic even I would recognize him. It was Ward Kimball, one of Disney's Nine Old Men, one of the greatest animators who walked the earth. You could not mistake Ward for anyone else. He had that round, pixie-like face, strands of hair straight back on his head, and those perfectly round, thick black glasses. This was the man that was, as the story went, the only "genius" Walt had ever tolerated on his crew.

I carefully slid into the small group of men and women surrounding him, hoping to catch a few priceless anecdotes. To my surprise, Ward thrust out his hand toward me. "Ward Kimball. Who are you?" He said. "Bill Kroyer," I mumbled. "from Chicago." It was then that I noticed Ward's T-Shirt, a blue shirt with the iconic "FORD" logo in the oval. Only that word in the oval written in cursive was not FORD. It was F*CK!! On a Disney legend!

Another celebrity at the dance was June Foray. June was the premiere female voice artist of animation, best-known for being the voice of Rocky the flying squirrel. June would become a living legend, earning the title "The Queen of Animation". When I met her briefly this night, I could not have imagined that we would be become close friends who eventually would fight side by side to keep the animated shorts on the Oscar telecast. That's a later story.

As luck would have it, I won the door prize at the dance that night. It was T-Shirt signed by all the celebs, including Ward, June, Fred Calvert, Adam Becket, and others. I still treasure that shirt. I also found out that one of the greatest Warner Bros. animators, Ben Washam, had just started teaching animation at his house in the Hollywood Hills. All you had to do was show up on Wednesday evenings...

9

Working My Way Back to Burbank

If you watch the old Warner Bros. shorts, you will see Ben Washam's name on a lot of them, especially those directed by Chuck Jones. Ben was a charter member of the famous "Termite Terrace" group, the contingent of animators that worked in a converted Quonset hut on the Warner's backlot. In true animation tradition, it got its nickname because it really was a termite-ridden dump. During WWII, when the Warner's lot was near the Burbank Lockheed aircraft plant, the management got in big trouble for painting arrows on the soundstage rooftops to tell the (expected) Japanese bombers that the studio was not the aircraft plant! This resulted in a cartoon of the Japanese commander chewing out his pilots: "I ordered you to bomb an ammunition dump, not an animation dump!"

The Termite Terrace gang cranked out classic cartoons at an unbelievable rate. When you watch them you will notice that the name at the head of the credits is Leon Schlesinger. Schlesinger was a relative of the Warner brothers and knew almost nothing about making cartoons, a fact that was duly noted by the animators.

Schlesinger would make one visit a day to the hut, entering the single door at the front and walking down aisle, looking in every office to make sure the animators were working diligently. In one of the greatest gags done by the Terrace

DOI: 10.1201/9781003558231-9

gang (and there were many), the animator in the very first office rigged an electric wire from his desk all the way down the hut, through every office. The wire connected to a small light bulb underneath each animator's drawing board. When Schlesinger walked in the front door, the animator would flick the switch, everyone in the building would know Leon was coming - and stop working!

Everyone had a unique way to goof off. One guy would read a newspaper, one would clean his shoe heel, one would smoke a cigarette. Chuck Jones would clean his ear with his pencil's eraser. And they would all do this every time Schlesinger walked through. In two years he never saw anyone doing anything but those actions. If you watch Chuck Jones' Oscar-winning short film *The Dot and the Line*, the narrator mentions that the Line "cleans his ear much too often". That's a reference to this gag.

That is the kind of story we just ate up when we had the chance to be around the old veterans like Ben Washam. Of course, the master storyteller was Chuck Jones, the Mark Twain of animation, the man who I credited with starting me on my career. Chuck was always supportive of young animators. We could visit him at his house in Laguna and he'd tell us stories and even draw a signed sketch. A small circle of the guys became very close friends and mentees of Chuck, earning the nickname "The Dover Boys" after a group of characters from one of his cartoons.

One of the Dover Boys, Rob Minkoff, would host "Chuck sessions" at his house in Eagle Rock. Because Rob was a typical animator with few pieces of furniture, Chuck would get the chair and the rest of us would literally sit on the floor at his feet as the Master would tell tales and spout wisdom. His thoughts ranged from comical to profound. He'd tell us "you can't caricature a fish" because they look so bizarre the job's already been done. He's also say that he believed "animator" to be a "gift word". By that he meant that the title of animator was so special that you cannot pronounce yourself to be one. The title can only be bestowed upon you by others who respect your work.

Years later, when Chuck passed, Rob and the Dover Boys recreated a Chuck session by renting the backroom at the old Tam O' Shanter Restaurant. We sat at a long banquet table with a large, framed portrait of Chuck propped on the chair at the head of the table. And we told Chuck stories.

I started going to Ben Washam's house on Mt. Olympus Drive every Wednesday after work. It was only a twenty-minute walk from Spungbuggy. I'd join a group of other hungry young animators to get wisdom from the veteran animator. We'd sit in Ben's studio, watch films, and listen to Ben talk about animation. He had tons of artwork from his days at Warner's and MGM. He'd flip original scenes of Bugs and Daffy. The most valuable thing he did was create exercises for us to do.

Using those classic characters, Ben would us assignments, like Bugs tasting a bit of soup or Daffy pounding a nail into a board. We'd go home, animate the scene, then bring it back for a critique. Ben sent our scenes to camera and paid for those tests out of his own pocket. We'd all watch those pencil tests, and stand over Ben's desk as he went over each student's work. I would not be exaggerating to say that it had a Renaissance-era feeling of master and apprentice.

It was here that I learned new and more advanced concepts of stylizing action and individual drawings. Things like multiple images, stretch/blur frames, character contortion, and tricks of motion were fascinating to experiment with. As an example, if you were going to hit a character on the head with a heavy club, you didn't actually have to have the club touch the head! You could start the club downward, then, instead of contact, have both the club and the head suddenly spring in opposite directions. Viewed "at speed" it looked like a hard hit. That's the kind of trick that opened my mind to illusions of motion.

As my animation at Spungbuggy improved, I started to get the feeling that perhaps I was ready to try again for the brass ring. I applied for the Disney internship program. Instead of submitting the portfolio they still required (which I never bothered to create), I submitted a 16 mm reel of my best commercials.

To my surprise and delight, they told me I could take the "entry exam". This exam was a test scene of a little rabbit character from the film *Robin Hood*. The character was supposed to examine an arrow. That's it. The lack of direction was, I suppose, meant to test the creative imagination of the animator. I worked very hard on that test for the week they allowed, working after hours. I had the little rabbit look down the shaft of the arrow, then do a quick thrust of his arms so his baggy sleeves would hike up his arms. That thrust caused the arrowhead to fall off, surprising the rabbit.

After a tense waiting period, I got the incredible news that I had been accepted into the Disney training program. Although this was February, they asked if I could wait until June so I could start with the rest of the trainees, most of whom were coming from Cal Arts, the Disney-sponsored animation school. They explained that the training program was not a guarantee of being hired. It involved two more four-week trial test scenes. I agreed to everything. For a chance to work at Disney, I would have agreed to anything.

I had loved my Spungbuggy tenure. Frank Terry was sorry to lose me, but quite proud I had made the move. Since I had three months before I needed to report to Disney, and had money in the bank from working two years at Spungbuggy, I decided to fulfill another dream. I was going to Europe!

Animation across the Pond

My Polish grandparents came to America in the 1890s, and my German grandparents came over around 1905. Since that time, not a single member of my family had gone back to Europe. I have always been a travel addict (I visited forty-four states in that Ford Falcon van) so a European trip was a must for me. In the pre-internet age, it wasn't as easy to research or plan such a trip, but I did find the one explain-it-all guidebook for young travelers. It was called "Let's Go Europe", and it was the paperback bible for seeing Europe on $5 a day.

Before I left I bought my roundtrip airfare, BritRail Pass and Europass for train travel, and packed a small duffel bag. When I landed in England it was exhilarating. I noticed every difference about the culture of the "Old World". It was my start at becoming a mega-Anglophile. I was especially surprised and delighted when my Bed & Breakfast lodging that was costing me a mere four pounds a night ($5) *included* a fabulous "English breakfast" of eggs, sausages, bacon, beans, potatoes, and toast.

The first thing I did in London was head for Soho Square. I did not know much about London, but in 1977 every animator in the world knew that London was the center of the European animation community, and Soho Square was its heart. That's because Soho Square was the address of Richard Williams Animation.

DOI: 10.1201/9781003558231-10

Richard Williams was a young Canadian animator who had, from a very young age, been destined for greatness. His draftsmanship was astonishing, but his passion for animation was even greater. After winning awards in Canada, he crossed the pond because London was the unquestioned hotbed of animation within the commonwealth. In a few years, he had established his own company and dominated the commercial business. His commercials and animated movie titles were brilliant, hilarious, and sometimes jaw-dropping in their scope and detail.

I walked into the office on Soho Square without an appointment. I introduced myself as an animator from L.A. and asked if I might meet Richard Williams. To show you how small and informal the industry was at that time, Dick came right out! He greeted me and we chatted. He had heard of Spungbuggy. I mentioned that I had brought a reel of my commercials. Was I applying for a job? I said no—I just would love for him to take a look at my stuff and give me some pointers. He handed the reel to his receptionist.

Dick then took me on a tour of the studio. In addition to the many young animators, Dick had hired some of the old veterans. I met legendary characters like Emery Hawkins and Art Babbitt working at their desks.

Art Babbitt was not just one of the greatest animators in history. He was also the most notorious, having been the guy who led the cartoonists strike against Disney in the 40s. He and Walt Disney actually got into a fist fight at the front gate. I recalled years later when Babbitt was invited to speak at Cal Arts, the Disney board informed the college that if Babbitt came to campus the school would never receive another dollar from Disney. This was twenty-five years *after* Walt had died! What a vendetta. It was the classic case of Irish Alzheimer's: you forget everything but the grudges.

Dick Williams was devoted to the history and legacy of the artform, so he hired these older guys even if they were past their prime. Rumor had it that Dick would stay after hours and secretly fix their scenes so the work would pass muster. On this day, Art Babbitt was animating a scene from what was going to be the very first animated feature film from the Williams Studio. It was tentatively titled *The Thief and the Cobbler.*

Art's scene was a nice, simple character shot. Down the hall, Dick started pulling folders from a "scene stacker", a tall rack with shelves and showed me some of the more complex shots from the film. As he flipped these stacks of drawings, I could not believe what I was seeing. There was a scene of a wizard magically shuffling a deck of cards. All fifty-two cards were flying through in the air in magical patterns, and each card had the full face of the card in full detail. Remember - this was hand-drawn! The huge amount of "pencil mileage", as we nicknamed line work, was astonishing.

Another scene showed the Thief character navigating his way through a giant machine. Not only were their girders, beams, and rotating gears - the entire thing changed perspective as the Thief moved through it. In this case, the feat of drawing geometric shapes with such solid precision defied belief. This was ten years before computer graphics would make this type of shot possible. I was speechless. I had never seen animation like this. No one had.

Sadly, tragically, *The Thief and the Cobbler* would be a colossal nightmare for Richard Williams. His brilliance on short films and commercials did not translate to the demands of a feature-length production. He poured most of his company's profits into the film, but fifteen years later, he still did not consider it ready for release. Computer imagery diminished some of the amazement of shots like the moving machine and playing cards. And the film lacked a solid story structure. He finally accepted outside money from Warner Bros. Studios to finish the film, and exactly what he had feared happened. The people with the checkbook took over the film and completed it without him. You can still find copies of his personal version on-line, but the experience took its toll - as I will relate later.

But this day in 1977, none of that could be imagined. At the end of the studio tour, Dick took me to the projection room on the top floor. The entire studio staff was assembled. "Are you doing dailies?" I asked. "No," Dick said. "We're watching your reel!" I was terrified. But Dick William, the world's greatest living animator, was the world's greatest living animator because he had an insatiable hunger for learning. He wanted to see what was coming out of a Hollywood commercial house. Compared to what I had seen downstairs, my work felt pedestrian. But the crew applauded politely.

I spent the next few days popping into other London animation studios. Oscar Grillo, the talented Argentine animator, had just opened his own studio and would eventually do *Seaside Woman* for Paul McCartney. The biggest studio in London at the time was H&B. It was not the American H&B, Hanna-Barbera, but the British H&B, Halas and Bachelor. Founded by John Halas and Joy Bachelor, it was similar to its American counterpart in its large production slate of simpler fare.

H&B was best known for its failed attempt to challenge Disney in the theatrical arena by doing its big-budget production of *Animal Farm* in 1954. Whoever thought George Orwell's supremely dark and vicious story would ever make a great children's film had obviously not thought deeper than the idea: "Hey - it's British, it's famous, and it's got talking animals!"

Once again, thanks to the quaint nature of the animation industry, all it took for me to get a personal meeting with the legendary John Halas was just showing up at the office. He was a true gentleman. I still have his iconic book, *The Technique of Film Animation*.

Eventually, I made it all the way to Italy where my technique of barging in announced was equally successful. This time, it was the studio of Bruno Bozetto, perhaps the greatest Italian animator. Bruno was the creator of the famous character Signor Rossi. I had met Bruno very briefly in Los Angeles in 1976 when he showed his new feature film *Allegro Non Troppo* at the Nuart Theater. I loved that film. Bruno was, and is, a hilarious and brilliant man.

I returned to L.A. at the end of May. It was time to live the dream: Walt Disney Feature Animation.

At the Feet of the Master

In the history of the world, if you wanted to learn the art of character animation in its highest incarnation, you could not choose a better place and time than the Walt Disney Studios in Burbank, California, in the year of our Lord 1977. Hyberole?

First, it was *The Disney Studio*, the place that produced the first significant sound cartoon, *Steamboat Willie*; the studio that produced the first Technicolor cartoons with *The Silly Symphonies*; the studio that crystalized personality animation with *The Three Little Pigs*; the studio that revolutionized animated effects and camera work with *The Old Mill*; the studio that changed film history with the first animated feature film, *Snow White and the Seven Dwarves*.

Snow White had been produced a few miles to the East at the old Disney studio on Hyperion Avenue, but the profits from that film (it was #1 at the box office that year) allowed Walt to create his dream studio. The Burbank lot had soundstages, office buildings, a theater, and a backlot, but the centerpiece of the facility was the Animation Building. It was not just the physical center of the lot. It was the acknowledged heart of the entire Disney empire.

Despite the tall tale that Walt had designed it so he could convert it to a hospital if he ever had to sell it, the building was the ideal structure for animation the

 DOI: 10.1201/9781003558231-11

Disney way. Eight wings (A-wing, B-wing, D-wing, etc.) spread East-West from a central hallway. That meant that the offices on one side faced South, the sunny side, and had outside adjustable awnings and interior adjustable Venetian blinds so the artists could control the light. The offices across the hall faced North and had the ideal North (indirect) light.

Each wing had a receptionist desk to control access to the wing and supply clerical support to the artists. The building was state-of-the-art when it was built in 1940. It had pure copper pipes for its plumbing, heating and air conditioning. No matter what the weather outside, when you stepped through the doors of the Animation Building, the humidity and temperature were always perfect. Fifty years after it was built, the system still functioned flawlessly.

Most importantly, this building contained the people who were the legacy of the first Golden Age of Animation. Four of the original Nine Old Men still worked in the building, but much of the aging layout, assistant animation, and in-between crew remained. That mission of preserving the Disney legacy that I sensed during my first visit two years before was still in force. It was the reason I was now being allowed to audition for a part in the magic.

Malcolm Gladwell's best-seller *Outliers* made the case that there are certain precise times in history that provide unique conditions for change or innovation. The Disney training program would have supported his theory. After forty years of resisting to recruit and train replacements for the all-star animation staff, the toll of time had made this recruitment essential for the survival of Disney animation. The great Disney animators were now in their 70s. Remarkably, there were almost no Disney animators in their 60s, 50s, or 40s! There was one who was 39: Don Bluth.

Coinciding with this need, a new school, Cal Arts, had been founded by Disney a few years earlier, and as moths are drawn to a flame, every young student across the United States who had discovered that addiction to animation that I had discovered enrolled in the animation training program. I had mentioned earlier that I have often been inexplicably clueless about things I might be expected to know, and Cal Arts was one of them. I never heard of the school until I was in L.A.

That said, the talent that was to come out of Cal Arts would change the industry. It was a bizarre and blessed Gladwell-like confluence that they were there to fill the Disney vacuum. My timing was perfect. I would slide in with this group. Had I applied to Disney any time in the last fifty years, there would have been no training program accepting young talent. Thank you Malcolm.

Years later Annie Leibovitz would do a famous group shot of these superstar Cal Arts graduates for the cover of *Vanity Fair* magazine. In 1977, these artists were not yet famous. They were to be my new roommates.

On that fateful June morning, I checked in at the Disney front gate and was directed to Ed Hansen's office. I was hoping he had forgotten my comment about the clothesline layout. Of course, he had not. Ed forgot nothing he could potentially use on you. As he greeted me, he had that tone that always bordered between nice and something else. "You know you are the only trainee we have ever accepted who had no art school or portfolio?" he said. Was that *good thing*, I wondered?

Ed walked me upstairs to the second floor. At the very end of C-Wing was the large corner room where the trainees sat. There were six classic Disney animation desks, a few scene stackers, and—as reminder that this room was once used by background painters—a wash sink!

I met the five other trainees, four of whom would be my lifelong friends from this day forward: John Musker, Brad Bird, Henry Selick, and Dan Haskett. The fifth guy, Arlon Barron, would not pass the entry test. He would leave the studio, and I would never see him again. The rumor was he went back home to the East coast.

There was another training room across the hall, occupied by another new hire, Jerry Rees. Jerry would also be a lifelong friend, but this day, he wasn't doing trainee tests. Although technically a trainee, he was so talented he had already been pulled into production and was doing key drawings on the studio's current film, *Pete's Dragon*.

That's when I was told that, instead of starting my training test, I was to take an "in-betweener test" to see if I was capable of working on *Pete's Dragon*. Apparently the production was so far behind schedule it was all hands on deck. Since I was Mr. In-between from Spungbuggy, I passed this test easily and spent the next few weeks drawing the dragon. There has always been a delicious rumor that Brad Bird and John Musker intentionally flunked their tests to avoid working on the movie, but they both deny this.

The Disney Studio was a very odd juxtaposition of talented, naturally independent artists working in a curiously rigid and formal structure. We punched a time card on the time clock at the studio gate (just like construction workers!) and had to be in at 8:00 AM. We worked until 10:00 AM, then had our first fifteen-minute break. During this break, everyone went across the lane to the Ink & Paint Building to the "Donut Room". That's exactly what it was called, and what it served. It seemed like one of those old "Walt traditions" that you just did.

We worked until noon, had thirty minutes for lunch at the studio commissary, then worked until 3:00 PM when we had another fifteen-minute break. The workday ended at 5:00 PM when we punched out. We were not allowed to stay overtime.

As you might guess, after the rigors of the commercial world, this 35 hour/week schedule was like a vacation to me. I did pick up a bit of freelance after work, and I managed to complete a project I had started before the Disney test: an animated educational short film with the inspiring creative title *Making Change for a Dollar*. It was the last project I did for the folks that got me started back in Chicago, The Loop College Educational Media Department.

As you might guess from the title, the subject could not have been more mundane, but because it was an animated film and I was the complete creator, and because I like to throw parties, I decided it deserved a world premiere.

I invited my friends, including my new Disney buddies, and projected the film on a bedsheet hung from the walls in my backyard in West Hollywood. The guests sat on the grass and drank bottled beer. I rented a tux (my first!) and arrived with a blonde on each arm and a big cigar in my mouth. The mediocrity and small scale of the film was a perfect compliment to the overdone pomposity of my celebration. My friends ribbed me about *Making Change for a Dollar* for decades!

After that, I gave up doing freelance and focused exclusively on my Disney work. This was somewhat of a sacrifice. When I left Spungbuggy I was making $400/week. My salary at Disney, both during the training period and if I got hired, would be at the Union In-betweener rate of $187/week. But as I told my students years later, don't take a job for the money. Take it for the experience.

We finished production on *Pete's Dragon* and the day arrived when I would start my first test. This was the make-or-break two months of my life. I'd have to create two original animated shorts films, and if they got by the review board, I'd be hired.

For those eight weeks I was officially a Disney trainee, and as such, I would have the privilege of being critiqued and tutored by one of the greatest Disney animators, Eric Larson. Eric was seventy-two years-old but sharp as a tack. He had started at the studio in 1934 and had worked on every Disney classic film. He is perhaps best-known for his animation of Peg, the glamorous dog in *Lady and the Tramp*, voiced by Peggy Lee.

Eric occupied a room adjacent to our trainee room. He did not lecture us. We could knock on his door and ask him to look at our drawings. To this day, I consider those moments of standing over Eric's shoulder, watching his pencil magically transform my mundane work into something better, to be the most wonderful moments of my career. I do not exaggerate when I say that this was the equivalent of being tutored by Monet or Raphael.

For my first test I was given exactly four weeks to create a pencil test of a character. That means the final test would simply consist of my pencil drawings; the test would never be colored or completed. They just wanted to see if I could animate.

It was a bit intimidating because the subject was to be completely of my own choosing. They did not supply a layout or any direction. The other guys in my group were doing their own character designs, so I had to come up with something. Finally, in the "write-what-you-know" vein, I designed a human character that looked a lot like me trying to operate a film projector.

Here's the idea I had: he would thread the projector, click the switch, and wait - but the projector would not start. He would examine it, click the switch a few more times, and finally, out of frustration, pound on the device. When he did, it would jar loose the unplugged power cord, which would dangle below the stand. He would sheepishly plug in the cord and start the projector. With this story firmly established, I started to draw.

My little projector guy passed the test! For my second and final four-week test I decided to do an entire short film. I created a story about an alarm clock that has trouble waking up his human kid for the first day of school. For this, I had to create multiple layouts of the bedroom and dresser, and animate about twelve separate shots. That seemed ambitious to my fellow trainees, but compared to how I cranked out commercials, it did not seem hard to me.

When we had a shot ready for pencil test, we'd put it in a folder and a production assistant would pick it up at 5:00 PM and take it to camera. At Disney, with their own camera department, your film was always finished and waiting for you on your desk when you came in at 8:00 AM the next morning. We would wait for Eric Larson to arrive, then we'd ask him to view our tests.

Even if you didn't have a test that day, you would still join the crowd around Eric for the critique of the tests. It was a chance to see the master at work.

Eric had a huge moviola. Unlike the green commercial moviolas you saw in the rest of Hollywood, this one was custom-built in the machine shop at Disney. It was black, and had a gigantic screen that made the image easy to see. It had a foot pedal to make the film run, and a hand-brake and switch to make the film run in reverse.

Eric would hunch over this screen and run our tests. They were "on a loop", meaning the film, which was never that long because our tests were only a few seconds long, had been spliced end-to-end. The shot would just run and repeat indefinitely. Eric would let it run, watching the shot at least six or seven times before he would say anything. It was here that I had my most dramatic lessons in the vital importance of timing.

Eric would suddenly stop the film. He'd point to the image. "Add two frames here," he might say. Or, "cut one frame here". You would not think that 1/24 of a second would make much difference, but by God, we would change our exposure sheets, send the test back to camera, and darn it - it looked amazingly better! That is one of the differences between good animation and A-list animation.

Years later, when my fellow trainee Brad Bird became a very successful director, he was directing the Tom Cruise film *Mission Impossible - Ghost Protocol*. There is a shot where the villain plunges thirty feet and lands on the hood of a car. As Brad's veteran editor Paul Hirsch told the story, Brad instructed him to remove *one frame* before the guy hit the hood. Skeptical, the editor cut the frame - and felt the impact improve. "I had never in my life had a director ask me to cut one frame", he said. I like to think that came from our days learning from Eric Larson.

12

The Rat's Nest

John, Brad, Henry, Jerry, Dan, and I all passed our second trainee test and were told we would begin to do actual production work. We would be moving out of the trainee room and down to D-Wing, an actual production wing. D-Wing had the nickname "The Hall of Kings" because the greatest animators, like Milt Kahl and John Lounsberry, had offices there. We would be moving into the suite of offices that had been occupied for the last three decades by two of those legendary artists, Frank Thomas and Ollie Johnston, or, as everyone knew them in the business, "Frank 'n' Ollie". In fact, I would inherit Frank's desk.

I used to joke that when I went home at night and turned out the lights, that desk glowed in the dark from Disney magic.

Frank and Ollie had been with the studio since *Snow White*, were two of the "Nine Old Men," and had been leaders on every classic Disney feature. Since they finished their work on *The Rescuers* a few years earlier, they had been devoting all of their time to writing a book about animation. They were not secretive in saying that their goal was to impart everything they had ever learned in fifty years of animating into this one book. And they did. It is the Bible for animators. It's called *Disney Animation; The Illusion of Life*. It covered every principle of animation, with wonderful illustrations and great personal stories.

DOI: 10.1201/9781003558231-12

It was very exciting to be able to drop in on these two larger-than-life legendary artists and get a sneak peek at their work, talk about studio history, or even ask for advice on a scene. Whenever we had a chance to show some of our work to any of the older veterans, we hungered for blunt, true criticism. We were aware that, being nice guys, they tended to be a bit more gentle in their comments than we deserved.

Brad Bird had learned a lesson years before when, as a Summer intern, he showed his work to one of the most curmudgeonly of all the animators, Milt Kahl. Brad discovered that the one true response he could get from Milt was watching Milt's face the very first time he flipped Brad's scene. Milt's "micro-expression", be it irritation, disdain, or pleasant surprise, would be his true opinion of the scene, no matter what he said to Brad.

I showed one my shots to Frank Thomas one day. He made a few suggestions, but I was surprised when he mentioned my shot in a lecture. He was speaking at the Cartoonist's Union, giving a talk on animation, and the place was packed. I was there, of course. No young animator would miss it! Imagine my shock when he said this: "I was I my office today and a young animator named Bill Kroyer comes in and show me a scene he's working on. He says, 'Frank, do you think I should add this extra bit of business to the shot?'"

Frank then joked that my question was typical of a young animator. "When you're young, you want to put EVERYTHING into each shot. When you get older, and lazier (he joked) you just want to put in what *must be* put in. And that's a good thing. Because you want the important thing to be what the audience is watching."

So my personal contribution to a Frank Thomas lecture was about how NOT to animate a scene! That said, I did remember the lesson.

My future wife Sue had a genuine connection to their book. Frank 'n' Ollie called her one day and asked her if she would read their text. "Why me?" she asked, surprised. She was just an assistant at the time.

"Because you're the person we're writing this for. The young person who wants to learn!" Each week they gave her a new chapter to review. Sue and I eventual got copies signed by the authors.

The studio decided that we brand-new animators should cut our teeth on something less demanding than a feature film. Brad, John, Jerry, Henry, and I were assigned to a Christmas-themed short film called *The Small One*. The title referred to the small donkey that carried Mary to Bethlehem. Eric Larson had been slated to direct this, but after some apparent backstage maneuvering Eric had been replaced by the department heir apparent, Don Bluth.

Don was a very talented animator, but his taste and creative direction immediately conflicted with our little group. When he could, he would ask us to copy or follow motion that has been done in previous Disney films. Even more irksome, he began to lean heavily on a technique called rotoscoping, where live actors were filmed and we were supposed to closely follow - even trace - their movements.

The Disney studio had filmed live action actors since *Snow White*, but the footage had been used only for motion reference. No one ever asked, or expected, the animators to literally copy it. And they never had.

Worse, Don would not hire real actors to film. He would just choose artists at the studio to dress in biblical costumes and act out the scenes. In one case, one of Don's "actors" was delivering the line "But Small One is old, my son," and because he was sweating in his woolen robe, chose that moment to wipe the sweat from his forehead. Don insisted that the gesture be traced exactly.

"Look at that gesture," he beamed. "Who would have thought of that?"

Uh..no one, Don, because it has nothing to do with the emotion of the dialogue!

This process was completely at odds with the thing we had all grown to love about hand-drawn animation. Animation should be "designed movement". It shouldn't copy reality. It enhanced acting through imaginatively designed graphic images and motion. Eric Larson had one saying taped to his animation desk. If Eric Larson had *only one saying* taped to his animation desk, you could bet it was important. That saying was this:

"In animation, you should make the action stronger than it could be in real life. To do so is to take full advantage of our medium."

Notice that Eric did not say the action should be "wilder", or "bigger", or "crazier". It should be stronger. It might be slower, or emphasized by a powerful pose, etc. And he said it was *"our medium"* We felt that. Animation was our passion.

So even when we were instructed to copy live action, we did our best to make it feel like *real* animation.

Despite this ongoing friction with our director, life as novice Disney animators was living the dream. The atmosphere of the Disney Studio lot at this time was like an artist's version of Camelot. We had no production managers hovering over us with clipboards. We could freely wander the halls, visit our fellow animators, and look at their work. We could roam the studio backlot, which still featured the sets of an Old West main street and the Spanish-themed village from the *ZORRO* TV series.

At lunch you could sit on the grass and enjoy a live performance of the Firehouse Five + Two, the Dixieland Band comprised of Disney artists, including Ward Kimball on trombone and Frank Thomas on piano.

In the true spirit of the artists' salon, we had drawing classes in the soundstages. We were given life-drawing instruction by the legendary Elmer Plummer, and T. Hee (his real name) gave us instruction in design and caricature. T. Hee was not just a terrific artist, but, like Chuck Jones, a highly intellectual, renowned philosopher. One day he had us drawing using sticks of charcoal instead of pencils. When his stick became dull, he asked if anyone in the class had a pocketknife. No one did - except me. I carried my Dad's old pocketknife as a small memento. I handed him the knife, and he held it up, showing it to the class. "This," he said, nodding at me, "is a creative person." Why carrying a small knife would indicate that wonderful trait was never explained.

The most humorous incident of these classes happened a few years after I left, when they brought a live lion on the stage to be sketched by the animators working on *The Lion King*. Although the lion was supposedly old, very tame, and very sedate, it had to be dragged from the soundstage when it made aggressive movements toward one animator, Tony Fucile. It turned out that Tony had eaten Kentucky Fried Chicken for lunch and had not washed his hands. And that lion *loved* the smell of chicken!

Because we were still technically apprentices in training, the studio gave us time to revise our shots to perfection. To assist us, we had the greatest resource any animator has ever had, or will ever have: the Disney Studio "Morgue".

The Morgue was the nickname given to what is now referred to as The Research Library. This was a huge room in the basement of the Ink & Paint Building where every drawing of every scene of every past Disney production was stored. In our room, we had "drafts", or logbooks, of every film that listed a description of the scene and the scene number. We could make a list of the scenes we wished to study, give it to a production assistant, and she would return an hour later with a dolly stacked with a dozen priceless scenes. A stack four feet high of animation!

We would open these scene folders, and in our hands we held the greatest shots every made in the medium. We would flip the scenes, or carefully place the drawings on our pegbars and meticulously roll the drawings, examining every detail of how the animator had crafted the pose, designed the arc, or cheated the eye with some illusion. Here was the reason we looked at rotoscoping as sacrilegious.

We examined the shot from *Snow White*, were Grumpy, the cantankerous grouch who belittled Snow White, turns his back to the camera and weeps uncontrollably at her death. All you can see are his shoulders quivering. It was the most powerful emotional shot ever done in animation up to that time.

We looked at the shot from *Lady and the Tramp* where Trusty, the Blood-hound, lifts his head after he is told by Scotty, "Everyone knows you have lost your sense of smell." We studied how Ollie Johnson, the animator, had drawn the dog's face to create that profound expression of devastation and defiance.

I was able to study Bill Tytla's master work from *Dumbo* when Dumbo visits his imprisoned mother and nestles his head in her trunk and cries. I loved this shot so much that I briefly entertained the idea of getting the scene and sequence number tattooed on my arm, but decided against it.

Years later I was attending a screening at the Motion Picture Academy where the Visual Effects Supervisor was introducing the film with the state-of-the-art CG-animated *King Kong*. "For the first time, you will see animation that will make you cry". My friend Barry Weiss leaned over to me and whispered, "Hasn't this dolt ever seen *Dumbo*?"

As I reflect on those original drawings, I am still astounded by the exquisite artistry. Mark Twain once said that the difference in impact between the right word and the *almost* right word was the difference in impact between lightning and lightning bug. We were taught, and could see with our own eyes, a similar principle in the Disney animation drawings. The difference between a good expression and a great expression could be the width *or even the weight* of a pencil line.

Photos don't seem to do these drawings justice. If you ever get a chance to see original drawings of the classic characters, from Snow White through Peter Pan through Malificent, I think you will understand. Unfortunately, there are few places to do this.

I hope you can imagine the desire we had to try to approach the artistry of these scenes. We fully appreciated how blessed we were to have this resource. That Disney Morgue remains the greatest repository of hand-drawn animation that will ever exist. Sadly, today's animators don't have the access we did. It is even questionable what Disney will do with this irreplaceable treasure.

When *The Small One* finished, we were assigned to the new feature production, *The Fox And The Hound*. This movie would have *three* Directors; Art Stevens, Rick Rich, and Ted Berman. None of these men had been particularly notable in the glory days, but because all the A-listers were retiring, they were the veterans who were in the line of succession, not so much on merit as endurance. Nice people, but again, their creative tastes were clashing with these youngsters who, it would turn out, were mega-talented.

And lo and behold, Don Bluth, who was the Senior Supervising Animator on the picture, wanted to use rotoscoping in this movie! Our room in D-Wing became somewhat of a hangout for the artists who were against roto. I felt that the conflict was a bad thing for the animation department and wondered if the management was aware of it. I decided to do what no one in our department had ever done. I would go to the third floor and ask for a meeting with the President of Disney, Ron Miller. For a trainee animator, this was a bit like visiting *OZ: The Great and Powerful.*

Ron Miller was a former football player for the Los Angeles Ram who had married Walt's daughter Diane. He was an imposing figure, and admitted he had little studio experience when he took the job. He seldom mingled with the artists, so he seemed unapproachable. But when I asked for a meeting, his receptionist said, "Come back at 2:00 PM tomorrow."

The next day I met with Ron in what had been Walt's own office. It was almost unchanged from Walt's day, and it was hard for me to focus as I imagined the meetings that had been held there. I found Ron Miller extremely likable. We joked about football. Finally, I asked if he was aware of the "conflicts" in the animation department. He asked what I meant by that, and I explained our resistance to rotoscoping. I said that, if anything, the Disney Studio should be exploring some of the exciting stylization that was happening in hand-drawn short films. Ron asked me to set up a screening to show me some of the films I mentioned. I said I would do that, and left.

A few days later, we were all working at our desks in the D-Wing Suite when the door slammed open and Don Bluth charged in. He was quite upset that we had "gone over his head" and "bad-mouthed" him to Ron Miller. We explained that no one had made a personal attack on him - but we were against using rotoscope on Disney films. Don felt we were the "ringleaders" of a movement against him.

"This room is a Rat's Nest of dissent," he said, and stormed out.

We were momentarily stunned by the confrontation. But as we thought about it, we liked the nickname. John Musker's girlfriend (and eventual bride) Gale Warren painted a sign with beautiful calligraphy that she hung over our door. It said: "THE RAT'S NEST. The only thing necessary for the triumph of evil is for good men to do nothing."

I would certainly never think of Don as evil, but he was right about one thing. D-Wing became a rallying point for the anti-roto group. In contrast, Don was accumulating a group of artists who were being converted to his style of filmmaking. We started to call these folks "Bluthies", because to us they had an almost cult-like devotion to Don. Soon Don would leave Disney in a famous exodus and thirteen of these artists would follow him.

In retrospect, no matter our differences, Don Bluth changed my life. When my wife Sue moved to Los Angeles and sought work in animation, her Aunt informed her that her cousin's-wife's-sister's-husband's-brother was in animation. That person was Don Bluth. He let Sue work (for no pay) on his garage film titled *Banjo the Woodpile Cat*, and he subsequently got her into Disney. When I was evaluated by the Disney review board from admittance to the training program, there was reluctance to hire someone like me who had no art school or portfolio. "But he has a reel of animated commercials!" Don argued. So he got me in. And the rest is history.

We anti-roto animators labored away on *The Fox and the Hound*. I spent months animating the chase scene where the dog, dragging a huge barrel, chases the baby fox around the barnyard. For the young animators, it was struggle to try to elevate their animation to a "classic Disney level" when the story and direction were not inspiring. It was about this time that the unthinkable happened to me. I considered leaving Disney.

13

The Miracle of the Pencil Stub

Even if *The Fox and the Hound* was not going to be the greatest movie ever made, we continued to study scenes from the Morgue, and we supported each other with incredibly blunt criticisms of each other's shots.

We also had tremendous fun. I suppose that when a person spends their life thinking about and drawing cartoon characters, it might be an inevitable result that they retain certain childlike tendencies. One might say that people with tremendous imaginations that tend toward the comical and absurd would logically be natural comics and pranksters. That description fits the Disney animators.

My (future) wife Sue was the only girl in her suite, so she was the target of jokes all the time. She brought in a potted plant to add warmth to her desk, but it quickly disappeared. She began to get ransom notes made with pasted cut-out letters. The "kidnappers" showed they meant business by sending her a severed leaf wrapped in a handkerchief. She eventually got it back from the culprits: Brad Bird and Jerry Rees.

Tim Burton was a fellow animator who did not fit the Disney mode. He would pitch bizarre and macabre ideas for stories, and they would always be shot down. He would leave Disney and become a world-famous director of such monster hit films as *Beetlejuice* and *Edward Scissorhands*, but when I knew him as a young

DOI: 10.1201/9781003558231-13

animator he had a pent-up energy that produced outrageous gags. He once stood for hours like a corpse, silently, in an animator's closet to scare the guy when he opened the closet door. When Tim had his wisdom teeth pulled, he came straight to work from the dentist and walked up and down the tile hallways of the Animation Building dribbling a trail of blood!

Sue and I would often have fellow animators over for dinner and play board games. While most people simply enjoyed the games, Tim always reacted as if they were alien rituals he had just been introduced to. His "world view", even then, was totally unique.

We *Rats* started a gag that has become somewhat legendary. For some reason, and I do not remember what motivated this, the animators started talking about showing up for work one day dressed as pirates. We even picked a day. The plan was to put costumes on in your room and meet at the Rat's Nest at 4:00 PM on a Friday. For weeks we joked about "Pirate's Day" and wondered who would actually have the guts to do it.

Lo and behold, the Friday came at 4:00 PM almost everyone in the department showed up dressed as pirates. We sang pirate songs (*Whale of a Tale* from 20,000 Leagues) and started rampaging around the studio. We actually went into the Department Manager's office and held a cutlass to his throat! Everyone thought it was funny. We left work right on time at 5:00 PM and went to a restaurant to continue the party.

We came in Monday morning and discovered that our prank was not appreciated in the upstairs executive offices. Our manager told us that Ron Miller had said that if the animators had enough extra time to waste marauding around, perhaps we did not need as many animators. We shook our heads and accepted the critique. Then we had a thought. Why not show a bit of contrition and show up next Friday wearing suits and ties?

We did that. If you can believe it, that really infuriated the management. Now they thought we were ridiculing them personally! Fortunately, we got through the episode with no one losing their jobs.

Perhaps the most unique and special aspect of the 2D animation culture was the art of caricature. These were not just some of the world's best artists; these were some of the world's funniest and wittiest artists, and they could capture and caricature a person's appearance or behavior in the most hilarious ways. Every office had caricatures pasted to the walls. It seemed that the more extreme and vicious the portrayal, the more flattering to have been the subject! Because I was one of the few guys to go on dates on the weekend, I was always being portrayed as a ladies man - the human Pepe Le Pew.

The King of Caricatures was John Musker. To this day, he cranks them out, and the way he captures a person's signature features is amazing. Almost everyone in the studio did caricatures, so finally, Musker decided to showcase this with a yearly display in the studio library. This became the "Disney Caricature Show", and its three-decade history provides an incredible visual record of the animation department done in the most unique format. What is interesting to observe is how much more benign those caricatures got as the years went by. Not only did drawing skills recede with the coming of the computer, but the "woke" aspect of unintentionally offending someone dampened the content. Those changes could be considered a reasonably accurate measurement of how the animation culture would be changed by the computer age.

One rule that we all found absurd was the studio's policy of supplying us with art supplies. We were given one pencil at a time to draw with. When that pencil got too short to hold, we had to attach it to a pencil-extender and draw with it until it was a 3-inch stub. Only then could we take our stub across the building to Art Props and exchange it for a new pencil. Imagine a billion dollar corporation wasting hours of artists' time exchanging pencil stubs! John Musker did a hilarious caricature of this situation when he did a picture of the Art Props manager manning a machine gun, propped behind a wall of sandbags and barbed wire protecting his pencil supply.

This ludicrous policy, however, did change my life in the most profound and important way imaginable.

Stuck in line with my pencil stub, I started a conversation with that lovely young assistant animator Sue Evans. We had passed in the hallway many times but had never really spoken. I was having a party at my house that Saturday. I would rent a 16 mm projector from the studio (they did that in those days!) and borrow one of the Disney feature films, then project it on a bedsheet in my backyard. Since this was before video it was a great way (i.e. only way) for us addicts to study the films. If a bomb had dropped on one of my parties the history of animation would have changed, because I had most of the future Disney and PIXAR directors sitting on my lawn.

Despite this pitch, Sue Evans declined my invitation. I was quite used to being turned down by girls, but this time, for some reason, I was doggedly persistent. After seven refusals, I got a "yes." Sue came to the party, and we started to date. I had always avoided having romantic relationships in the workplace, but with Sue I could not resist. As it turned out, that conflict would soon go away.

One day a young guy named Steven Lisberger walked into our suite in D-Wing. He had a visitor pass, and knowing Steve, I am sure he charmed the studio into letting him in. What was rather astounding was that he was pitching us on his new project, and trying to recruit us. In our own office!

The project was *Animalympics*, and it was to be a feature film showing the Olympic games with animal contestants. Steve had a small studio in Boston doing commercials, but had sold this idea to NBC (it was also to be broadcast on the network) and he had just relocated to Los Angeles and needed artists. I immediately liked Steve. He exuded energy and a sense of exploration.

Disney's next project was *The Black Cauldron*. This was the film I had seen in development years before. There had been some incredibly wonderful and original design work done by Tim Burton, but all his work had been rejected. I did not feel positive about spending the next few years working on this picture.

Three years later, Walt Disney's nephew Roy Disney, Jr. and the film's Director, Joe Hale, would invite that year's Freshman class from Cal Arts to come to Disney and have a sneak preview of *The Black Cauldron*. After the screening, Roy and Joe asked what the students thought of the film. There was a long silence. Finally one hand went up in the back of the room. It was a young student named Ralph Eggleston.

Ralph was blunt. "Why does the film suck so much?"

Stunned silence. Roy and Joe walked out of the room, and Cal Arts students were no longer invited to studio screenings.

Years later, Ralph Eggleston, by then an Oscar-winner and famous Production Designer of the biggest PIXAR films, attended an awards dinner and sat at a VIP table next to Roy Disney. "Do you remember me?" Ralph asked Roy cautiously.

Roy was not sure, so Ralph reminded him that he was the Cal Arts student that had spoken up at the screening and said that Cauldron "sucked".

Roy thought for a moment. "Yes, I remember you," he said slowly. "And you were not wrong."

But this day, in 1979, I had only suspicions about the film, but I had seen enough to know that it probably be more fun animating animals doing surfing and gymnastics. I gave my notice to Disney. Our group of rebels had a farewell party for me. The suite at D-Wing was jammed with well-wishers, and John Musker did a monumental caricature of me that included the whole gang. They all signed that picture, which I have to this day.

Off I went to work for Lisberger Studios in Venice, California. An immediate benefit of this change was that I could continue to date Sue Evans without the conflict of the workplace. That worked out well. We were married a few months later. Sue Evans became Sue Kroyer, and we have been together ever since!

14

Things You Could Never Imagine

Venice, California, in 1979, was the last beach community between San Diego and Santa Barbara where you could still live cheap. And it felt like that. Although it was trying hard to gentrify, for every new, hip, modern house, there were four old adobe duplexes with peeling paint and bars on the windows. It was still a rough neighborhood. The fact that it was the Southern California headquarters of the notorious outlaw motorcycle gang Hells' Angels said something.

Steve Lisberger rented a warehouse at 1510 Andalusia and set up shop. If the entire scope of 2D animation production could be compressed under a single roof, Lisberger Studios was the perfect example. This may have been the last time in the United States that an entire animated feature film was produced in one building.

At a big studio like Disney, there were separate departments for storyboard, design, layout, animation, and clean-up. At Lisberger's, animators had to storyboard and layout their own sequences. Steve simply assigned each animator their own personal assistant who doubled as in-betweener and clean-up artist. We had five background painters cranking out color paintings, and my old Spungbuggy friend and industry icon Aurel Pebley had her own Ink & Paint department that colorized the entire picture. We had one camera stand that worked twenty hours

DOI: 10.1201/9781003558231-14

a day shooting pencil tests and final color footage, and Steve had one editor and one moviola to put it all together.

As often happens in guerrilla filmmaking, our crew bonded quickly, and we had a blast making the movie. Since I was the "Disney veteran" Steve appointed me as Animation Supervisor of all the animators, and the industry being as tiny as it was, I had an all-star crew. Darryl Rooney and Bruce Woodside would become successful directors of TV series and movies, Dave Stephan (my assistant) would be an A-list story man, and Roger Allers would end up as co-director of the most successful 2D animated film of all time, *The Lion King*.

When my Rat's Nest roommate at Disney, Brad Bird, was unceremoniously released from Disney due to "creative differences" I immediately offered him a position. The future Oscar-winning director of *The Incredibles* and *Ratatouile* sat at his desk on the balcony and created a gem of a sequence on figure skating. A bit of animation trivia: this is the only sequence on film that Brad conceived, storyboarded, layed-out, and completely animated by himself.

Animalympics was unusual for the time because it was fully-animated and done in an old-school, cartoony style. For me, it was the purest exercise in that magical process of "creating life" through animation that had hooked me years before. I got to invent and embody a variety of total different personalities, including a bobsledding team of Italian squids called The Calamari Brothers, an uptight karate duck named Bruce Kwakimoto, a raucous hockey-playing Canadian canine, and a new-age surfer-otter named Dean Wilson, voiced by Steve Lisberger himself.

All great animators have a desire to keep learning the craft, so as Animation Director, I tried to help by having guest speakers on Friday nights. Our crew would gather in the conference room and listen to an industry legend. Disney's Ken O'Connor amazed us one evening by explaining the thought and detail that went into designing the "Dance of the Hours" sequence in *Fantasia*. I had never noticed how the round shapes of the hippos were augmented by their circular dance movements, and the angular design of the alligators mirrored their linear movement.

I will never forget the lecture by Ruth Kissane, one of the greatest women animators in Hollywood. She stood at the end of the table with a stack of blank, white animation paper in front of her. As she talked, she peeled sheet after sheet off the pile, crumpled it into a wad, and tossed it on the floor. Finally, she paused to explain the message. Paper means nothing. Never stop revising your drawings until you have reached perfection.

One Friday, I invited famous Disney Art Director Walt Peregoy to speak. You would recognize Walt's work; he designed that modernistic, semi-abstract style of the backgrounds on the original *101 Dalmations*. Walt was a known curmudgeon but a fantastic designer, so I was a bit disappointed when he showed up at the studio with empty hands. I thought he would bring some of his artwork. Instead, he stood in front of our group and shocked us.

"You missed it. It's over." He said. He went on to say that the greatest animation had already been done. The Golden age had passed. We could never match it, so what's the point of trying? It will never be surpassed.

Needless to say, this was not the motivational visit we were expecting. But then - a voice from the back of the room. Steve Lisberger, who did not usually attend these talks, stood up.

"You are wrong," Steve said to Walt. "We're going to put things on screen that you could never imagine."

At that time, we appreciated the sentiment, but we weren't sure what Steve was imagining. That's because we had not yet heard of the project that was germinating in his brain. It was a movie called *Tron*.

15

It Will Remind of You Something You Have Never Seen Before

As soon as I finished my animation tasks on *Animalympics*, Steve told me about his idea about a gamer being sucked into one of his own computer games. Computer games were exploding into the cultural consciousness at that time. The Video Game Arcade was becoming as iconic as the Western Saloon. Like everyone else in our studio, I had played games, but I had never touched a computer. That didn't matter at this time. Storyboards were still hand-drawn!

Steve found a co-writer, Bonnie MacBird, and they began cranking out script pages. Steve hired commercial designers Peter Lloyd and Chris Lane to do conceptual art. Following their visual ideas, I started to storyboard the sequences in the script.

Tron had originally been conceived as a totally animated film. One of our animators, John Norton, did some hand-animated shots of the character designs. Instead of tracing and painting these characters on cels, as we did for *Animalympics*, each drawing was photographed and printed on a kodalith sheet. A kodalith was an acetate sheet with a black coating of emulsion. You would "develop" that sheet like a film negative and end up with a negative image of the drawing you photographed. In other words, instead of black lines on white paper, you would have clear lines on a solid black surface.

DOI: 10.1201/9781003558231-15

That kodalith was placed on the camera stand and lit by a light under the camera stand, or "back-lit". By placing colored gels under the kodalith it produced colored lines. By putting special filters on the camera lens, those lines could appear to glow, or sparkle, or do other effects. Using this method, John's characters appeared as "electric beings" made up of glowing neon lines. We didn't know it at the time, but this "kodalith process" would end up being the most monumentally gigantic task in the movie.

These first animation tests were interesting to watch, but it was apparent to us that a character made only of neon lines would not be able to convey subtle facial acting. Steve moved forward with the idea of making *Tron* a combination of live actors and animated effects.

Slowly, rumors got out about Steve's project. In a phenomena that would increase as the project leaked out, computer visionaries from around the country would flock to *Tron* like bugs to a nightlight. One of the first to show up at our Andalusia Street warehouse was Alan Kay. Alan was one of the "five APPLE fellows" who created that company. He was light years ahead of us. At the time, he told me that he was designing a computer that would be the size of a book. It would be small enough to sit on your lap; a *laptop* computer.

"How can that possibly work?" I asked. I knew there were no computer screens that thin, or batteries that small. Alan explained that his job was to imagine things that would be needed that did not currently exist so someone would invent them. He had complete confidence that by the time all the design and production issues had been worked out, those inventions would exist. It was my first experience with that kind of futuristic planning.

Eventually I would encounter plenty of examples of the opposite paradigm, i.e., the technology would already have been invented and no one had yet figured out how to apply it creatively. Both of those conditions would happen on *Tron*. With Alan's commentary and suggestions on the technology, the story developed with new technical sophistication.

The mood at Lisberger Studios was dampened a bit when President Jimmy Carter announced that America would boycott the 1980 Summer Olympics. Because of that, NBC cancelled the airing of *Animalympics*. Although our Winter Olympic portion of the feature had aired as a half-hour special, the entire feature was never to air on American network TV. By contract with NBC, it could not be released in American theaters. *Animalympics* became a very fun, lightly viewed relic that has only recently become widely available thanks to streaming.

The disappointment of the TV cancellation was quickly followed by good news. Steve sold *Tron* to Disney! This was hard to believe, but some changes had happened in Burbank since I had left the company. The Disney live action films had been performing very poorly, so Ron Miller took a chance and hired a confident young executive named Tom Wilhite to energize the division. Tom immediately sparked to Steve Lisberger and his bold, visionary project called *Tron*. Lisberger Studios would close, and a select few of us would be moving to Disney.

For me, that news was almost too good to be true. I'd be returning to the dream factory with a dream project. When the Disney animation manager was told that I would be returning to Disney, he informed Steve that I would have to resume employment at the Union pay scale I had when I left, i.e., an assistant's salary. Steve informed the manager that I was his Directing Animator, a pay scale far higher.

"That's not how we work here," the Disney guy said. "It takes years to advance to that salary." Disney was about to get one of their first lessons in dealing with the young upstart Lisberger. I got the raise.

I moved into a large story room at the end of A-Wing in the Animation Building. The first thing I did was try to recruit talent to work on the project. For starters, we just needed another story man to help me board the picture. To my surprise, most of the animators were reluctant to sign on to a "computer film." It was such a new thing that suspicions were very high. One animator that had no reservations was Jerry Rees, that master draftsman who was also a Rat's Nester. Jerry embraced the new technology and its challenges, would stay with me throughout the picture, and then go on to a career as possibly the most innovative and productive Director in the history of the Disney theme parks.

A "story room" in the Disney system was a large room with flat desks in the middle for drawing, and all the walls lined with corkboards for mounting artwork. These corkboards were framed with wood and called 4-by-8's because (surprise!) they were four feet high and eight feet wide. Each board had hooks on the back so they could easily be hung from metal "rails". The rails allowed the boards to be slid left or right without lifting them off the rails. This system had been unchanged since *Snow White*.

Jerry and I drew on pads of paper that were the same ratio as the film frame. We'd pin these on the boards using metal push pins. A small note of animation trivia: since these push pins had been used by story men for decades, some developed a skill at throwing them like darts. You could only do this curling the pin in the crook of your first finger and spinning it forward with an underhanded throwing motion. We became skilled at hitting targets with this method. In the age of digital storyboards I doubt there are five people in America now who have this "skill".

Jerry and I had only been drawing for a few days when our new teammate arrived. You cannot imagine our shock and delight to discover that we were to work side by side with one of the world's greatest artists, the legendary Jean Giraud, a.k.a. Moebius! Moebius had achieved cult status in Europe for his illustrated novels, especially the *Lt. Blueberry* series. He was one of the most astounding draftsmen I have every encountered.

Moebius quickly arrived at an economical, yet inspiring, drawing style for our storyboards. We would draw with soft Blackwing pencils (we were used to that) but quickly enhance the drawings with quick splashes of cool or warm gray magic markers. We only had six or seven shades of gray, but when used creatively they made the drawings appear more atmospheric and *dimensional*. That last feature, dimensionality, was critical and important because *Tron* had taken a new direction.

As noted, Steve had originally conceived *Tron* as a 2D animated film, then switched to a live action film with animated effects. Now he was actively investigating a truly ground-breaking approach. Perhaps the imagery in *Tron* could be made by computer! Although it seems hard to believe, *Tron*, the landmark film in computer animation, started as a project that did not consider using computers. If you knew the state of computer imagery in 1980, you would understand why.

At that time, the highest form of CG-imagery was the rotating TV logo. CG objects were simple geometry, and the motion was basic. More critically, the "resolution" or clarity of the imagery was suitable for a low-resolution TV screen but far too grainy for the big screen of a movie theater.

But that "bug light attraction" effect started to attract not just artists, but studios. Steve began receiving sample reels of CG animation from computer studios all over America. There were not a lot of such studios, but as he met with the owners, Steve was being convinced that CG animation for the big screen was possible.

Steve convinced the Disney management that using true CG animation for certain sequences was the right approach. What is truly remarkable about this is that he could not show the management any examples of what the imagery would look like, because, as 1980 began, *it could not yet be created!* Steve promised that they would invent the medium as they made the movie. To paraphrase, he was proposing to jump off the cliff and build his wings on the way down.

To do that, he would build a team that would, for the next two years, perform tasks on a daily basis that no one had ever done before in the movie-making business. One of the first artists that came into this fold was the creative director of one of the computer companies that had convinced him it could do the work. The company was Information International, Incorporated, nicknamed "Triple-I", and the artist was Richard Taylor. Richard was one of earliest pioneers of using light effects for entertainment. His Rainbow Jam company did light shows for the biggest rock bands. He had migrated to TV commercial work with Robert Abel & Associates and invented the "candy apple glow look" made famous by his commercials for 7-UP. He had readily embraced the challenges of adapting his creative vision to the digital world of Triple I.

When Steve met with Richard he found the partner he believed could produce the imagery he could not yet fully describe.

"I get it," Richard told Steve in an early meeting. "It will remind you of something you have never seen before." That phrase would become a guidepost for the production.

16

Board Certified

Once the decision was made to use CG animation in the film, it presented a new challenge for our storyboarding process. We were always being reminded that *Tron* was being done on a very tight budget, so it was not just important to create storyboards that told a good story - it had to be a story that could actually be made!

Although it is not often mentioned in the job description, the storyboard artist has tremendous power. One of the dirty little secrets in Hollywood is how shockingly few of the "filmmakers" and power brokers who make key decisions on a film have any ability to visualize the film they are making. This is especially true with live-action directors, who avoid the request to visualize beforehand by saying they prefer to arrive on the finished set and make "inspired decisions" on the spot.

That's why a storyboard artist who can take the script, along with some vague notions from the director, and transform it into the exact visuals that look like a film, can have a profound influence on a project. "YES! That's what I mean!" Directors will say! Quite often an original idea that the storyboard artist whips up with his pencil will be followed exactly by the set designer, effects director, etc., to the cost of hundreds of thousands of dollars. In the twenty-first century,

DOI: 10.1201/9781003558231-16

that power of visualization has now been extended beyond the storyboard to the art of "previsualization", where the CG artist creates a quick CG simulation of the proposed scene. It is remarkable to watch the side-by-side comparison reels of how faithfully the final film has followed the look of the storyboard and the "previs."

I had this situation occur in one of my *Tron* sequences. The script described an incident where the hero Tron was forced to fight, and vanquish, another character in a game. But the game was not described. It had been left for us to invent the game in the storyboard. I came up with the idea for "The Ring Game" where the players would stand on platforms made of floating rings. Each player would try to destroy the rings of his opponent. When your rings were gone, you would fall to your death. I just came up with this idea with no research or prior knowledge of anything similar in video games (and as it turned out, there were no precedents). Not only did my game concept make it completely intact into the film; it was also used in the *Tron* arcade game.

Jean Giraud/Moebius was moved out of his storyboarding tasks and switched full-time to designing the film. Steve felt that his soft, organic shapes were ideal to convey the feeling of the good guys, their world, their costumes, and their vehicles. In contrast, the bad guys would have a sharp, geometric tone, and for that Steve turned to the designer who had already been christened with the title of "futurist", the incredible Syd Mead. Moebius and Mead would fill our corkboards with designs of vehicles and environments, and Jerry and I would begin to incorporate these designs into the actions described in the script. But an important detail remained a big question mark. How could things move?

As someone once said, with great power comes great responsibility, so Jerry Rees and I understood that successfully producing the visuals on *Tron* had to start with us conceiving *producable imagery* in our storyboards.

We convinced Steve that we desperately needed to understand the rules of this new medium ("a man's got to know his limitations!") and started to have personal meetings with CG artists. Steve had decided on four companies: Triple I in L.A., MAGI Synthevision in Westchester, NY, Digital Productions in NYC, and Robert Abel & Associates in Hollywood. Each company would be cast to a specific portion of the film that best suited their technical capabilities.

This evolved into what I called the "symbiotic relationship" between our art and their technology. We'd draw something like a character grabbing another character by the sleeve and they would tell us, "Forget that. We can't do fabric. We can't even do wrinkles."

But then we would notice that in one of their tests, one solid object could pass right through another solid object. "Is that hard to do?" we would ask. "No," they would answer, "it's very hard NOT to do. We have no program for collision detection." We ended up incorporating that discovery into a character called "The Bit." It was a Tinker Bell-like companion to *Tron* who expressed emotions by transforming shapes — done with the exact "interpenetration" that the CG folks considered a weakness.

Robert Abel's company had a comparatively primitive technology compared to the other companies. Rather than render final images in the computer, they animated geometric shapes that appeared as white vectors on a black screen. They would photograph these to create the kodaliths I described earlier, then re-photograph those on a traditional animation stand using gels, filters, etc. Since that was the only imagery they could create, we cast them to do the entry into the gaming world, and carefully storyboarded a graphic sequence that matched their capabilities.

Jerry and I divided the script into sequences. It fell to me to do a major action sequence involving the vehicles we called "Lightcycles". These were futuristic motorcycles. Designed by Syd Mead, they were assigned to MAGI, because their simple geometric shapes were possible to create with MAGI's 'synthevision" process. MAGI had been founded by Dr. Phil Mittelman, who had invented the MRI machine, and Phil realized that if he made light bounce off surfaces the way waves bounced off bones you could make pictures. All of MAGI's models were constructed of mathematically-described shapes: a sphere, a block, a cone, etc. By assembling these shapes, interpenetrating them, or even subtracting them from other shapes, you could make an object. That's how they built the Lightcycles.

On my first trip to MAGI's offices in New York, I got a lesson on how things were built, and how they could be made to move. One thing that jumped out at me was the completely alien idea that an object could change direction in one frame. In other words, it did not need to curve around a corner. It could just switch directions 90 degrees in one frame. That seemed to fit the other-worldly nature of the computer world that we were trying to convey. I worked that into my storyboards for the Lightcycle chase.

Jerry and I worked for nine months storyboarding *Tron*, constantly revising sequences as Steve rewrote them or gave us new notes. Word was getting around about the film, and we had a stream of visitors in our suite. One of my idols, Kirk Douglas, walked in one day. I was so excited I could barely pitch a sequence to him. Moebius, although not boarding, was still our roommate. He liked being with us even though he did only design work. The actor Martin Cove (Cobra Kai) stopped by to see Moebius because he had been cast in a proposed film based on Jean's character Lt. Blueberry. If you ever compare a picture of Blueberry to Martin Cove, you will see the close resemblance. Unfortunately, that project never made it.

There was one famous visitor that I desperately wanted to meet. Peter O'Toole was to meet with Steve Lisberger about playing the film's villain, Sark. I considered O'Toole to be one of the world's greatest actors, and one of my favorites. I pleaded with Steve to bring him up to our storyboard room. I'd do anything just to meet him. On the day of the meeting, I sat anxiously waiting for the door to open and my idol to walk in. Instead, the phone rang. It was Lisberger.

"Get a cup of cold water and come to my office right away, "Steve snapped. He clicked off. I immediately grabbed a cup of water from the water cooler and dashed downstairs. I knocked on Steve's door.

The door opened and I was face to face with Lawrence of Arabia! I was momentarily speechless. I held out the cup. "Uh...did you want some water?" I asked.

O'Toole snatched the cup from my hand. "Actually I think I just needed to be burped." He smiled and closed the door in my face. I had had my brush with immortality!

17

Animation by the Numbers

Once we had finished storyboarding the movie, it was time to move into phase two: animation. After all, this would be the first time that anyone had attempted to create full CG-animation for the big screen, and in 70 mm, no less! This would be a bigger challenge than anyone had anticipated.

It's hard to believe now, but in 1981, there was no such thing as animation software. Technologists had learned how to build models, color models, texture models, light models, and finally, to "render" and film models. They knew how to position them on Point A and Point B. But nobody had yet given much thought to how to make them move with anything resembling natural, or complex, movement.

There were no external controllers, like dial boxes or a mouse, to help the animator position the models. Objects could be moved only one way: by rendering their positions in space frame-by-frame.

Even after you had "defined" its motion, you could not even watch a solid object move on a computer screen. Solid objects require more data computation than a computer could do in real time. The technology could only move vector lines.

DOI: 10.1201/9781003558231-17

These were some of the limitations we were learning as we approached the task of animating the twenty-odd minutes of 100% computer-animated footage on *Tron*. To add to the complexity, there was no standardization of technology between the four CG companies hired to make the imagery. They not only had completely different, unique, in-house software but completely different hardware!

MAGI, as mentioned, had their synthevision process that resembled an MRI machine. Robert Abel only had the vector-monitor system. Triple-I had the system that most resembled the future of CG. It worked with a modeling system that used polygons, so they could create much more complex shapes than MAGI. Their motion was still undeveloped, and they had their own homemade, unique central computer called THE FOONLEY. When the FOONLEY crashed, everything stopped until someone figured out how to reboot it. Digital Productions in NYC was similar to Triple-I on a smaller scale. And none of these companies could share any data.

Add to this the slight disadvantage that neither Jerry or I had ever owned or operated a computer of any kind. What we did have, and this proved to be critical, was the essential skill that all 2D animators had: the ability to completely visualize what we intended to create. When you sat down at your animation desk, and were about to spend days creating forty or fifty drawings that had to flow together as a seamless performance, you didn't just plow ahead. You thought it through—thoroughly. Shamus Culhane, the legendary Fleischer animator, said that no matter how much time he was given to animate a shot, he always spent 50% of that time just thinking about the shot. Knowing what you were trying to achieve was the surest way to achieve it.

So Jerry and I applied that age-old wisdom to our approach at computer animation. In 2D animation, the animator usually visualized his plans by creating small, quick drawings called "thumbnails." These small drawings, quick to make and easy to change or discard, were a good way to make sure that the idea in your head actually worked as a drawing. We did that for every scene.

For *Tron*, we extended that precision to our storyboards. Since the computer companies had no way to offer any kind of "preview" of what they would be building or animating, it put increased importance on us to make storyboards that were very close to what the final imagery would be. Not only did this allow Steve Lisberger to have confidence that what he was seeing in the boards would be what he would be seeing on the screen, but it also allowed everyone on the crew to be on the same page as far as what the shot entailed.

If you go online and watch the side-by-side comparison of my storyboard reel to the finished color version of the Lightcycle chase, you will see how closely the computer animation followed the drawings.

Those storyboards were especially useful to computer companies, who needed a clear visual direction of what they were being asked to create. Jerry and I were a bit shocked and intimidated to find out that the storyboards would be the only visual "animation" we would be asked to supply to the computer companies. Additional drawings were basically useless to them. All they could use from us was *numbers*.

As I mentioned, the CG companies could build the Lightcycles, Recognizers, Tanks, and other models, but they had no software to make them move. To make them move, you simply had to define where they were on every frame. In other words, to create one second of animation for a Lightcycle, I had to supply twenty-four sets of numbers, one set for each frame (remember—film runs at twenty-four frames-per-second).

What was in each set? The "world" of the computer operated within a space defined by the cartesian coordinate system. That meant there were three axes emanating from an absolute zero centerpoint: the x, y, and z axes where the X-axis defined left/right, the Y-axis defined up/down, and the Z-axis defined forward/back.

In addition, we needed to define how each model turned, so we had three more values for that: YAW defined turning left/right, PITCH defined rotating up/down, and ROLL defined leaning left/right.

I would have to supply a number for each of these six values for every frame. Therefore, for a three-second shot, I would need to supply three seconds × twenty-four frames × six values = 432 numbers! And that was for one vehicle! If there were two vehicles in the shot, double the number.

Since *Tron* was projected to have about 20 minutes of animation, we were looking at supplying over 172,000 numbers! There was no way to get around it.

I was beginning to understand why my animation compadres downstairs were not feeling the allure of this new medium of computer animation. The 2D animator lives by, and thrives on, his ability to draw. Drawing is not just a means of illustrating an image. It is a free, almost magical exercise in the exploration of visual possibilities. Since you are immediately connected to your pencil, and thus the imagery, with no intervening "interface" the creation is immediate. As you draw, you discover little changes or tweaks that seem inspired.

Almost every animator experienced what I experienced when animating in 2D, and that was getting "into the zone". That was an almost unconscious state of mental flow where you are in the world you are drawing. You feel the space and volume, you completely visualize all the actions you are creating for every moving part of the shot. It can be addictive.

What I was facing with computer animation was the opposite. The act of imagining the action was still required, but I would now have to analytically dissect that action and translate it into a form that had no spontaneous possibilities. It would be lists of fixed numbers.

18

Computer Image Choreography

Jerry and I divided the sequences on the film and began the task of animating. As mentioned, animated drawings were useless. Numeric values were the tools.

To figure out where and how a vehicle would move through a scene, we hand-drew the paths of action of the vehicles on graph paper, then placed dots or "hash marks" on the lines at precisely even intervals. Those intervals represented the frames of the shot. For a two-second/forty-eight-frame shot, you would have forty-eight hash marks on your line. Then, it was just a matter of using the graphs to give you the x-y-z coordinates for each frame.

For the rotation coordinates (YAW/PITCH/ROLL), we would supply the CG company with a "model sheet" of the vehicle that would define exactly how those rotation values would affect the positioning of the model. We would just have to guestimate the rotations on a per frame basis.

If there was additional movement on the model, like the rotation of a tank turret, we had to supply extra numbers for that.

In most shots, we had a moving camera. This was one aspect of computer animation that instantly and dramatically set it apart from 2D animation. A moving camera was not just dimensional; it made you feel like you were traveling through

DOI: 10.1201/9781003558231-18

the world. We moved the camera almost all the time, and as such, had to supply the six values of motion per frame for the camera.

We would send our graphs and numbers to the computer technicians, and they would manually copy all those numbers into their own software system. The CG company would render a series of uncolored, "wire frame" pictures on a high-resolution monitor (like a very fancy TV screen), which would be filmed by a camera. Since *Tron* was to be a 70 mm film, the very first motion test on which we could view our animation was in 70 mm! We would stand on the soundstage at Disney and watch our animated "tests" play on a gigantic screen. Steve Lisberger would view them with us and make comments.

I have to admit, seeing that CG animation at that scale, some of it unlike anything any 2D animator had ever created, was a thrill. This was motion we couldn't flip in our hands or shoot roughs to preview. We had to wait for it. And it was worth the wait.

It was a testament to our extremely careful planning that we had very few second re-takes in *Tron*. I cannot remember any scene that had three re-takes.

As we worked, the numbers were, excuse the phrase, adding up. After a few shots, we were wondering how we could ever complete the movie, not just for the sheer amount of data, but because the precision of the computer imagery required very accurate data for curves, acceleration, deceleration, etc. We were "guesstimating" these values. We had no computer to help us. It was remarkable to think that there was not a single computer inside the Disney animation building.

Something occurred to me. There was *one* computer on the lot! It was in the camera department. Just a year before, a clever technician named Bill Tondreau had developed a system to calculate camera movement for the Oxberry animation stand. If you recall, the Oxberry's tabletop moved back and forth and left and right, riding on gears controlled by dials. For decades, the cameramen operated those dials by hand, but Tondreau had the idea of replacing the dials with servo-motors driven by software. The cameraman would enter the start-and-stop values into the computer, designate the number of frames contained in the move, and the computer would automatically calculate the values of all the frames within the move. You could have those values represent a linear movement or one that had an ease-in or ease-out pattern using a B-spline.

This was our salvation! Instead of calculating every single frame of value on my animation graph, I would only calculate the "key" frames. I could then type those values into the Tondreau computer, hit the button, and in an instant, the computer would list every value for every frame - with perfectly smooth accuracy.

There was the slight problem that the Tondreau computer had no way to print out those values. I had to sit and hand copy them! Later, to expedite things, I started taking Polaroid pictures of the screen and just sending that to the CG companies. We never could have made the movie without that device. But how fitting! It was, after all, *computer animation*.

The Lightcycle sequence was one of the first sequences I worked on. As it turned out, this would be one of the most iconic scenes in the film. In the sequence, Flynn, Tron, and their friend Ram must battle three of the bad guys in a game where their cycles create walls. Through clever maneuvering, the player tries to force his opponent to crash into a wall and disintegrate.

As I mentioned before, the initial tests of the motion would be viewed in 70 mm, with the bikes represented as black-and-white vectors. Standing on the soundstage and seeing the bikes rush past, or viewing the shot where our point-of-view takes us through the maze, everyone on the show started to get the idea that we were creating something very new, and very special.

Since this was one of the first sequences in production, it was actually preceding the final decisions on the design of the live-action footage that would be incorporated into the shots. At the time, the thinking on the show was that the good guys (Tron, Flynn) would be colored with "warm" colors like red and yellow, because warm is friendly, while the bad guys would be "cool" colors, like blue and gray, because cool is not friendly. Admittedly, this was a somewhat intellectual rationale.

Because of that, when it came time to generate the final color footage for the Lightcycle sequence, we colored the good guy bikes as red, yellow, and orange and the bad guy bikes as blue. Months later, after numerous tests, Steve decided that the good guys' costumes looked much better with blue neon lighting than red lighting. That's why, in the Lightcycle sequence, Tron and the good guys have blue costumes but ride red bikes, and the bad guys wear red costumes but are in blue bikes.

We were constantly improvising and inventing on *Tron*, and a few other problems surfaced in this first sequence that required solutions. The computer only does what you tell it to do. In the case of the Lightcycles, the action takes place upon a grid that is simply white lines on a black surface, so the computer rendered all those white lines with the same brightness, making the grid look miniature. We wanted it to look vast. The MAGI technicians wrote software to create a technique they called "depth cueing". It was quite simple. The further away from the camera, the dimmer the illumination of the line. This made the grid appear to diminish into the distance.

In the opening shot of the sequence, the Lightcycles are supposed to magically form beneath the legs of the riders. The CG models of the bikes, which were built using MAGI's solid geometry system, could not do this, so a clever solution was used. The MAGI bikes were positioned in the scene, and that frame was printed out as a hard-copy photo. Using that photo as a guide, a visual effects artists named John Van Vliet, who specialized in light effects, hand-drew the bikes as polygonal models. These were transformed into kodaliths, backlit, and revealed using mattes to create the effect of the glowing polygons assembling into the final shapes. Then a dissolve switched them to the MAGI bikes, which accelerate out of the shot.

About half-way through production, we finally got a tool that you would have assumed we had all along. We got a computer! It was the Chromatics 9000, a device that, it turned out, could really do only one useful thing for us. It could provide vector images of our key frames.

The Chromatics had a cradle on top holding a standard telephone. We would get a phone call from one of the CG companies telling us they had our key frames to review. We would place the phone in the cradle, and it would begin to emit a series of beeps. It was like a telegraph; it was emitting beeps that corresponded to the pixels on the scan lines of the monitor. Like an Etch-a-sketch, it would literally sketch, dot by dot, an image on the screen. This took quite a few minutes, but we would end up with low-resolution vector images of our shots. These images would include the background model and any vehicles. In this way, we had one more intermediate way to confirm the staging of our animation. We had become so good at planning our shots that the Chromatics imagery was more of a validation than a game-changing tool.

What might really make you laugh was the way we saved these images. We had no way to save a "Jpeg" or "screen capture" the image. We had that trusty old Polaroid camera that we would just point at the screen and take a picture!

There are some images of me and Jerry in front of the Chromatics, but the one photo that has a notable historic footnote is the one of me alone sitting in front of the machine, my hand on the joystick, pretending that the joystick has some useful purpose (we never used it for anything). That photo made it into the cover story article on *Tron* in *Cinefex* magazine. *Cinefex* was the industry encyclopedia of visual effects.

From that day to this, seeing CG artists and technicians sitting in front of their computer screen has become as ubiquitous as seeing a couple holding hands in their wedding photo. What is notable about the photo of me sitting in front of the Chromatics is that it is the *first-ever photo of a person using a computer* ever published in *Cinefex*. What is also notable is that they got the caption wrong! They identified me as Frank Serafine, one of our sound effects guys, and had my name under the photo of Frank sitting at his electronic keyboard. Fame is so elusive.

As simplistic as it was, having a computer in our office at Disney, a computer *showing pictures*, not text, was still quite the thrill. One of the Cal Arts trainees started hanging out with us constantly, sitting behind me as I worked, asking questions about everything we did, enamored with the way the Chromatics could draw pictures digitally. You could tell he was really getting hooked on this idea of animation by computer. Sparking interest in that young animator may have been the most significant legacy of our production. That trainee was John Lasseter, who would create PIXAR.

Despite the lack of advanced animation tools, we felt we achieved some pretty decent animation in the film. Jerry did a shot of the Recognizers bouncing off a wall, and the boomerang action looks perfect. He also did an amazing shot of the Recognizer rising from a dump heap and assembling its parts, all with a rotating camera.

Some of our more beautiful shots were the easiest to animate. The Solar Sailor, designed by Moebius, traveled in a straight line on a beam of light. That was easy to calculate. Despite that, one of the more important shots in the film, where the Solar Sailor escapes from its hangar, had a mysterious delay. We sent this shot to Triple-I, who did all the polygonal models, and waited for the shot. And waited. Why was such a simple shot taking so long?

Finally, the shot arrived. The Triple-I guys were beaming with pride. The wall of the hangar, which had been designed as a sleek, metallic edifice, had been replaced by a distorted rock face that looked like crumpled aluminum foil.

"What happened to the wall?" we asked.

"THAT", the Triple-I guys said, "is cinema's first fractal wall!" It had taken them two months to write the custom code. They were quite disappointed when Steve told them to get rid of the fractals and restore the original design.

Following an old animation tradition, Jerry and I did sneak a few "Easter Eggs" into the film. These are little visual inside jokes. Early in the film, Pac Man makes an appearance in Sark's headquarters. When the Solar Sailor glides on its beam across the "Sea of Simulation", if you look carefully you might notice that one of the craters is an exact silhouette of Mickey Mouse.

As we finished our animation, the question arose about our screen credit. Since we were arguably the first artists to create feature film CG animation, how should our credit be listed? After some discussion, we thought it might be cool to distinguish ourselves from "just animators" to something more profound. The credit we chose was "Computer Image Choreographers." That seemed accurate at the time. It was, however, a title that never caught on. Although we were the first animators to receive the credit "Computer Image Choreographers", I think we are, to this day, the only animators to receive the credit "Computer Image Choreographers".

There was another publicity shot that had some unexpected symbolism. It showed me sitting at the Chromatics computer, Jerry standing beside me, and in the background, dimly lit, the traditional green film moviola. The moviola almost appears to be fading into the darkness, and it was. If *Tron* was the harbinger of the digital age, the device for viewing 35 mm film on celluloid strips was soon to be obsolete. In the 2010s, I would ask my film students if they recognized the green device in the back of this photo. None of them knew what it was.

19

Get Me 100,000 of Those

Although it may not be, in the strictest sense, "computer animation", the majority of the footage of *Tron*'s CG world was created using another process that was so bizarre and unique that I cannot resist explaining it.

Although the scenes "within the electronic world" purport to be a world of the computer within the computer, the only computers used to create that world were the ones attached to the animation stands that used the Tondreau software. Everything else about that production process was insanely hand-made.

Steve wanted to place live actors in a world that appeared electronic. After much experimentation, the solution he chose was to shoot the actors on black sets which would later be replaced by fanciful paintings. The actors would wear costumes that were white with black piping that looked like circuitry. All this would be photographed using a 65 mm camera. The electronic lighting would be achieved by re-filming every frame on an animation stand using that dreaded kodalith backlit process.

A curious detail was that the camera used on *Tron* had also been used to photograph David Lean's classic *Lawrence of Arabia*. The rumor that there was still sand in the camera case has never been verified.

DOI: 10.1201/9781003558231-19

The plan was to print every frame of the film on 11×17-inch kodaliths and re-photograph them on an animation stand to create the electronic, glowing look. By making positive and negative prints and selectively painting "hold-out" and "reveal" mattes, any number of different colors or different glowing effects could be used in the shot.

Of course, this meant using a set of kodaliths and mattes for every frame of the shot. Typically, there would be a minimum of ten separate pieces of artwork per frame. A typical shot would have the background painting, a protection matte to hold out the painting as you photographed the character, the character level, and all the mattes that would selectively colorize the shot. This meant thousands of individual pieces of art to shoot a single ten-second scene!

The process of preparing that art for camera was arduous. After the scene was shot, the "master kodalith" that showed the entire shot was placed on a light table, and a group of Art Directors we called "Scene Coordinators" would have to break down the shot into all the separate passes from each separate color. They had to write a "wedge test" for each color to test not just the color but the filter and exposure. I am trying to be simple with this explanation, but the process was intensely complex.

AND—after the Scene Coordinator had defined all the levels to be shot, the entire scene had to be shipped to an animation studio in Taiwan, where an army of Chinese artists would follow those guides to paint all the mattes for each shot. Most of what they painted was just black paint on black kodaliths. How boring!

When you watch the final screen credits on *Tron* you will see rows and rows of Chinese characters. These are for the Chinese matte painters. Because of that, years later, rumors started that *Tron* had been animated by Chinese animators in Taiwan. Fact check: Jerry and I did all the animation. All these folks did was just apply black paint to kodaliths.

Would you like to know how crazy this process was? Those black 11×17 kodaliths were acetate cels with a black emulsive coating. In the first month of doing film tests of the process, there was a very subtle flicker in all the shots. No one could figure out why. Then someone realized that the problem was with the kodaliths themselves. They were produced by dipping clear acetate into a "bath" of black ink. With every dip, the solution was slightly, imperceptibly diluted. You could not see it with the naked eye, but kodalith #50 would be 3% less dense than kodalith #1. You would not notice that if you shot the kodaliths in the progressive order, they were dipped, but if you shot kodalith #15 right after kodalith #42 you would see a flicker!

The solution was to number the kodaliths in the box and always, always shoot them in order. To make sure we had enough to do the film, they had to order 300,000. They initially had only 200,000, when they asked for the extra 100,000, Disney did not blink an eye. As the only major Hollywood studio that made animated films, Disney was used to ordering tens of thousands of cels.

Another odd problem with shooting the film for this process was that everything in the shot had to be in perfect focus. Normally, in live action photography, there is a limited depth-of-field where you focus on the main character and other things are soft focus. Since the characters in this film would be colorized using those kodaliths with mattes, all the lines had to be sharp and in focus, no matter where they were in the shot.

To do that, you had to have an infinite depth-of-field, and to do that, you had to "stop down" the camera aperture all the way, and to do that, you had to have a tremendous amount of light on the set. That's why the soundstages on *Tron* had a gigantic lighting grid. They drew so much electricity that they twice crashed the Burbank municipal electrical grid (the only time that ever happened in history).

Shooting every scene in the film with twenty or more levels for every frame ran up huge camera bills. Richard Taylor, the effects supervisor, would sit in dailies every day, surrounded by his Scene Coordinators, and pick out the problems that must be fixed. Because of the tremendous complexity of producing these shots, he searched for the simplest solutions. One was rationalizing that that any light pops or glitches might be attributed to the fact it was the nature of the electronic world. Richard had an overriding rule: "When in doubt, black it out".

Despite these challenges, the final imagery of these sequences was beautiful. Unlike future productions with digital light, these scenes captured natural light on film emulsion, giving them a richness that made them elegant and distinct. That insane process of filming in 65 mm, then re-filming every frame using kodaliths and mattes, had never been done before—and has never been used again.

When Richard Taylor presented *Tron* to the Motion Picture Academy's Visual Effects branch, he asked if there were any questions about the production. Dead silence. Even to the wizards of cinema, *Tron* was hard to comprehend. *Tron* failed to win any awards for its visual effects. We learned later that many of the industry pros thought we had somehow "cheated" by using computers.

Now, with the benefit of hindsight, it is remarkable to see that *Tron*, although receiving a cool reception on its release, achieved two things that very few films have ever done.

First, it had a completely unique look. To this day, you can view almost any single frame of the film and instantly recognize it as *Tron*. How many films can say that?

Second, it has progressively, continuously grown in stature not just as a pioneering achievement in film history, but as a created world that continues to inspire new projects. These include an exciting spin-off TV series, two theatrical sequels, and multi-million dollar thrill rides at the Disney theme parks.

Those thrill rides, as you may know, feature the Lightcycles, the sequence I storyboarded and animated. In a business where much of your work disappears, I have always felt incredibly fortunate that one of my key creations remains famous and memorable. When we go to a restaurant, and the hostess tells us there are no tables available, my wife (jokingly) nudges me and says, "Tell her you did the Lightcycles in *Tron!*"

20

Let the Digital Age Begin

The mood at the *Tron* wrap party was very upbeat. Steve had asked us all to dress only in black and white. I bought a black Japanese kimono for the event (which I still have in my closet). Jeff Bridges, who had been the coolest guy during production, showed up and held court.

I got to know Jeff a bit hanging out on the Disney sound stages during the shoot. He became a video game virtuoso by playing the arcade games Lisberger placed around the set. Jeff gave me a signed kodalith with his famous phrase: "Greetings, programs!" Little did I know that seven years later I would meet another Hollywood character that would have a profound effect on both of our careers.

We all felt we had made a movie that would usher in a new age of cinema. The first disappointment was the box office receipts. In a competitive field that featured *E.T.*, *Bladerunner*, *Raiders of the Lost Ark*, and *Star Trek: The Wrath of Kahn*, our film performed OK, but was not considered a hit. Worse, Disney showed no interest in using computer technology. My only option was to go back to the traditional animation department, where they were still animating *The Black Cauldron*.

DOI: 10.1201/9781003558231-20

For me, *Tron* was a very special experience because every day I showed up for work, it was conceivable that I would be doing something, or creating something, the likes of which no artist had ever done before. That was absolutely thrilling. I felt that CG animation was a new frontier. I wanted to be part of it. I left Disney again, hoping to work with one of the CG companies we had used on the picture.

John Lasseter, however, who had haunted our room during production, caught the bug just as badly as I had. He wanted to stay and force Disney into the new age. John knew that computers were not yet capable of doing character animation with the sophistication Disney required but had other capabilities. He conceived of a short film using characters from Maurice Sendak's book *Where the Wild Things Are* (Disney had optioned the rights) that would combine the two mediums. He would build the house in the computer, use his computer camera to fly through the house in a dramatic, dimensional motion, then add hand-animated characters to the shot.

Disney reluctantly funded the test. John used MAGI for the CG work, and drafted Glenn Keane, perhaps the best of the new young animators, to do the characters. In the cartoon, a little boy searches for his puppy under the bed, then chases the dog through the hallway and down the stairs. In a remarkable advancement for the time, they even figured out a way to scan Glen's pencil drawings and color them in the computer. The test worked and made a charming film.

But Disney was not excited. After the test was screened for the execs, Ed Hansen, the Department Manager called John into his office the very next day. "Well John", he said, "now that the test is done, I guess we won't be needing you anymore". And with that, he fired John Lasseter—and a billion dollars in future box office walked out the door.

Phil Mittelman, owner of MAGI, had a completely different opinion about the prospects of computer animation. He believed that Hollywood was ready for CG. He opened a branch office of MAGI in Santa Monica. I did freelance animation on a few commercials, animating vehicles similar to our *Tron* models. Then MAGI tried to make a big leap into film production. They convinced Disney that they could create a photo-real CG model of a steam engine, train cars, and train station for a live-action film *Something Wicked This Way Comes*.

One of the reasons our animation on *Tron* was successful was because we exploited the things the computer could do, and we avoided the things it could not do. In this case, MAGI bit off more than they could chew. Their software was not ready to create photo-reality. After huge expenses, and losses, the project was abandoned. This not only shuttered the Santa Monica operation. It had a chilling effect on the enthusiasm for the new medium of CG effects in film. All the studios knew about the fiasco, and decided that CG was not ready for the big screen.

It also had a chilling effect on my employment. There were not many opportunities for a freelance CG animator. Although paying gigs were getting tougher to find, it was clear that the interest in this medium was still growing. Because of my work on *Tron*, people were curious about the CG animation I had done.

I got an invitation for an expense-paid trip to the University of Calgary to give a lecture to their film students. I put together a 35 mm slide show and headed up to Canada. I arrived at the campus and asked to check out the classroom to make sure the projection was set-up properly.

My host assured me that the projectionist could handle things. He showed me the room. It wasn't a classroom. It was the school's main theater—and there were 400 people inside. A packed house, every film student in the school!

"Is this for me?" I asked. He said it was. Only for me.

An animator, as you may realize, is primarily an actor because the essence of the artform is to give a performance on screen. To do that, we do all the prep, all the thinking, all the visualizing that a live actor does. The huge difference is that we don't act in front of an audience. We act in the privacy of our own rooms, hunched over a drawing board or computer keyboard. The nature of that private focus tends to attract, or even create, a person who is by nature more of an introvert.

I had never really considered myself an introvert. I never had any trouble speaking to group of co-workers, or a classroom full of students. But I will admit that facing the prospect of taking the stage in front of a huge crowd gave me pause. I got stage fright.

I headed to the men's room, retreated to a stall, and tried to calm my nerves. As I sat there, I had a revelation. This thing I had worked on, this thing called computer animation, done the way we did it on *Tron*, was so completely new to the world that no one in that audience could have any idea how it was done. I could basically say anything I wanted and no one would know if I was right, or wrong, or anything in-between. That realization instantly calmed my nerves. In fact, that same thought permanently removed my fear of speaking in front of crowds.

Good thing, because it wasn't long after the Calgary talk that I got another invitation to speak in front of a much more intimidating group. I was invited to speak at the Lawrence Livermore National Laboratory in Livermore, California. This is the lab where they do some of the most intense research in the world on lasers, atomic particles, fusion, etc. They host many technical conferences attended by the world's most brilliant scientists.

A sequence in *Tron* was filmed at Lawrence Livermore. It's the one where Flynn is blasted into the computer. They have a huge laser that was the perfect set for that scene. Perhaps because of their connection to the movie, they invited me to speak at the conference. I was scheduled to go on right after the lunch break.

I attended the morning session and could not believe the dense and difficult topics being presented. At lunch, I confessed to our hosts that my talk, with my 35 mm slides about light cycles and recognizers, might be rather rudimentary for this crowd.

"That's why we scheduled you after lunch, to ease into the afternoon session", they told me. "You're the comic relief". My talk was well-received; I think even smart people like a little show-biz silliness once in a while.

I was lecturing about the computer revolution but was having a tough time finding work in it. I had to bring in some income, so I picked up freelance work doing storyboards. No matter how the medium evolves, there will always be a need for storyboards. It remains the quickest and most efficient way for ideas to be transformed into imagery. I storyboarded a rock video for Sammy Hagar, and the director, a first-timer named Gil Bettman, followed my board's shot-for-shot. Whenever I'd see Gil in later years, he told me I jump-started his career.

My next rock video gig was somewhat mysterious. I wasn't told who the artist was or what the song was. The director told me to bring my sketchpad and pencil to an agent's office in Beverly Hills. A small team of us gathered around the coffee table when the mystery artist made his entrance. It was Prince! At the time, he was the hottest thing in music, and his eccentricities were considered the byproduct of true genius. I happened to believe in that evaluation.

I was surprised how small he was in real life. He spoke so quietly that even in a room that was dead silent, he was hard to hear. Prince and the director started discussing visuals, and I frantically sketched away, trying to keep up. Prince would look at my drawings and suggest corrections, which I hurriedly supplied. After a few hours, the meeting ended and I went home waiting for the next step. Prince decided against the concept so that video was never produced. As a storyboard artist you hope that the project didn't fail because of your lousy drawings!

I was hired to storyboard the action sequences for a film titled *Malone*, starring Burt Reynolds. It was very exciting to be invited to Burt's estate in Beverly Hills, which was hidden behind massive 8-foot tall hedges. Burt was one of my favorite stars, and although I thought if him primary for his roles in *Deliverance* and *Smokey and the Bandit*, I was surprised to see the extensive collection of cowboy and Western memorabilia in his house. He loved that genre. Unfortunately *Malone* was nothing like that. He didn't seem excited about the movie. When it was released the audience felt the same way.

The post-*Tron* film business may have been reluctant to embrace computer graphics, but the TV business seemed ready to give it a try. Donald Kushner, the producer of *Tron*, managed to sell a TV series idea to Glen Larson, television's most successful and prolific creator. Glen was the man behind mega-hits like *Magnum P.I.* and *The Six Million Dollar Man*. The networks would pretty much green-light anything Glen told them would work. That's why ABC gave him a thirteen-episode order for Donald's concept called *Automan*.

The character of Automan was basically *Tron* brought to life—on a lower budget! Automan was an "automatic man", i.e., a computer-generated A.I. character created by a nerdy computer programmer named Walter Nebicher. Walter was played by Desi Arnaz, Jr. son of TV legends Lucille Ball and Desi Arnaz. Automan would pop out of the computer screen on command in the form of a hunky blond human actor wearing a spandex suit that made him look "digital".

In the movie *Tron*, those glowing lines on the suit were done by a very labor-intensive process. That wouldn't fly in TV, so they came up with a cheaper solution. Automan's suit had big patches of a reflective fabric made by 3M.

In post-production, the editors simply "keyed" a star field into those reflective areas. It made Automan appear to have a see-through body in front of a glowing field of stars. It sort of looked like a magical digital effect.

There was another character in the show that was also a rather direct rip-off of the *Tron* movie. It was called "Cursor", and it was exactly like "The Bit". It was a little glowing Tinker Bell-like sidekick that flew around and helped Automan solve crimes. Like the suit, it required a much simpler process to create. That's why Donald called me. I was to animate the Cursor. I would finally be animating on a TV series.

The idea we came up with was to have the Cursor appear as a rotating, glowing, faceted jewel-like fairy. We created a twelve-frame rotation cycle of such a character using computer graphics, but then printed those twelve frames as colored cels that could be photographed under the camera stand.

To match the Cursor's action with the live actor's action I used a device called a "beam splitter". That was a light that you would attach to the camera to project "a beam of light" through the camera lens. It basically reversed process; instead of photographing what was on the tabletop, it would project the image on the film on to the tabletop. I would project the live-action footage and then literally draw the "path of action" of the Cursor on the paper displaying the projected image. Then, I would frame-by-frame use a control box to move the tabletop to match the moving position of the Cursor on each frame. The cameraman would "cel-flop" my twelve frame cycle of the Cursor image as the tabletop moved the image along the path I had pre-recorded. The two shots would then be composited. Creating the Cursor using those techniques was tedious work. It did the job, and it was sort of "innovative", but flying a glowing ball around the room barely qualified as character animation.

The most fun about the project was that I got work out of a bungalow on the Fox Studio lot. In a bit of bad timing, the series *Mash* filmed their last episode the very same week I started, so I never got to visit that set. It was still exciting to be around live-action soundstages and film crews.

I also got to work with Michael Scheffe, the legendary vehicle designer. He had designed the NIGHTRIDER car, the DELORIAN in *Back to the Future*, and now the cars in our show. One day, Michael and I were invited by a friend to have lunch at another famous location: the studio commissary on the MGM lot. Like the Fox lot, MGM had a lot old sets still standing, and there were movie stars to be seen. The MGM commissary had a fancy executive section at the back, but we were dining with the regular crew folk in the main dining area. I was just starting to cut my fried chicken when I sensed a definite *hush* in the crowd. I looked up and there, walking toward me down the aisle between the tables, was the vision of Cary Grant.

I say "vision" because he did not seem to be part of the real world of the commissary. He wore a perfectly fitted three-piece gray suit that perfectly matched his silver hair, combed in a perfect wave that outlined that supernaturally tanned face. He glided forward, took the hand of his luncheon guest, turned, and disappeared into the Executive Dining Area. I felt the distinct impression that everyone in the room had responded as I had. We were in the momentary presence of history, class, grace, and elegance, embodied in that rarest of beings, a screen legend. I wonder who could elicit such a response today—or if there is an audience that would appreciate it.

Returning to the real world, my next freelance job came from a very unexpected source. My wife's sister, Karen Johnson, had an animation company in her hometown of Racine, Wisconsin. She had been doing reasonably well doing traditional animation on local commercials when she stumbled on a new market—scoreboard animation. This was the time when stadiums and arenas were installing "dot matrix" scoreboards to flash names, scores, and statistics. These scoreboards were basically just rows of bulbs. They usually only displayed type, but Karen had met the scoreboard operator of the Milwaukee Brewers baseball team and she learned that they could also display images if they were programmed correctly.

Karen started animating for scoreboards. She created some now-iconic imagery, like the screaming home run ball. You can see some of her work in the animated scoreboard sequences in the feature film *Major League.* Soon, she had almost thirty big-league teams as clients, creating animation for baseball, basketball, and hockey arenas. It was one of those clients who recommended her for a special assignment, the scoreboard in the L.A. Coliseum for the Opening Ceremonies of the 1984 Summer Olympics.

There were two huge boards in the Coliseum, a black & white dot matrix board and a color video board. The color board had been preparing imagery for months when someone noticed that the B&W board looked terrible sitting there empty. It was only three weeks from the show when Karen got the call to prepare something for the Opening Ceremonies on the matrix board.

Because we lived in L.A. it was an obvious choice for Karen to seek help from me and Sue. The three of us worked frantically for the next few weeks to animate, on paper, some animated images and the word WELCOME in twenty-five languages. The process required us to scan all these images into the Coliseum's computer. This was computer animation at its most primitive. The matrix board had a hundred rows of bulbs, but the scanner could only scan seventy rows at a time. We had to double-scan and "stitch" any image that needed to use the entire board. We tried, when possible, to use only the top or bottom or middle seventy rows of the board!

Worse, this very basic computer was not made to run imagery sequentially. It had been designed to just show still images, like typed scores. Every time we ran our animation, it ran at a different speed. It would not synchronize with the music of the Opening Ceremonies. We tried every trick, but it failed every time, including the dress rehearsal. There was discussion to not use it all in the real show. Finally it was decided to run it because it would be better than a black void on the screen.

There is a scene in the movie *Shakespeare in Love* where the manager of the Globe Theater, after enduring disaster after disaster, is asked why he remains optimistic. He shrugs and says that he does not know why, but no matter what happens, somehow, in the theater, it all comes together in the end.

We turned off the troublesome computer at the Coliseum and did not boot it up until five minutes before the Opening Ceremonies. We hit "start", and for the one and only time, it played perfectly with the music.

21

Animating with Crayons

I was hoping to find some opportunity to animate something more challenging than dots. Just across town, two *Tron* veterans were setting up a new venture to do just that.

John Whitney, Jr. and Gary Demos, the visionaries behind Triple-I, had broken off and founded their own CG studio called Digital Productions. DP had, without a doubt, a dramatic advantage over every other CG studio in America. It had the industry's only super computer, the CRAY-XMP.

How did that happen? John's father, John Whitney Sr., could be called the father of computer animation. In the 1950s he adapted one of the world's first computers, a US Air Force M-5 anti-aircraft gun director, into a device for generating CG animated geometric patterns. He made beautiful short films featuring hypnotic, complex graphics that no human could have drawn. The most famous of these films was *Arabesque*, a kaleidoscope of colored patterns. John Sr. had maintained a close relationship with the military, and, the story goes, convinced them that there was value in devoting one of the rare and valuable CRAY-XMP machines to something other than a military application. It should be used to make pictures.

DOI: 10.1201/9781003558231-21

The CRAY, as we called it, was unlike anything Hollywood had ever seen. The central processing unit was housed in a casing that looked like series of multi-colored refrigerators linked in a half-circle. In a bizarre design twist, a naugahyde-covered bench surrounded the columns. Because the circuitry ran extremely hot, the machine was cooled by liquid freon that ran through tubes around the circuits. To pump this freon and cool it, a huge 'heat exchanger" the size of a dumpster sat just outside the building.

The CRAY was so unique and so specialized that the manufacturer, CRAY RESEARCH, supplied a team of specialists for every machine. They were called CRAYONS. Their sole purpose was to keep the machine running.

The CRAY could process 3 billion calculations per second. With that kind of processing power, it seemed the potential for creating images was limitless. Of course, there was one limitation. Someone had to write software that would exploit that speed and still be usable by artists.

I got a call from John Whitney to come to their warehouse and see what they were doing. Remember how I said that no one had yet written software for animated movement when we did *Tron*? John and Gary were very excited because that is what they had now done. They had new animation tools, and they wanted to move beyond animating simple machine parts. They wanted to animate characters by computer. And I was to be the test pilot!

They sat me down at my new "workstation", a huge TV-like monitor called an E&S machine. E&S stood for Evans & Sutherland, the inventors of this device. It was the same one used by Robert Abel & Associates on their *Tron* sequence because the E&S machine was still the only computer that could show motion moving in "real time". The only thing that could move in real time were vectors, so any object I animated would have to be made of only vectors.

I would not be working on the CRAY. I'd be creating the animated movement of objects that would then be rendered in magnificent complexity by the CRAY.

DP was one of many companies in the world trying to expand the capabilities of CG animation. The discoveries and advancements made there were also being made by others, but with its visionary owners and unmatched computing power, DP was leading the way.

The first piece of software I was asked to use as their new "hierarchical software". This was the most basic, most essential tool for animating a character because it mimicked the motion of a connected skeleton. It's like the old sing-song "the foot bone's connected to the shinbone, the shinbone's connected to the knee, the knee's connected to the thigh bone," etc., etc. Although this may seem ubiquitous now, in 1983, it was a big deal.

The modelers had created a simple humanoid figure they called "block woman" because she was exactly that: a collection of vector cubes and boxes linked by an invisible skeletal structure. I could manipulate each box, and keeping true to the principles of a hierarchy, if I moved one box, all the boxes connected to it lower in the hierarchy would move with it.

In the model, the top of the hierarchy was the character's chest. My first request of the modelers was that they change the "center-point" of the hierarchy to the box that represented the hips because, as every animator knew, that's the center of gravity on a human figure.

The so-called "animation software" they were so excited about was still very primitive, and not very artist-friendly. To select a box to manipulate, I had to type in its name. These were abbreviated: UAL for Upper Arm Left, LLR for Lower Leg Right, etc.

Then I had to type in the frame number I was setting the key on (frame 1, frame 24, etc.). Then, and this was the most non-instinctual part, I had to *type in* the rotation values of the box. As in *Tron*, that was three values: YAW, PITCH, and ROLL.

I could not see the position of the box until I typed in all these numbers and hit RETURN on my keyboard. Then the box would pop to that position. If I wanted it to be two degrees less of a turn, I had to re-type that and hit return. It was truly "hunt-and-peck" animation!

It would take quite a while to manipulate all the boxes into what appeared to be a human pose, and then a similar time to do the next pose, and the next. The computer would quickly calculate the in-betweens, but always in a linear speed. To achieve variable speeds, like slow-outs, I had to manipulate the poses to change less between keys.

Another rather astounding limitation of working on the E&S machine was that it could it did not run exactly at twenty-four frames per second like film, but varied its speed depending on the number of vectors.

We solved this problem in the most mechanical way. I would set up a 35 mm camera on a camera stand behind my chair, pointed at the screen, then click through my scene one frame at a time as I clicked the shutter of the camera one frame at a time. We had a "developer bath" at DP so I could instantly develop my film and watch it on the projector. It all sounds amazingly primitive today.

It took me a few weeks to animate my first "block woman test". To give it some pizzazz, I decided to animate the test to the soundtrack of a new Mick Jagger tune called "Just Another Night". I had block woman strutting, walking, clapping, bouncing her hips, pointing, etc. It actually looked pretty cool. It was kind of earthshaking to see an object so distinctly inhuman (vector blocks) dancing in such a human way.

The test blew everyone away. This was a milestone - human figure animation by computer. John and Gary started to bring guests, clients, and investors to the studio and the first stop was my workstation. They would stare in amazement at my motion tests. "What kind of SOFTWARE is that!?" they would ask. "Key frame software" Gary would blandly reply. As if it was the software doing the animating.

Then my Block Woman/Mick Jagger test was seen by someone who really sparked to the idea of a CG woman.

That someone was Mick Jagger.

22

She's a Hard Woman to Please

MTV—Music Television—revolutionized the music industry when it started running "rock videos" in 1981. There had been very few animated videos in those early years, and none with CG animated characters. That may be why Mick Jagger believed he could make a splash if he used our new technology for a single from his first solo album.

I could hardly believe it when they told me that Mick wanted us do this. I had been a Rolling Stones fan from the beginning. When I moved to L.A. in 1975, I had hitchhiked to the Fabulous Forum in Inglewood to see the Stones perform because I felt that this might be their last concert tour. At that time they had been touring for twelve years. How much longer could they go?

We had a saying in animation: "If you can't make it good, make it loud and fast!" It was an old trick we used to cover up mistakes or weak work. I knew that our technology was still quite basic, but set against the fast-cutting and boisterous energy of a Mick Jagger rock'n'roll tune, it would work.

That's why I was a bit concerned when they played me the track of the song we were to use. It was called "Hard Woman", and it was *slow*. It was kind of a lost-love ballad. How would this work?

DOI: 10.1201/9781003558231-22

Our owner, John Whitney, immediately made himself the Director, even though he had little experience directing. I believe that he sold Jagger's people on the idea that this new technology could only be realized by a person who understood it. But John had some interesting ideas. He decided to set the action against a Southwestern design style. Like many videos, it wouldn't have a distinctly straightforward narrative, but be a collection of scenes that evoked the mood of the lyrics.

This was a project that was led by the designs, not the storyboards. John hired Peter Lloyd (one of the original *Tron* development artists) to conceive the backgrounds. The toughest design challenge we faced was the Hard Woman herself. As I mentioned, the only objects that could be animated in real time were vectors. Our solution: make the Hard Woman a "vector girl". Peter designed a female character that was a clever assemblage of just colored tubes. She was like a wire sculpture come to life.

I would still animate her as vectors on the E&S machine, but they had written some software code to capture the coordinates of those vectors and re-render them as solid colored tubes in the final imagery.

I did a storyboard for the video and we used it to breakdown exactly what live action footage would be needed for the short. This was the exciting part. We would be filming Mick himself for the video.

We rented a soundstage in Hollywood with a full camera crew. The stage had no sets. It was just a "green stage" with green screens. Mick would be shot against green so his figure could be easily isolated and matted into the animated environments. These sessions are expensive. Typically, the crew has a 7:00 AM "call time", and once they show up, they are all getting paid whether you use them or not. As they say in the business, "the meter is running".

So there we were, 7:00 AM, all set to go—but no Mick. 8:00 AM came and went, no Mick. 9:00 AM, 10:00 AM...no Mick.

It turned out that the previous evening he had been in Philadelphia, on stage, performing at the LIVE AID concert! It was a minor miracle they had gotten him on the plane to L.A., but he was pretty tired and had a hard time getting started on our shoot day. Mick, accompanied by two of his "mates", walked into our soundstage just after 11:00 AM.

Once there, however, he was a pro. We'd show him the storyboards for each shot, he'd discuss some ideas until he and John agreed on the final approach to the scene, and film would roll. We'd play the song over loud speakers and Mick would mouth the lyrics.

John had instructed the crew that only he should be giving instructions to Mick, but there were some shots where Mick would have to closely interact with the character I would be animating, so John would include me in those discussions. There was one shot where the Hard Woman would be shoving him, so I started shoving Mick Jagger until we agreed on the proper shove! Now, I thought, I can include the credit that "I once personally shoved Mick Jagger" on my resume.

One thing I remember about that day was how different Mick was between takes. When on the set, he was all business, a proper Englishman. When he'd take a break with his mates at the craft service tables, he'd revert to that cockney punk you knew from the 60s. To me, there was something life-affirming about that.

There was a key shot in the film where Mick plays his guitar, dances with the Vector Girl, then throws his guitar into the sky. I had had an idea for that scene that ended up working beautifully. Why not make the guitar appear to be a "vector guitar"? I remembered that on the very last scene in *Tron*, where the helicopter lands on the roof to meet Flynn, Steve Lisberger had put reflective tape on the helicopter to make it glow like a vector helicopter. We did the very same thing with the guitar, striping it with reflective tape.

With the late start, we struggled to get all the footage we needed. We did get all the shots, but in one key scene we only captured one take, and Mick happened to blow the lyric. He was supposed to say "dealing the final blow", and if you watch the film, he is mouthing something different.

Back at Digital Productions, we chose the takes of Mick's performances that we would use for each scene. This is where the production entered unexplored territory.

The usual process for incorporating a character on green screen into another environment followed one of two processes. For film, you would use an optical process to create a matte from the green portion of the frame, then use that matte and its reversal matte to composite the images in a device called an optical printer. For video, you could "key out" the green simply by choosing that precise color spectrum.

DP was about to do something futuristic. The 35 mm footage of Mick was scanned into the computer. The green portions of the frame would be ignored by the software, and Mick's image would be *digitally composited* with the computer-generated backgrounds, props, and other characters. That meant that combining all the disparate images would be wholly done within the computer. That had never been done before.

Another first was the process of digitally *mapping surfaces*. The buildings in the Mexican village were built as plain, uncolored polygons. Instead of simply texturing the polygons with colors, John had Peter Lloyd hand-paint swirled, adobe-colored paintings, and these were scanned and mapped onto the surface of the polygons. Another innovation!

My job of animating Vector Girl was somewhat straightforward for most of the shots. I could not have an actual background to work against because the E&S machine could only process one thing at a time, i.e., the girl. So I would have to study the environment she would be placed into and carefully imagine how her movements would fit that environment.

They did give me a new tool that made my task a bit easier. It was called a "dial box", and it is exactly as it sounds. It was a small black box that had six dials, one for each of the values I had to define (x, y, z, yaw, pitch, roll). Instead of having to type a value, I could simply turn the dial. Better still, as I turned the dial, the object I had selected turned with it! This added a bit more spontaneity and "feel" to the posing process. I could fidget with a dial until the angle of the object was just what I wanted.

The most challenging shots were the ones in which Vector Girl was going to appear with the live footage of Mick. To make this look right, I had to find a way to match her motions precisely with his, both in time and space. We came up with a crazy solution to do this.

I had mentioned that to test my animation from the E&S machine I had to photograph it off the screen with a 35 mm camera that was mounted on a tripod behind my chair. I realized that this set-up could be used in reverse exactly the way I did it on *Automan*—with a beam splitter. I would load the original 35 mm film of Mick into the camera, turn on the beam splitter, and the camera would project Mick's body on to the E&S screen.

I could now click and advance Mick's image frame-by-frame and match my animated character frame-by-frame to his image. If Mick leaned forward, Vector Girl leaned back, etc. If he kissed her cheek, I could position her head so he could reach it.

What I was doing was a modern technological throwback to a process that had been used in animation since Walt Disney did his "Alice in Cartoonland" short films in the 1930s, i.e., matching a live actor with an animated actor. But no one had ever done it like this. And with the rapidly changing advancements in the technology, few people ever would again.

This was rather arduous work. When it became obvious that I could not finish all the animation by myself, I recruited my friend Chris Bailey to come to DP to help out. A brilliant 2D animator, Chris was one of the few that had no trouble at all switching to a digital work process, and did a great job.

Other than Vector Girl, I had one more set of characters I had to animate on the film. These were skeletons that surrounded the girl's swimming pool. John Whitney had the idea of doing them with a sort of street-dance. John hired a local L.A. dancer to show me his moves. He was a Hispanic guy who did a style of break dance where he appeared to pop his joints. That's why his nickname was "Pop'n'Taco".

That kind of pop-lock style looked amazing when a real human did it, and it turned out to be incredibly easy for me to animate. All I did was set the different poses and let the character "pop" into them with no ease-in or ease-out. It looked very fun on film.

We finally finished *Hard Wonman*. Despite the shortcomings that bothered us, we had created something with truly breakthrough techniques. Unfortunately for us, Mick's song did not catch on, and the video did not get the playtime we had hoped for. In another bit of bad fortune, we just missed the deadline to submit the film to SIGGRAPH, the world's most important film festival for computer imagery.

Although I had been immersed in this new computer thing since the start of *Tron* in 1980, I was still an animator who identified with the animation community more than the computer graphics community. I didn't understand the significance of missing the SIGGRAPH deadline. Much like my ignorance of the existence of the Cal Arts animation program years ago, I didn't even know what SIGGRAPH was. So when the next conference came up in 1985, I figured I had better attend.

23

The "E.T." You Haven't Heard of

Way, way back in 1947, when computers were just emerging from wartime secrecy, researchers had the good idea to start a "learned society" for the advancement of computer science. That society was the Association of Computing Machinery, or ACM for short. As computer science advanced in scope, special interest groups, called "SIGs" were formed within the ACM, and lo and behold, by 1967, with computers actually starting to *make pictures*, a new SIG was formed to study graphics. That group was called SIGGRAPH.

SIGGRAPH held its first annual conference in Boulder, Colorado, in 1974, and 600 people attended. By the time I attended my first SIGGRAPH in 1985, its yearly conference had grown to 27,000 attendees. And here's the amazing thing about that number. That was basically everyone on the face of the earth who had anything to do with computer graphics.

During the last half of the 1980s, SIGGRAPH became an event, a phenomena, a "happening" unlike anything we will see again. Why? For starters, as I said, everyone in the world doing computer graphics (CG) was there. That's how small the worldwide community was. Because this was before the internet, nobody knew what anybody else was doing until you came to SIGGRAPH.

 DOI: 10.1201/9781003558231-23

The convention floor was loaded with booths of every tech company, showing off workstations, monitors, scanners, film recorders, and every kind of software.

1985 was the year when it really hit that CG imagery was entering mainstream entertainment. SIGGRAPH, up to then a technical conference, was about to be invaded by—hold your breath—filmmakers. The next few years would see the explosion of tools that would make CG imagery ubiquitous in Hollywood movies.

The place where you saw those landmark milestones was in SIGGRAPH's film show, the Electronic Theater, or "ET". The ET played for three nights, Monday through Wednesday, and the opening night on Monday was the equivalent of the Cannes Film Festival and Christmas Morning for CG geeks. The ET audience was unlike any other audience on earth. No audience had the technical knowledge and intellectual brilliance to match the ET crowd. They applauded and cheered wildly, not for Clint Eastwood or Kathleen Turner, but for a revolving DNA strand, or a wavy silk curtain blowing in the breeze caused by fluid dynamics, or a crystal duck sculpture lit by ray-tracing.

The ET audience was uniquely tech-savvy, but they were also just *an audience*, watching movies. They fully appreciated the advancements in complex modeling, rendering, and lighting they were seeing, but one night I saw a remarkable confirmation of the simple magic of animation.

It involved one of the very first applications of what would come to be known as artificial intelligence. Some CG technicians had created a very simple character. It was literally just a row of eight little square blocks connected invisibly. They had pre-programmed the blocks to move with the motion of a caterpillar. It would bend and stretch and squirm along. But they had also pre-programmed it to deal with obstacles. If it ran into a wall, it would automatically feel its way along until it came to the end, then crawl around it. If it came to a step, it would crawl over it. This was not an animator manipulating the object. This was the little object *thinking for itself.*

After conquering a few obstacles, the ET audience started rooting for the little guy. The caterpillar finally came to a stepladder that had increasingly tall steps. The little guy made it up the first step, then the second. The last step was clearly at its limit. The ET audience watched it struggle, fall, and then struggle again to get over that step. You could tell that everyone had become riveted with this struggle. It was a faceless, colorless collection of blocks, but because of *how it moved*, the audience had come to believe in it! When the caterpillar finally made it over that last step, the theater exploded with the loudest cheers and applause I have ever heard.

What a lesson! In the show that followed, there would be films that cost a million dollars, made by some of the top computer graphics companies in the world, with extravagant models and special effects, and those films would be met with bored indifference. But the little caterpillar-block character brought down the house. That is the heart of animation—creating characters the audience believes in and cares about.

Animation hit SIGGRAPH big-time. John Lasseter's short films, made at the newly formed PIXAR ANIMATION STUDIO, became huge hits. The fact that

CG could make animation that truly entertained an audience was earthshaking. John's films like *Luxo, Jr.* and *Tin Toy* were greeted with wild enthusiasm. They proved to the tech heads that CG could make movies.

SIGGRAPH had days of technical conferences and seminars on every topic, many on creating animated characters and environments, but nothing on the performance of animation. For the next year I proposed a course called "Character Animation by Computer". My proposal was accepted, and for the next five years I chaired this course, which sold out a 300-seat auditorium every year.

If there was another moment when that moniker of "Mr. In-Between" could be applied to me, this was it. I found myself seeking to bridge the old world of classical animation with the new world of computer graphics. I balanced my course speakers with brilliant technicians mixed with classic animators. I even had Frank and Ollie, the greatest of the Nine Old Men, talk about how classic Disney character animation could be, and should be, created in then new CG medium. That was a quality of those greatest of animators. They never stopped having that desire to learn and improve.

SIGGRAPH was like the ultimate High School reunion, and the big Opening Night Party, held right after the Monday ET screening, was the must-attend event. It wasn't just the fact that the party allowed you to mingle with all the folks you only saw that one week at SIGGRAPH. It was usually held at a cool venue. In San Francisco, it was held at the Museum of Fine Arts, in Dallas at the South Fork Ranch, and in Orlando at the Disney World Hollywood Theme Park. But the most legendary party ever was at the 1987 SIGGRAPH in Anaheim, California. Since the party was hosted that year by ILM, famous for *Star Wars*, I suppose the managers of the venue they chose recognized ILM as a legitimate business. We were all surprised at the location they chose: The Richard Nixon Presidential Library in nearby Yorba Linda!

While many of these opening night parties could get a bit wild, there must have been something about this venue that brought out the "imp of the perverse". Everyone just went kind of nuts. When I arrived, being a Midwestern kid who still had touristy instincts, I grabbed the opportunity to actually tour the Library (open for free, of course) and see how they had brushed over the Watergate thing. When I came outside to join the crowd, it was wild. ILM had hired fortunetellers, sword swallowers, fire-breathing jugglers—every kind of street artist you could imagine. The rock band FISHBONE was playing live, blasting music from a stage. They took a brief break to allow the featured guest, counter-culture icon Timothy Leary, to read poetry about the wonders of LSD. Lots of liquor was being consumed.

The legacy of that party is that the Nixon Library never hosted a SIGGRAPH party again.

SIGGRAPH eventually grew to 40,000 attendees, but with the advent of the internet, where everybody could see what everyone else was doing, it eventually lost its show-biz luster and retreated back to what it is today, a primarily technical conference.

24

Outperforming a Muppet

After that SIGGRAPH convention of 1985, I returned to Digital Productions to see what John Whitney and Gary Demos would come up with next. We did a series of commercials that kept introducing new CG tools. One of the coolest was motion blur.

When you photograph an object in motion in live action, and it is moving fast, the object will be in motion during the 1/24th of a second that the film is stationary and recording it. The object will therefore blur the emulsion on the film. Oddly, this will not look wrong when you view the object projected at twenty-four frame-per-second. Your eye will accept the fact that the object is blurred. In fact, it will look natural.

This phenomenon was an early discovery in hand-drawn animation. If you wanted to make a character appear to move really fast, you drew the blur! That wasn't hard to do in 2D because the animator could draw anything he wanted on a piece of paper. The only limitation was his drawing skills.

That was not so easy in computer graphics. There was no real camera, and there was no film emulsion. Making the object itself take on the shape of a distorted, blurred object would have been a very difficult modeling task.

DOI: 10.1201/9781003558231-24

The solution was, as usual, a software application. Our programmers created a distortion filter to alter the bit map imagery to mimic a true blur. Basically, the program would "average" the image of the object on the preceding frames and stretch and blend those images into the current frame. Of course, it's more complicated than that explanation, but to us animators, it simply gave us a new tool to make our work look better. One of the first commercials I used it on was for a car engine. When I rotated the gears, they progressively blurred. That was cool.

The biggest challenge we faced was building realistic-looking, stretchable skin. We had punted on that problem when we did *Hard Woman*. You could make a character with solid arms, legs, and a torso, but when the limbs moved they would interpenetrate the other shapes. We had a term for this kind of model. We called it a "cans model", because it resembled a collection on tin cans mounted on an invisible skeleton. A cans model could never pass for an organic body.

That was why it was quite surprising to us at DP when John Whitney promised Jim Henson he could create a completely photo-realistic owl for Henson's new fantasy film, *Labyrinth*.

The reason John got this opportunity was almost comical. A snow owl was a prominent character in the film, and Jim Henson was determined to have that owl featured in the opening credit sequence. Jim's vision, and he would not let it go, was to have the owl fly through an invisible maze (labyrinth) and illuminate the opening credits as it flew past them.

Henson hired a big-time Hollywood animal trainer to provide the owl. They rented a soundstage, built a maze set, and hired a full camera and lighting crew. On shoot day, the entire team set up for the shot, the trainer released the owl, and the owl proceeded to fly all the way up to the ceiling of the soundstage and perch itself on a rafter. Despite the yells, whistles, and pleading of the animal trainer, the owl stayed put. Eight hours later, they gave up on shooting a live owl.

Henson then built a "muppet owl" in the Henson creature shop, but when it flapped its wings, it looked ridiculous. The wings looked like cardboard slats.

John Whitney heard that Henson was desperate for a solution, so he pitched the idea of a CG owl. Jim Henson was dubious that it could be done, but John assured him that Digital Productions could do it. John was going to jump off a cliff and build his wings—owl's wings—on the way down.

At that time, no one had yet attempted to build a CG animal that could pass for a real animal, but as we examined the owl footage we had for reference, we came up with ideas we thought would work. For one thing, other than the rotating head, the only thing that moved on a flying owl were its wings. The wings were really just the assamblage of the feathers. If the owl just had to fly, you could do that without having to create anything that resembled stretchy skin or fur.

For the attaching the wings to the body and attaching the individual feathers to the wing, we could let those "bones" intersect like a cans model and cover up the joints with an added layer of fluff.

It was my task as the animator to make this bird fly. In 95% of the bird animation you have ever seen, it probably consisted of just the upper and lower parts of the wing flapping with some overlapping action. I knew that for a photo-real action, I would have to be much more detailed.

I studied every video reference I could find of bird flight, especially owls. I got reference books from the library with terrific color photos of birds in flight. I even went to the Los Angeles Museum of Natural History and was able to check out a stuffed owl in a display case. By minutely examining the wings, I learned that an owl has eighteen individual feathers in each wing. Each feather not only rotates up and down at its base but also bends and rotates. During an owl's wing flap, the feathers connect to make a solid surface to push the air during the downward thrust, but the feathers actually separate, like venetian blinds, to minimize air resistance as the wing lifts back up. The wing also moves in a slight figure-eight motion. It is somewhat like a propeller. It doesn't just flap downward, but slides downward through the air to force the air backward, giving the owl forward movement. Whew!

I would have to animate each of the eighteen feathers individually on each frame of a sixteen-frame wing cycle, with each feather moving and twisting on every frame. What made this even more complicated was that the feathers were extremely close to one another. This would have been difficult enough to do if the feathers were solid, but I was still animating them *as vectors* on the E&S machine, so what I was looking at was an incredible maze of white lines. It would be like dropping a package of a kid's pick-up sticks on the floor and trying to see through them.

It took me three weeks to create one sixteen-frame wing flap. What saved me were the capabilities of the computer that were not available in 2D animation. For one thing, having finished the right-wing flap, all I had to do to create the left-wing flap was to add a negative (–) integer on the y-axis to all my coordinates. This automatically "flipped" all the animation of the right wing to the left wing. To make the wings flap and flap, I merely had to copy the sixteen-frame cycle over and over.

Another nice feature was the ability to make my wing flap faster or slower. To do that I, I just applied a mathematical formula to "extrapolate" all my values from sixteen frames to any length cycle I chose. These tricks worked perfectly!

To animate the flying scenes, rather than burden the computer with hundreds of feather values per frame, I built a simplified "preview owl" whose wings were just two flat plates. They would still flap with the exact same twist and speed as the full wing but render almost instantly. I flew the owl through all the shots with this simplified owl because it was quick and easy to adjust the motion. After everything was approved, we replaced the preview owl with the final model.

To turn my "vector feathers" into photo-real feathers, the modelers made polygonal models of each individual feather. Our painter then painted very realistic paintings of the feathers. Those paintings were scanned into the computer and mapped on to the polygons. Because an owl's wing has very light, fragile "fluff" on the edges of the feathers, we created a "transparency map" that would ramp that painting from 100% visible on the feather to gradually disappearing at the edge. We did similar paintings for the body, legs, and feet. All of these processes were state-of-the-art at this time.

The owl's head, however, was a special problem. In those days, computer models were built on an "encoding table". This was basically a big drafting table that had hundreds of wires arranged in a grid right below the surface. Everywhere these wires intersected, or crossed, was a "point". The modeler had hand-drawn design drawings of the object he was building. The drawings usually were a front view and side view of the object, so all the dimensions were visible. He placed those drawings on the encoding table and painstakingly used his "mouse" to click along the lines of the drawing, creating points in space that would then be connected as polygons. That was how you made a dimensional model.

To draw a front view and a perfectly matching side view of a simple object, like a cube or a barn, required precision. Trying to draw a complicated organic shape, like a real owl, was almost impossible.

We solved this problem by doing what may have been the world's first "3D digital scan". First, I commissioned one of my 2D animator friends, Kathy Zielinski, to sculpt a model of an owl head. We gave her the photos of a real snow owl, and she came in a week later with a beautiful plaster head about twenty-two inches high. We painted this sculpture flat black. We mounted it on a record turntable (remember how people used to listen to vinyl record albums?) and drew 182 little marks on the wheel. We took a 35 mm slide that was solid black and, using an exacto knife, slit a razor-thin line down the center. When we put that slide into the projector, it projected a straight, fine white line. When we projected that line on to our black owl sculpture, the white line distorted as it followed the contour of the head.

We pointed a 35mm camera at the sculpture with the white line projected on it. Then we proceeded to rotate the head to each hash mark and take another picture. We ended up with 182 squiggly white lines on 182 frames of film. Those 182 frames were scanned into the computer. The software guys wrote a program to have the computer take each line, rotate them two degrees each, and connect them from the top in 3d cartesian space. When that was done, we had 182 white lines in a vertical, circular pattern. It looked somewhat like a wire birdcage shaped like the owl's head.

Then, the software just divided the lines with horizontal lines and we ended up with a polygonal model of the owl's head. It was a perfect wireframe duplicate. But how to color it?

The guys wrote software to take those polygons and spread them out, using the top of the owl's head as the centerpoint. It was like smashing the model flat on to a table. That's why we nicknamed it "the road kill owl". We printed that smashed polygonal shape on to a big piece of paper.

Then our painter hand-painted an absolutely realistic painting of all the feathers, beak, and eyeballs of a real owl on to the paper, but distorting the color to fit the smashed, distorted shape. We scanned that "road kill" painting back into the computer. Another software program wrapped that painting around the polygonal model. Like magic, we had very organic, very complicated, very real-looking 3D owl head.

If you watch the opening titles of *Labyrinth*, and look carefully at the close up of the owl's head, you can see the radiating lines coming out of the very top of its head.

In motion, however, no one would notice those lines unless they were really looking for them. Jim Henson didn't notice them, and in the end, we provided the opening titles of *Labyrinth* with what historically could be claimed to be the first photo-real animal in the history of computer animation.

25

Dead on Arrival

Digital Productions was my first experience working on staff in a computer graphics company. I hesitated to call it a computer *animation studio* because Chris Bailey and I were the only two true animators on the staff of sixty people. There were some similarities to an animation environment. There were a lot of young people working around you—but there were no "old veterans". The industry was so new that no one over forty years old could be found. Most of the folks were technical. They were very smart but often rather "left brain" analytical and not as comical as an animator. No caricatures!

The environment itself was different. At DP, the warehouse was always freezing, because in those days even small computer workstations would overheat if they were not in a cool environment. We all wore sweaters, and we drank hot coffee constantly. I found myself getting the jitters from too much caffeine, so I solved that problem by just drinking cups of hot water. Plain hot water.

One very big difference between DP and an animation studio was the absence of the time clock. No one punched in and out. You were generally expected to show up sometime before lunch, but the simple requirement was to get your work done on time. This approach was possible because of, and benefited from, what continues to be a curious phenomenon.

DOI: 10.1201/9781003558231-25

Computers can be addictive.

I had not really experienced this allure in full force before I came to DP because, as I have described, much of my work was not actually working on the computer, but planning movements, graphing out movements, etc. When I started to actually sit at a workstation and have instantaneous feedback on the screen from every action I performed, I started to feel the hook. I was getting that "food pellet" feedback loop so widely recognized now. I noticed how few of my DP colleagues left their desks during work hours. They stayed hunched over their keyboards, mesmerized. It was easy, in fact the norm, to have no idea how much time you had been working since you last took a break. The fact that our warehouse had no windows or clocks (like a Vegas casino!) supported that habit.

When I was working on the owl wing, I was so immersed in my concentration on the vector images that I would sometimes work all night and hardly notice. I'd look at my watch and realize it was 4:30 AM. It became a ritual among us all-nighters to take turns running to McDonalds when it opened at 6:00 AM to fetch breakfast. My wife found this troubling, but it was obvious to her that I was not staying away from home because of any problem. I was staying at my workstation because I was experiencing, in my own way, those rare moments of artistic discovery that could be traced back to my winking snake so may years ago.

We felt we were doing magical things at Digital Productions. Imagine my shock when I showed up one morning and found the doors locked, with Security Guards telling me that the company was closed.

This was the great "crash and burn" of L.A. computer graphics.

In 1986, three companies dominated the CG animation business in Los Angeles. One was my employer, Digital Productions.

The second was Robert Abel & Associates. Bob Abel was an absolutely brilliant artist and commercial director but an even better salesman. He built his commercial studio into a juggernaut, hiring the very best designers, directors, and technicians to create ground-breaking imagery. He recognized the possibilities of the computer very early. His studio had been one of the four subcontractors on *Tron*. Abel had done the "entry to the computer world" sequence using his E&S vector workstations.

Bob Abel pushed into the CG arena by creating a new subsidiary called Abel Image Research (AIR). His crew was writing their own code to compete with Digital Productions. Although they were behind DP in technical tools, they made up for that with very clever and dramatic design and visual effects applications.

The third company in the mix was Omnibus Computer Graphics. This company was a bit of a mystery to us. Most of us at DP knew the Abel employees, and had even worked with them at previous commercial companies. We didn't know many of the Omnibus people. That's because it was a Canadian-owned company that had started in Toronto and only recently moved to L.A. They were isolated because their office was located on the Paramount lot. To visit them you had to get a pass to enter the lot, which you only did if you had business with them. No drop-ins.

I have never learned exactly what motivated them to do what they did, whether it was a misguided visionary or the glamour of Hollywood, but at the end of 1986, the Omnibus folks decided that the computer graphics industry was the future of Hollywood, and its complete domination was in their grasp. That's because both Digital Productions and Robert Abel had a lot of debt.

I hear that Bob Abel struck a deal to sell his company, but John and Gary would never have sold Digital Productions. The Omnibus people secured a multimillion-dollar loan from The Royal Bank of Canada and bought DP's debt. That gave them control of the company. I don't think John and Gary ever saw that coming. They were unceremoniously escorted from their own building, and when we showed up, the doors were locked and Omnibus was in charge. It was the end of Digital Productions.

The new owners decided to temporarily brand the new company with Robert Abel's AIR logo. Although they had not hired back any of us from DP, I did attend the press conference were Bob Abel proclaimed that this merger was a terrific thing. He said he "couldn't wait to get his AIR software running on that CRAY". Even I, who had the most rudimentary understanding of coding, thought that was the most naive statement I had ever heard.

Although I was now technically unemployed, I had been already invited to Monte Carlo to talk about the *Labyrinth* owl. This was at a conference called IMAGINA, which was the European version of SIGGRAPH. It would be a lot of fun, and I would get to meet Prince Albert of Monaco, so I went. When I checked into the Lowe's Hotel, and they asked for my company affiliation, I said Robert Abel & Associates since DP had been closed down.

When I went to check out five days later, instead of a free pre-paid room they presented me with a bill for $2500.00! How could this be? The manager explained to me that Robert Abel himself had attended the conference last year and never paid his hotel bill. Since I worked for him, it was now my bill!

Luckily for me, one of my close friends, Jeff Kleiser, was also at the conference. A real superstar CG guy, he was still solidly employed at Abel. I pleaded with him to take the bill because he had a good chance of getting the company to cover it. He did, and they did. Thank you Jeff!

Ironically, while I was away, the Omnibus people agreed to open the doors at the Digital Productions office and let the former employees inside for two hours to retrieve their personal belongings. The Omnibus people had refused to pay any of the back pay we had been owed when they took over. Chris Bailey went in to the office that day with a duffel bag, picked up the few personal items from his desk and mine, then quietly grabbed that *Labyrinth* owl head sculpture and dropped it in his bag.

When I returned from Monte Carlo Chris gave me the owl head. "The back pay they owe you", he said. I still have that owl head on a pedestal in my house.

Trying to consolidate the three biggest CG companies into one entity, particularly when none of the three was actually financially viable, quickly turned into a total fiasco. We had nicknamed the entity "Digital-Omnibus-Abel—D.O.A.".

Just a few months later Omnibus defaulted on the loan, went bankrupt, and closed the doors. The super-company was truly *Dead on Arrival*, and they managed to put all three workforces out of work! And Robert Abel never got his software running on the CRAY.

What now?

Some of the talented ex-employees were talking about starting over with small boutique companies. They would do that, and out of the ashes of D.O.A. would rise a number for companies that would do well, like Metrolight, Sidley-Wright, and Kleiser-Walczak. Until those got going, there were few options for a freelance CG animator.

I considered going to back to traditional animation at Disney, but things were not going well there. The new regime of Michael Eisner and Jeffrey Katzenberg had recently assumed control of the studio. Because of the financial disaster of *The Black Cauldron* they weren't sure they would even keep the animation division going. They had just kicked the animators out of the Animation Building on the main lot and banished them to warehouses in Glendale. Morale was not good.

I had never worked in series television, and I did not like the idea of working in a sausage factory like Filmation. Freelancing on TV commercials was a possibility, but my old connections to that business were long gone. One day I got a call from a friend of mine who was freelancing on an independent animated feature film being done in the San Fernando Valley. They were using a very basic computer system to animate spaceships. They were badly in need of a computer animator!

The film was called *Starchaser: The Legend of Orin*, and it was being produced by Steven Hahn, a Korean businessman who owned one of the largest animation studios in South Korea. It was blatant rip-off of *Star Wars*, and reviewers would one day marvel at the fact that Steve was never sued for plagiarism. But at that moment the only thought was finishing the film.

The software for actually animating the spaceships was very basic, in fact, much like the graph-planning I had done on *Tron*. It was a job, and it was computer animation, so I dove in. It wasn't hard to do. One unusual challenge was the fact that *Starchaser* was being done in 3D stereoscopic, so I had to do two different flight paths for each ship, one for each eye!

Because his Korean animators were not as skilled at acting, Steve Hahn was employing a small cadre of American artists to do some of the key characters shots in the film. One of them was my friend Steve Moore, the guy who called me about the job. Steve was immersed in a very difficult shot. It had the three main characters having a conversation, then turning and running, in perspective, down a long hallway. It's tough enough to animate runs, but to do three characters at once, running away in perspective while maintaining their size and action as they get progressively smaller, is a real drawing challenge.

Steve had been working on this shot for three weeks and was almost finished. He came to my desk one morning, looking distressed. "Have you seen my scene?" He asked.

Of course I had not. We went back to his cubicle. I asked where he usually kept the drawings. He said that he typically had them on the shelf above his desk, but because they had now become such a huge, heavy stack of drawings and were hard to handle, he had set them on top of his wastebasket so they were easier to grab.

"Oh my God Steve", I said. "The cleaning crew thought you put them there to throw out!"

Steve and I ran downstairs to the parking lot. The building's dumpster was in the back of the lot. We jumped up and looked inside. It was completely empty.

We must have looked crushed as we walked back to the building. The Janitor saw us and asked us why we were climbing the dumpster. We told him that we thought something important had been thrown away by mistake.

"Ya know", he said, "they empty our dumpster into the big one at the service station on the corner".

In a second Steve and I were running down the alley. We got to the gas station and sure enough, saw a gigantic dumpster the size of a truck. We climbed up and looked inside. It was full! We exchanged glances, then, without a word, dove in. After scrounging through bags and bags of trash, we found one that had tell-tale peg hole paper. Ripping it open, we found his scene! It was covered in ants, but other than that, in fine shape. This form of "data retrieval" is not possible in the digital age.

That remains, to date, my most successful dumpster dive.

Not long after I finished the *Starchaser* gig, I was contacted by a guy named Michael Bryant. Michael was a champion motorcross racer who had an idea for a kids' TV series called *Team America Supercross*. Michael was a very handsome and charismatic guy, and although he had limited Hollywood experience, he was the kind of positive personality you suspected was perfect for the business.

More than just that positive aura, his idea was a good one! *Team America* would have young racers, based on real-life motorcross champions, traveling the globe as crimefighters working undercover as champion racers. Michael had defined the characters and had some good episode ideas. He had also been smart enough to know that the only way to animate motorcycles in animation was to use computer graphics. When he asked around town for advice on who might be able to do something like that, my name kept coming up. Almost everyone knew I had done the Lightcycle sequence in *Tron*.

Sue and I met Michael and liked him, and the project, immediately. In one of those valuable moments of synchronicity, I had just met a computer programmer who could make those motorcyles. Tim Heidmann was writing software for a small visual effects company named R&B FX. I had met Tim when I did a small freelance job for R&B. The job had involved some hand-drawn animation, and when Tim scanned my drawings he mentioned to me that he had been dabbling with an idea to make computer animated models render as line drawings.

I immediately recognized how that invention would serve our TV series. Computers could not yet come close to doing human figure animation, let alone cartoon characters on a TV series budget. TV budgets could not afford to render motorcycles in color in a computer and then composite them with ink & painted imagery. But if you could make a computer draw those bicycles, you could treat them exactly like the drawn characters and run the whole production through a traditional TV ink & paint company!

I asked Tim if I could hire him to write this new software. He agreed. It would cost about 20,000 dollars. I only had a few thousand in the bank. Sue asked her Dad to loan us the rest. I had never borrowed a cent since I left home for college, but there was no other option. We had to roll the dice on such a good idea.

Michael and I developed the artwork for a "pitch package". We polished the treatment, the character descriptions, the episode ideas, and created illustrations for the characters and the futuristic motorcycles. We started to pitch the project around town. At that time, there weren't as many places to go. The first stop was the networks. All of them turned us down. We tried some of the animation production companies, but they declined as well, especially because we were proposing a production method that did not yet exist. I started to think that I had made a huge mistake funding software development for a project that I had not even sold yet. The classic cart before the horse.

I had just about run through all our money when I had a classic Hollywood moment. I distinctly remember lying in bed, unable to sleep, thinking about my situation. I was unemployed, in debt, without prospects, and would be unable to make my mortgage payment when it came due next week.

The phone beside our bed rang. That was unusual. No one called us after 11:30 PM at night. It was Michael Bryant. He had big news. He was at a Hollywood party, and he had just sold *Team America*.

26

Kroyer Films Ink

How else do things get sold in Hollywood? My friend Mike O'Hara once sold a TV movie idea by scribbling the logline on a napkin at lunch. In this case, Michael Bryant had been at a Hollywood party when he ran into a young guy named Jeffrey Scott. In answer to the obligatory Hollywood question "so what *do you do*?" Jeffrey said he was an executive at Stephen J. Cannell Productions who was charged with developing animated TV series. It took Michael Bryant about two seconds to launch into the description of the most exciting TV series idea in years, *Team America Supercross*. Not only was it a great idea, it would be produced using never-before-seen cutting-edge computer animation.

And waddya know—that was exactly the kind of cutting-edge, original idea that Jeffrey Scott was looking for. He asked Michael to bring his partner (me) to his office tomorrow. We arrived right on time, showed Jeffrey our pitch package, and he immediately bought it. We wondered—is this possible?

Jeffrey Scott, it turned out, was technically the most successful writer/producer in TV animation history. He had more shows produced than any other writer. I had never worked in children's TV so I had not heard of him, but Cannell certainly had. Along with my old *Automan* producer Glen Larson, Stephen J. Cannell was the other great force in TV series. He had created some of the biggest

DOI: 10.1201/9781003558231-26

hits on TV, like *The Rockford Files* and *The A-Team*, and having sensed there was money to be made in animated shows had hired the most successful guy he could find, Jeffery Scott, to open that side of the business. Jeffery had authority to make decisions. Sure enough, Cannel confirmed the deal immediately, and we were sent a contract.

Neither Michael or I had ever produced a TV series before. I did have a very good lawyer that I had met years before on *Tron*. Jim Schreiber of the Beverly Hills law firm of Leonard, Dicker & Schreiber was not just a top-tier Hollywood lawyer but had become a close personal friend of Sue and I. The first thing to do was to draft the deal between Michael and me. That was easy because we liked and trusted each other and thought alike (and still do!).

Then there was the detail of starting my own animation production company to produce the show. I had never owned my own company. Many years earlier, in my Chicago days, I had tried formalizing my animation work into a studio I called Aardvark Productions. The name came from my very deep and brilliant thinking that I would always be listed first alphabetically in any directory of art studios. I ran into one of my old Northwestern University professors, a highly paid-advertising guru named Stuart Henderson Britt. When I told him I had named my studio Aardvark, he got a very distant, disdainful look in his eyes. "I will never understand the point of weird names", he said. "If you named the studio after yourself, the reputation of both you personally and the studio grow together".

I never forgot that admonition, so now, fifteen years later, I followed his advice. The company would be Kroyer Films. Because we would make our name by filming drawings that would be inked by a computer-driven plotter, I briefly toyed with the idea of the pun-ish "Kroyer Films Ink". But I settled for the more traditional "Kroyer Films, Inc."

The contract with Cannell was far more complex, and a learning experience. It was more like an option deal, which is typical for series work. It provided us development money to get started, with the bulk of the money coming in steps as we hit benchmarks—like selling the show to a distributor.

The most interesting and unexpected detail of the contract was the require-ment to secure a toy deal. Kids' TV shows in the 80s were basically commercials for toys. The money you got from the distributor barely, and even rarely, covered what it cost to make the show. Profits came from toy sales. One of the first things I had to do was become a traveling salesman!

Cannell engaged a toy agent named Jay Roth to handle the sale. Jay was an old-timer who knew everyone in the business. At least that's what he projected, because every time we would mention a big shot at one of the toy companies Jay would say "He's one of my oldest friends". When I finally met these executives it turned out that they knew Jay, but oldest friends? Sort of—by the merit that they were old.

Jay and I went on a ten-day blitz of all the big toy manufacturers in America. It was agony. I did not own a suit at the time, so I had to buy one to do these sales pitches. Being Mr. Casual I forgot to buy a belt for my pants. The trip was so non-stop that I never had a chance to take a detour to a men's store to buy one. I made the entire trip belt-less.

We didn't have luck with the big companies like Mattel or Hasbro, but eventually, we got a good offer from a smaller, but supposedly innovative company called LJN. With that deal signed, Cannell felt confident to proceed.

We were delighted when Cannell said they would give is a suite of offices rent-free. Because Cannell's expansion had outgrown the office building that housed his headquarters, he had leased office space all over Hollywood. The "suite" we got was basically a storefront in a mini-mall at the corner of Hollywood Boulevard and La Brea. Our next-door neighbor was a nail salon run by Vietnamese ladies.

Our suite had just three offices and a workspace. I took the front office with a big window facing Hollywood Boulevard. My view provided non-stop entertainment. There were always call girls hanging out on the corner luring the tourists. A bearded guy wearing biblical robes would drag a full-size wooden crucifix on roller-skate wheels past our building every afternoon. My window had one-way reflective glass. Because of the mirror surface people would stop and check out their hair and make-up in my window, looking right at me but not seeing me!

Michael Bryant and Tim Heidmann took desks in the next room. Typically, a show like ours got development money to pay for our salaries, scripts, designs, etc. Our show had something Cannell hadn't encountered before: computer costs and software development. My initial investment to fund Tim's software had gotten us 90% of the way there, but we still had not gotten the system working. For that, we needed a computer. In 1988, there was only one computer that would do the job.

It was called the Silicon Graphics IRIS 3130. It had what was called a "graphics pipeline", a hardware configuration that allowed it to not just model and light objects but display them in motion. Computer animation in real time! The cheapest model that would work for our show costs $57,000.00. It had a whopping 4 MB of memory and a hard disc of 600 MB. That's about 1,000 times less than your smartphone. But it was enough to do what we needed. We could only afford one computer, so the whole show would have to be produced on it.

The second device we purchased was a Hewlett-Packard plotter-printer. Our computer would feed its images to the plotter, which would be loaded with pre-punched animation paper. The rapidograph pen in the plotter would whiz back and forth across the paper at lightning speed and produce the drawings. At least that was the plan.

To dramatize the unique motion capabilities of the IRIS, it came with a built-in "flight simulator" program. This was like a very advanced video game where you could fly an airplane through various landscapes and practice landings and take-offs.

One day a really strange, deranged guy walked in off of Hollywood Boulevard. We were usually able to intercept these walk-ins and send them away, but this guy was belligerent. He barged past me and went to the room with the computer.

Tim saw him and switched to the flight simulator. He managed to convince the guy we were a secret government contractor doing aircraft development. If he didn't leave immediately, the FBI would arrest him. After a moment of thinking, the guy complimented us on our "cool tech" and left peacefully.

Tim set to work debugging the software, configuring the hardware, and building the models. I had hired my friend Michael Scheffe, who had designed the famous NIGHTRIDER car, to do the final designs of our bikes. A few weeks later, I came into the office and Tim handed me a piece of animation paper with a drawing of one of our motorcycles. I can hardly express my relief seeing that drawing! Our entire show depended on that process, and Tim had done it!

Michael and I were meeting with Jeffrey Scott, creating the outlines for the thirteen episodes that would compose our first season. We were surprised to learn that Jeffrey planned to write every episode. He was a writing machine. TV work is somewhat formulaic, and Jeffery had that down to a system. No one would consider his scripts to be Oscar material, but for kids' TV, they seemed to fit the bill. Among the tweaks we made was a name change. Instead of the somewhat nationalistic title TEAM AMERICA SUPERCROSS, the show would now be called ULTRACROSS.

After the first script was delivered to us I began to storyboard the show. I was a fast storyboard artist, and I also had a sense of the strengths and limitations of the technology we planned to use. It was critical that I design the show around that. About this time, Tim decided that his work was finished. He wanted to move along to other software development work. Eventually he would do amazing things, including designing the magical first-down line you see superimposed on the field of every NFL football game.

Tim introduced me to his friend Brian Jennings. Brian was a computer expert who immediately absorbed all the intricacies of Tim's system. Brian would model all the bikes, stadiums, and props we would use on the show. I would be doing all the animation myself. That was by far the most efficient way to control the creative look and maintain the schedule and budget. At this time, I probably had more experience on CG motion than almost anyone. I was one of the very few CG animators with Disney-quality training, and since I knew exactly what I wanted, why not just do it myself?

My company would create the designs and storyboards and do all the CG animation of the bikes, but we still needed a studio to do the thousands of animation drawing of the characters. At this time, most of the 2D hand-drawn animation production was going "off shore". The idea of sending work to lower-cost overseas studios had started in the early 1980s. This was labeled "runaway production", and the Animation Guild, formally known as the Motion Picture Screen Cartoonists Union, had actually tried several labor stoppages to prevent it. But because of those lucrative toy deals, children's television had become extremely profitable, and was even more profitable if you could produce the shows for half the cost of doing them in Los Angeles. As it turned out, the guild could not stand up to that kind of financial incentive.

Ironically, it was a fight they were lucky to lose. What happened was that the studios sent all the "grunt work", like in-betweening, ink & painting, and photography, overseas but had to keep the "skill work" in America because, thankfully, no one could write and design shows that would appeal to the American audience like American artists. As a result, the Union did lose most of those lower-scale, lower-paying jobs, but because of the profits, TV animation production skyrocketed. The Union added double and triple the number of higher-paying jobs for directors, designers, layout artists, etc.

Japan had been the original provider of these offshore studios, but other countries quickly saw the opportunity and jumped in. Korea and the Philippines started studios, but the biggest 2D studio in the world would pop in Taiwan. It was called "Cuckoo's Nest", founded by James Wang.

James had come from a well-connected family in Taiwan, but for some reason had gotten the bug for animation. To his credit, he decided to learn the business from the ground up. He got a work visa for the United States and signed on as a lowly in-betweener on the animated production of *Raggedy Ann and Andy*, being done in New York City. The American artists (including my wife) liked this quiet, unassuming, hard-working Chinese kid. One day, James invited a dozen of his fellow artists to lunch at a rather fancy Chinese restaurant in Manhattan. Imagine everyone's surprise when they walked in the front door and found the restaurant's owner, chefs, and entire staff lined up to bow and greet Mr. Wang. That's when they got the sense there was something special about this guy. As it turned out, James was a member of one of Taiwan's most powerful families.

James told me that he named his Taiwan studio "Cuckoo's Nest" because the Cuckoo is the one bird that will accept chicks that are not its own into its nest, and care for them. That is the metaphor he thought best expressed the care he would provide to the animated work from other studios sent his way. Eventually, I would send work from my company to Cuckoo's Nest.

But not ULTRACROSS. There was another foreign studio that Cannell liked, one that was just as economical but a lot closer. It was called NELVANA, and it was located in Toronto. Its president was a guy named Michael Hirsh. He was an unusual character. It was not uncommon for people in animation to be somewhat colorful and eccentric, but Michael's way of doing that was unique. He always wore a suit and tie, but his suit was wrinkled. I don't mean it had a few wrinkles. I mean it looked like he had crushed it into a ball and left it in a bag for a month.

Michael Hirsh wanted Nelvana to get a lot of that lucrative American sub-contracted work. We traveled to Canada, met him and the Nelvana team, and he sold us. Nelvana had good animators, had a great reel, and promised that our show would get their A-team. We went back home and started to prepare the storyboards, layouts, and designs that Nelvana would follow. Since it takes time to do the animation, we would send pre-production materials for the first seven episodes to Nelvana before we got finished animation back for the first episode.

Then, disaster struck.

We had been working on the show for about three months when we got the call. I honestly cannot remember who told us the news. It was probably Jeffrey Scott. LJN, the toy company doing our merchandise, had cancelled our deal. They had been bought out by a conglomerate that was restructuring the company. Cannell would sue for some damages, but the bottom line was that without the toys, producing the show made no sense. And while the lawsuits played out, the copyright on the show would be in limbo so it could not be set up elsewhere.

Needless to say, we were stunned. We had just gotten our first pencil tests of finished animation from Nelvana. I had already animated thousands of frames of CG motorcycles. It was just starting to feel like a real production. Now, it was a pile of useless paper. ULTRACROSS was gone. It would never be resurrected.

If that wasn't a dark enough day, I received some very sad news from my friends at Disney. My mentor from the Disney training program, the legendary Eric Larson, had passed away. A group of us young animators, some still at Disney, some elsewhere, attended the funeral. None of us felt like we had the right to say anything at the service, having only known Eric for a few years. His old friends and fellow artists gave their eulogies, and the thing that struck me most at the time and has remained in my memory to this day was the tearful, unrestrained sorrow these grown men publicly displayed. Such was the pain felt by those who were fortunate enough to know this kind, gentle, giving, talented genius.

I still own a wonderful caricature of Eric that he signed for me when I left the studio. He wrote, "Bill—remember the staging". He wanted me to remember that it's not just the animated movement that touches the audience. It's the way you present the image. Every picture tells the story. No one told a better story than Eric Larson.

I had lost my mentor, and had lost the only project that was funding my company - and my life. What now?

27

The Technological Threat

With the cancellation of ULTRACROSS we had no work. What were we to do with our fledgling enterprise, Kroyer Films, Inc.? We had developed this incredibly cool, unique, innovative way to combine computer animation with hand-drawn animation. Nobody understood what we had because nobody had seen anything like it.

To his eternal credit, Stephen J. Cannell (or whoever advised him) was incredibly generous to us. We didn't have to refund any of the money we had been paid to date. Since we had been advanced funds to cover the next two months, we had a bit of a financial cushion. Incredibly, they let me keep the IRIS and all the other hardware and software. To add to that, they told me I didn't have to vacate our office. They didn't need the space at the moment, so we could stay rent-free until they did.

I suppose there are times in all success stories when a moment of special circumstances changes the tide. This was our moment, thanks to Cannell.

We had the team, we had the space, we had the technology, we had a bit of money. The choice was obvious. We would make a film that would show the world what we could do! But we had to do it fast.

DOI: 10.1201/9781003558231-27

The toughest thing to do in any production is to create the story. You can't do anything until you have figured that out. The primary requirement of the story we must create was not that it be just entertaining but that it demonstrate our unique production capability. In other words, it had to be a story that required computer-animated characters to act alongside hand-drawn animated characters. That situation had to feel natural.

As we mulled this over, and threw out ideas, something occurred to me. During our three-month stint of ULTRACROSS production, when I was cranking out the computer animation of the motorcycles, we had a constant stream of friends visiting our office. When I took my animator friends into the back room to watch the Hewlett-Packard plotter at work, I noticed their reaction. The plotter's pen raced across the paper and in less than ten seconds and created a perfectly drawn motorcycle. It spit that drawing into a tray, loaded a new piece of punched animation paper, and cranked out another perfect drawing. It was not just a perfect drawing. It was drawing made with such precision and detail that it would have taken my animator friends over an hour to create something like it, and it would not have been as good.

I got the distinct impression that as they stared down at the plotter, they were really staring into the abyss of their own obsolescence. How could they compete with this? They didn't yet understand, as I did, that the computer had limitations. To them, their jobs were under threat.

Technological Threat.

I pitched that idea to our little team. We would make a film about computer workers replacing normal workers. And to make the essence of the characters fit the story, and also provide a wonderfully ironic metaphor, we would animate all the "normal" workers with hand-drawn animation and all the computer workers with computer animation.

There are times when an idea is so solid that the story flows off your fingertips. This was one of those times. Working with Sue and our one remaining artistic employee, a recent Cal Arts grad named Rich Moore, I quickly outlined out the basic scenario. It would be an office with rows of desks populated with cartoon wolves, busy doing repetitive clerical work. We liked the idea of wolves because they were so quintessentially identified with cartoons. It was a bit of homage to Tex Avery.

One by one, these cartoon wolves would be replaced by computer workers. One vital feature of our production process was the ability to combine hand-drawn details with computer precision, so we designed these computer characters to have geometric body parts that the computer could do well but enhance each drawing with hand-drawn eye expressions that would have the organic subtlety the computer could not do. Because the CG characters were basically pyramid-shaped heads sitting on a block and sphere body, supported by a pencil for a neck, we nicknamed them "pencil-necked Geeks".

I ripped through the storyboards quickly and we felt confident we had a solid little film. One by one, the wolves would fall through trap doors and be replaced by the computer workers. Even their boss would be replaced by a computer boss!

The last wolf standing would rebel. He'd go nuts and start destroying the computer workers. I left some leeway for the animators of these scenes to create gags about exactly how the wolf would do that.

Designing the CG "Geeks" was the first task we finished. The design direction was driven by the requirements of their functionality. They had to be made of relatively simple geometric shapes that could be animated easily. That's why the structure of a rolling sphere mounted on a cube fit the bill. They still needed personality, so adding eyeglasses and bug-eyed innocence made them feel like mindless clerical workers.

There is a saying in our business: "There are no cigarette butts in animation!" That has nothing to do with health consciousness. It refers to the fact that unlike a live-action film, where the camera photographs everything on the film set—including a cigarette butt casually discarded by a worker—in animation, *nothing* appears on the screen if you have not intentionally designed it and built it. Now that we had our Geek co-star, everything else in the movie had to be designed.

As a matter of luck or destiny, that lone rookie employee, Rich Moore, happened to be incredibly multi-talented. In future years he would become famous as the Director of some of animation's biggest blockbusters, like *Zootopia* and *Wreck-It-Ralph*. Rich could direct, Rich could animate, but lucky for us, he could also design.

Rich quickly created model sheets for our wolf characters. We didn't hide the fact that they were classic cartoon designs. The office environment was the bigger question. We wanted something futuristic but industrial. My wife Sue had always loved Frank Lloyd Wright's famous "Great Room" at the Johnson's Wax headquarters in her hometown of Racine, Wisconsin (fun fact: Sue's family's construction company had built Wright's famous "research tower" on the same property!).

Sue showed Rich photos of the Great Room, and you will notice his design in *Tech Threat* pays homage to the famous columns. We liked the idea of a somewhat colorless, sterile environment, but Rich came up with the brilliant idea of adding a splash of color to the backgrounds by using a "sponge technique". He would literally dip a sponge into a pool of paint, then dab it on to the background to give a speckled array of color. Very un-computer-like!

Brian built the models and I started posing the layouts and animating the geeks. Because we had such a tight budget, I asked some of my animator friends to help by animating one shot—for free. I ended up with a credit list of future superstars, including Rob Minkoff (Director of *The Lion King, Stuart Little*), Greg Vanzo (Director of *The Simpsons*), and Chris Bailey (director of *Kim Possible*). Sue and Rich animated most of the wolf shots. Sue did the scene of the wolf stuffing pencils in his nose to stop him from sneezing, then sneezing, shooting the pencils into the head of the wolf next to him. To this day that shot gets the biggest laugh in the film.

The one shot that caused debate was the most important shot in the film. It was the finale. I had always had the idea that the wolf and the geek should, in the end, defeat the bad boss and end up as victorious partners. My wife Sue had a totally different idea. She saw the film as a metaphor for technology replacing art. In that struggle, it was important for art to retain the upper hand. As they stood over the hole in the floor, the wolf knocks the geek into the hole. Art wins! We came to realize how right she was to fight for that ending.

We finished the animation in just two months. We had a completed pencil test that played well. The next big hurdle was getting it painted, photographed, assembled, and scored. I had only about 8,000 dollars left, which was not nearly enough to have that done in Los Angeles.

I called Steve Hahn, the Korean producer I had helped on the *Starchaser* movie. Steve had one of the biggest animation companies in Seoul, South Korea, HAHNHO LTD. Once again, angels seem to be watching over us because Steve agreed to color and shoot the film. If I deducted what I'd need for the score and the edit, I only had 6,000 bucks. Steve agreed to do it for that. Basically, a miracle!

I flew to Korea with two huge suitcases crammed with all the paper animation and painted backgrounds from *Technological Threat*. It was organized well, each scene clearly labeled in its own scene folder with the accompanying exposure sheet that listed all the shooting instructions. I thought we were fairly well organized at Kroyer Films, but I was blown away by the efficiency of Hahnho. I watched as my scenes were unpacked, checked, sorted, logged, and sent into the Hahnho production pipeline. All the pencil artwork was sent to xerox, where it was copied to acetate cels, ready for painting.

Typical for an animated production, we had prepared color models of the characters and props. The Hahnho Ink & Paint supervisors translated those colors to the colors used by their painters and distributed the shots. It was humbling to see forty ink & paint girls hunched over their desks feverishly painting my movie. We had over 7,000 individual cels. I was told they would have everything painted in four days!

That gave me a bit of free time to see Seoul. This was 1988, thirty-four years after the Korean War had reduced Seoul to a massive pile of rubble. When I looked out the third-floor window of the Hahnho Building, I could see the modern skyscrapers marking the downtown business district. Construction cranes were everywhere. An unusual feature of the landscape was the proliferation of large, netted tents. They seemed to be every six or seven blocks. I learned these were golf driving ranges! The Koreans had fallen in love with golf, but few people could afford to travel to, or play at, the expensive private golf courses outside the city.

Directly beside the Hahnho building was what you might call a "shanty town". These have disappeared today, but in 1988 they were still some dotting the city, makeshift homeless encampments for people who had not been able to afford real housing. You could see the smoke from the cookstoves seeping up through the tented rooftops.

Housing was still in tight supply. As I met and befriended the young Korean animators at Hahnho, we would go out for beers after work. We would almost always go to a "lounge" that invariably consisted of a basement apartment that was like a pub. Instead of looking like a tavern, it looked exactly like an apartment living room. I learned that almost none of the young people could afford their own apartments. They all lived at home, so to socialize, instead of inviting anyone to their own over-crowded house, they would meet at these fake apartments.

That may have explained why these Korean workers were the hardest working people I had ever seen. Having been born in the 50s and 60s, these kids had grown up in a ruined country with few amenities. The chance to have a job, save money, and buy the nice things their parents could never have had was a driving force. You did not have to offer incentives to these kids to put in a ten or twelve hour day to get that bigger paycheck.

As I walked the city I noticed that there were almost no old structures. I expected to see a pagoda or some such ancient historic building, but because of two wars they seemed to have been wiped out. I eventually found a few that had been reconstructed. My explorations led me to the biggest shopping mall in town, the immense Lotte World. This super-modern shopping mecca had an animation theme. Every day at 4:00 PM, there would be a parade through the mall featuring floats that contained all the Disney Princesses. This was years before the "Disney Princesses" became a "thing" at Disney in America. I was quite taken aback at this set of princesses because although they had the exact clothing, hairstyles, and make-up of Snow White, Cinderella, and Sleeping Beauty they were all Korean girls. Pioneers in cultural appropriation.

On my fifth day at Hahnho, I was stunned to learn that my film had been completely colored and photographed. I could not believe that could be true. I was led into a screening room, accompanied by Steve and the managers from all the departments, each with a notepad. "For changes", Steve said.

Sure enough, when they ran the film, there were dozens of mistakes! Colors popped, colors changed, spaces were left unpainted, cels were shot of order. Almost every mistake you could make when you rushed through production had been made. I was about to panic when Steve explained the plan. According to the way production worked at Hahnho, it was far more efficient to jam everything through the pipeline as fast as possible, then target the mistakes, than it was to do it slowly and carefully. He told me to just step through the movie and call out every single "fix" I wanted done. We switched to the editorial room, where I could scroll through the movie frame-by-frame. With the managers scribbling behind me, I called out the fixes.

Lo and behold, I came in the next morning and was told the next version was ready to view! How could they fix and re-film 7,000 frames of film in 24 hours? You can do that when you have fifteen camera stands and 700 people working at it.

I viewed the film and most of the mistakes and been corrected. But not all of them. I was told that was typical. We repeated the process of me naming fixes. Sure enough, the next morning, we viewed the film and it was almost perfect. Just a few more tweaks and I could head home.

Now that I was able to view my film its completed form, I felt there was something missing. I felt that it needed just one more moment, a moment of smug victory for the wolf. I had the idea to have him smile, stick the boss's cigar in his mouth, and hit the button. Being the computer animator, I had not done any of the hand-animated wolves on the film, but this time, there was no time for anything else. I sat a desk and animated the shot in an hour. The Hahnho team cleaned up my drawings and sent them through the pipeline. That scene made it into the final reel.

After just nine days in Korea, I headed to the airport with the only existing version of *Technological Threat* under my arm.

28

From Korea with Love

On the flight back to L.A., I held the film can in my lap. I didn't even trust putting it in the overhead compartment. What if I dozed off and someone stole it? That film can held my entire fortune, my entire future! It contained the original negative to my film. To understand what that means, you must know that in the days of celluloid film, the film stock that was shot by the camera, the absolute original imagery, was the negative. To view that, you "struck" a print from the negative to create a positive print, and that is what you loaded into a projector to display on the screen.

It wasn't a disaster if the print got scratched or damaged because you could always strike another print from the negative. It wasn't as easy as it would be in the digital age, when you could simply hit "copy" and drag the data from one hard drive to another. To make a print, you had to have the film lab carefully clean the negative, thread it into the optical printer, and make your copy. Every time you did that you risked scratching or damaging that precious, one-of-a-kind negative, so one of the very first things you did was make a duplicate negative, called an inter-negative. Or many inter-negatives. Once you had the inter-negative, all the prints would be struck from that, saving the original negative.

DOI: 10.1201/9781003558231-28

That original negative was so irreplaceable, so valuable, that there were negatives stored all over Hollywood at the various film laboratories. If you walked through the shelves of a famous lab you would look side to side and see film cans with the titles *Gone with the Wind, The Sound of Music, Jaws*—the greatest films very made, their actual source material sitting inches from your face.

The one similarity my little negative had with those classics was that it was equally vulnerable and irreplaceable. All the work we had done designing and animating, and all the work the hundreds of workers in Korea had done to color and shoot the art, was now contained in this small film can. If anything happened to it, the chance of re-prepping and re-shooting those stacks of painted cels would be nil. I certainly would not be able to pay for it.

I landed at Los Angeles International Airport, passed through immigration, and picked up my suitcase from the bag carousel. As I walked past U.S. Customs, as was my usual routine, an officer spotted the film can. It was covered with the labeling that Hahnho had stamped on the can.

"Let's see that", he said. I reluctantly handed him the can. He glanced at it, studied the label, and placed it on the table behind him. "You can pick this up after it clears customs", he said.

My heart went to my throat. "Wait a minute", I said. "I can't leave that. I'm hand-carrying that! Can't you just check it here?"

He was adamant. The can was a commercial product being imported from Korea. It had to go through the customs office. No exceptions. After a moment of desperate pleading, during which I sensed he was about to call the Airport Police and have me hauled away, I relented. I walked away from the desk, leaving my future behind.

I walked toward the exit door to the terminal. I was distraught. For some reason, I decided to go back and make one more plea. I took a few steps back toward the customs area and was shocked to see my film can resting on top of a briefcase, sitting on the floor of the terminal. No one was around it!

I considered grabbing the can and making a run for it. I stood there, trying to decide what to do, when a voice broke through my distracted attention.

"Don't worry, I'm watchin' it". It was the customs guy who had taken my can. He was checking some other bags a few feet away. He gave me the thumb to get going. I slunk out of the airport and went home. It was Friday night. Worse, it was Friday night of a three-day holiday weekend. That meant that the customs office would not re-open for public access until Tuesday morning!

I got home and told Sue about the disaster with the film can. She suggested that I call the customs office before they closed for the weekend and make sure that the guy had safely dropped off the film. I called and actually got through. I described the film can and asked if it was there. The guy put down the phone and was gone for a good four minutes.

He came back on the line. "Nothing like that here", he said.

I nearly choked. It had to be there, I cried! An absolutely disinterested voice told me to check back Tuesday, and hung up. That three-day weekend was the longest weekend of my life. Some people say that a stressful situation like that will give you nightmares. I did have one of the most vivid dreams I have ever had. I dreamt I was in the customs office, sleeping on one of the shelves. I was sleeping on my side, curled up, and safely tucked against my stomach was my precious film can. Talk about a hopeful delusion!

Tuesday morning I headed into Hollywood early. My plan was to get to the office and figure how I could get my film out of the L.A. Airport Customs Office. I had no idea how to do that. I was still sick to my stomach about the whole thing. When I got to the office, the door was open because our assistant Leslie had already beaten me to it, as usual. I walked into my office and saw a box on my desk.

To my utter shock, it was my film! Beside it was a bill from a Customs Agent. It turned out that Steve Hahn had failed to inform me that Hahnho had filled out all the proper paperwork, stamped it on my can (in Korean so I couldn't read it), and registered the imported item. The local L.A. agent that handled all the Hahnho imported work made his usual early visit to L.A. Airport that morning and picked up the can with the other Hahnho stuff. He unceremoniously had delivered it to our office. My nightmare was over.

Out of curiosity, I called the Airport Customs office to ask about the mystery of where my film had been over the weekend. I was told that the agent who took it from me could tell that I was extremely anxious about it, so he had placed my can in the locked vault. Apparently, the guy I spoke to on the phone Friday night did not have access to that vault, hence the missing can. Whew!

The first thing I did was to take the film to the Deluxe Lab. I ordered an internegative and a print struck. We used that print to do the final "mix" of the soundtrack. We also created the opening title and the final 35 mm credit sequence.

Although I had carried the pencil drawings to Korea, once that art was painted on cels it was considerably more bulky and heavy. It had to be shipped back to us in L.A.. When the boxes started to arrive, we noticed that the labels identified our project as "Are were hero—Wolf". We couldn't figure out how that happened. A phone call to Hahnho solved the mystery. We had jokingly labeled the model sheets of our wolf character as "Our Hero". Apparently, when asked how to title our project, a Korean secretary had read "Our Hero, Wolf" and it had been misunderstood and transcribed as "Are were hero—Wolf". We gave special thanks to that label in the final credits.

With titles and sound, *Technological Threat* was ready for its close-up!

That's me on the left, with my back to the camera, listening to the great Eric Larson lecture to us trainees in the Disney training program in 1977. The blond guy on the right is Henry Selick who would direct *Nightmare before Christmas* and *Coraline*.

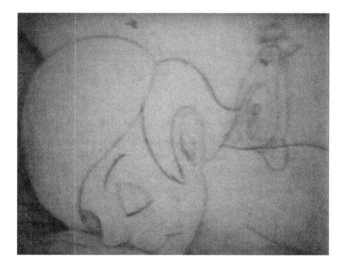

Sorry for the poor photo, but this is a "screenshot" of my Disney trainee pencil test where a little clock character tries to awaken his master on a school day. This test got me into Disney!

The Rat's Nest

Taken thirty years apart, these photos show my lifelong friends from Disney: L-R: Henry Selick, me, Jerry Rees, Brad Bird, and John Musker.

Don Bluth called us "a rat's nest of dissent" when we disagreed with him about using rotoscope in our animation, and we embraced the name.

If you check the credits of this group, you will see the controversy did not hurt our careers.

John Musker stayed up all night drawing my farewell card when I left Disney. There are a lot of famous animators in this shot, including my wife Sue (holding the guitar). Eric Larson's farewell message: "Remember the staging."

The farewell celebration. The guy in the center, enjoying the cake, is future PIXAR director John Lasseter.

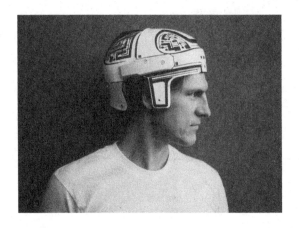

1982, posing in an authentic helmet from *Tron*.

I didn't work on the live action, but the process was crazy. Those black stripes on the helmet would be made to glow "electronically" through special effects.

My photo posing in front of the CHROMATICS 9000, the only computer Jerry and I touched on *Tron*. This photo has some notoriety, being the first photo of a "guy working at a computer" ever published in CINEFEX – and they got my name wrong!

BELOW: Some of the diagrams I created to make the animated movement of the *Tron* cycles.

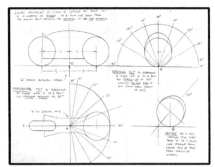

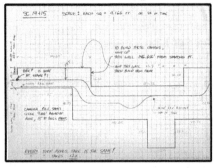

When I animated this "Block Woman" at Digital Productions in 1984, it was one of the very first "hierarchical figures" to be animated on a computer.

Mick Jagger loved the Block Woman test and hired us to do his rock video "Hard Woman". Like Block Woman, a computer could still not create bendable, flexible skin, so we created "Vector Woman"!

Technological Threat

My Oscar-nominated short film, historic for combining hand-animated characters with computer-animated characters. Rich Moore designed the film. Sue insisted that the cartoon guy defeat the computer guys!

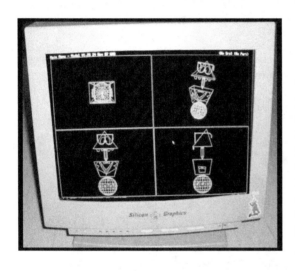

The SILICON GRAPHICS IRIS 3130 was the only computer at the time that could display real-time motion. It cost $57,000, so we could afford only one! Here you see the computer-created "Pencil Necked Geek" being modeled from four views.

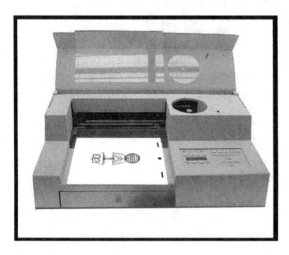

Our big innovation, made possible by Tim Heidmann's unique software, was rendering our three-dimensional character to look like a two-dimensional drawing. Then, we printed the image onto regular punched animation paper, so we could ink and paint it just like the hand-drawn characters.

FernGully: The Last Rainforest

Our small crew on the scouting trip in Australia for *FernGully*. Ralph Eggleston, lower right, became a full-fledged Production Designer on this movie.

The *FernGully* crew at Kroyer Films in Van Nuys, California. Sue and I are behind the sign. We took over the old Stroh's Brewery and had over 170 employees at this site – but more workers in Toronto, London, Seoul, and Taipei.

In 1982, Sue and I, both unemployed, mortgaged our house and took a trip around the world. In China, we were the first Western animators to visit the Shanghai Animation Studio. I'm pictured here with the two directors. Despite the largest social and cultural gap imaginable, we found instant rapport with our Chinese animator counterparts. They joked around just like...animators!

In 2009, the Academy sent us back to China to accompany Academy President Sid Ganis on a cultural goodwill tour for the film industry. Remarkably I was able to return to the Shanghai Animation Studio. It was cleaned up – in more ways than one. Instead of the innovative small personal films they did in the 1980s they were now doing outsourced TV work.

In my three terms as a Governor of the Motion Picture Academy, I got a lot of perks, attending the Oscars, the Governors Awards, and the Nominees Luncheon. I was able to take my Chapman students to some events, like SHORTS NIGHT, where they met KOBE BRYANT and GLEN KEANE, nominated for their short film *Dear Basketball*, which won the Oscar!

As a Governor, I was invited to St. James Palace in London for a reception honoring all past British Oscar winners. Sue and I had a chance to meet the future King.

We were surprised and delighted to find that Prince Charles loved animation, and personally knew many of our animator friends in the UK.

SOME LEGENDS: Pictured on the couch at our Christmas Party, on the left are our role models, Bob and Cima Balser. No one loved art and artists more than they. On the right, THE QUEEN: June Foray, the voice of Rocky the Flying Squirrel and the strongest voice fighting for the Animation Branch of the Academy. They don't make 'em like this anymore.

Mo and Dick Williams at the St. James reception. Richard Williams will go down in history as perhaps the greatest animator/draftsman ever.

My *Tron* buds. L-R: Director Steven Lisberger, *Tron* himself – Bruce Boxleitner, Disney publicist Howard Green, me, *Tron* PR master Mike Bonnifer.

The man some consider to be the Japanese Walt Disney, Hayao Miyazaki. Despite the dominance of computer animation in modern production, Miyazaki-san is the last, great disciple of hand-drawn animation. I met him first at the Governors Awards where he was given a special Oscar for his career work. The next time I saw him he was at his animation desk.
Drawing.

When I say that animation has been the foundation of my life, I mean it, and nothing in the world of animation was more important to me than the fact that it cast its spell on a young artist from Wisconsin named Sue Nelson Evans. Sue arrived in L.A. the same month I did in 1975, but it would take two years for our paths to cross at Disney Animation.

She was an exceptional animator, seen here working on Brad Bird's hilarious short film *Family Dog*, but her true gift was recognizing great potential and discovering some of the industry's top talent.

And then, there was that little thing of marrying me and making me a success, and a very happy husband.

The Eggman

1965–2022

No person had a greater impact on our lives or careers than Ralph Eggleston. We hired him when he was just a kid out of school and watched him develop into one of the most honored and accomplished artists in the history of animation. He was family.

29

Chasing Awards

I didn't know much about the world of animated film festivals. I had worked in studios that made feature films or commercials. Film festivals were primarily showcases for short films.

Most film fans know about the big live-action festivals, like the Cannes Film Festival, the Venice Biennale, Telluride, Park City, and the like. Those fests had short film programs, but the big stars, and the big publicity, centered around feature films. In the 1980s, there weren't enough animated feature films being made to merit a festival. But short films? That was another story.

I had a friend, Ron Diamond, who produced a show each year that was a collection of the year's best shorts. To find them, he attended most of the important festivals. I turned to Ron for advice, and he helped me enter *Technological Threat* in some festivals. The first one I entered was the most important animation festival in the world, The Annecy International Film Festival.

Annecy was started in 1960. It originally occurred every two years, alternating years with its "sister festival", Animafest Zagreb in Yugoslavia. The idea had been to make it possible for animators behind the iron curtain to meet and mingle with their Western counterparts. As I have mentioned, the unusual personal traits that made artists immerse themselves in an imaginary world of moving

DOI: 10.1201/9781003558231-29

drawings gave such artists a commonality that it overpowered cultural and political differences. The year I made *Tech Threat*, it was Annecy's year, so off to France we went!

I had never heard of the town of Annecy, and I think the French may have been intentionally hiding it from American tour guides books. It was the most idyllic setting you could imagine. The town was on the shores of Lake Annecy, with views of the French Alps. It was surrounded by Alpine foothills dotted with historic castles and mountain chateaus. There was an old Medieval town center laced with charming canals lined with old shops and unbelievably great restaurants. That region was famous for a dish called raclette. It consisted of a half-wheel of cheese mounted on a tabletop stand. A candle slowly melted the exposed half of the wheel, and you would scrape the melting cheese onto fresh bread. It was heavenly.

Annecy also had a dock with rental boats to view the lake, and beaches that had topless sunbathers. That was a stunner to the American animators. The film festival was held in small theaters around town, but all the main events took place in the main Festival Hall. There was a big lawn on the lakeshore, and every night, there would be an outdoor screening of animated films. Thousands would sit on the lawn, drink fine (yet inexpensive!) French wine, and watch movies under the stars surrounded by their animation brothers and sisters from all over the globe. It was an animation paradise.

On advice from some festival veterans, Sue and I had taken lodging in a 500-year-old former rectory right in the middle of the Old Town. In Annecy, everything is a short walk. During the festival, the town is completely taken over by animation people. At every restaurant, you just had to look at the table beside you to strike up a conversation. You would meet artists from Europe, Asia, and Australia—everyone was there. Unlike Cannes or Venice, where the big stars stay at ritzy private hotels, in Annecy, even the best-known animation artists walked the streets and hung out at the cafes with everyone else.

At that time, the most experienced festival attendee in the world was John Lasseter. PIXAR was focused on proving that computer animation was the medium of the future. Although the company was losing money, being supported by Steve Jobs, they funded a short film every year and sent John on a PR blitz to the most important festivals. In addition to being a filmmaking genius, John was a most gregarious and eloquent ambassador for the new medium. He was also an emerging epicure. He knew the best places to eat and drink.

That is how I had my first experience at a genuine 3-star Michelin restaurant. I did not know what that designation meant when John took a group of us to the village of Talloires to eat at his favorite place. The luncheon took three hours for eleven courses, four of them dessert! I will never forget that moment when the waiters set dome-covered-dishes before us and simultaneously lifted the covers.

I would run into John at future festivals, but the funniest incident related to his gourmet tastes occurred the next year at the IMAGINA festival in Monte Carlo. Sue decided not to go with me because our dog was sick, so I took my seventy-five-year old mother! My Mom had never been to Europe, so this was a wonderful treat for her. In Monaco, we were staying at the Lowe's hotel, as was John Lasseter. The three of us were sitting together at breakfast, and John had ordered a soft-boiled egg. When it came, John poked it with his spoon and decided it was too hard. He sent it back. The egg came again and this time John felt it was too runny. He sent it back again. The next egg came, and he felt it was too hard. On the fourth try, he deemed the egg acceptable. This made such an impression on my mother that for the rest of her life, when I would mention John Lasseter, who had won two Oscars, who had created PIXAR, who had guided the most successful animated film studio in history, she would always say "John Lasseter? Is that that friend of yours who is so fussy about his eggs?"

Our first visit to the Annecy Film Festival turned out to be a thrill, because *Technological Threat* won a very big prize. It didn't win the Grand Prize, but it won THE APOLLO AWARD, a new prize for innovative filmmaking. The perception was that we had come in a very close second to the winner, a film called *The Hill Farm*, that would sweep the world's festivals that year. The Annecy award was a huge attention-getter. Although I didn't attend most of the other festivals, *Tech Threat* started racking up awards.

Back in Los Angeles, I was surprised when Ron Diamond called me one morning and said he had heard a rumor I should like to hear. *Tech Threat* might have a chance to get an Oscar nomination! I wasn't sure how to respond to that. I had no idea how that might come about. Was I supposed to do something? Ron said that our film had a "good buzz" and that I should immediately fill out the entry forms for the Academy and submit a print. I did that immediately. And waited.

Our free rent at Cannell's office was about to expire. Cannell said we could stay, but we'd have to start paying. I could not afford to pay Rich Moore, so he had left. I could not let Brian go, since he knew our computer process better than anyone. My finances were stretched very thin. Once again, the fates of Hollywood had good timing. We got the Oscar nomination.

With that publicity, and the aura of validation that comes with the recognition of our new animation gimmick, I was able to make some inroads and land some small jobs. Sometimes they would be just tests, but funded tests, like Richard Taylor asking us to do a chorus line of twenty 7-UP bottle caps dancing like the Radio City rockettes. I felt that we just had to keep the doors open until the Academy Awards. If we could win an Oscar, our future had to be secure—right?

In future years, the Academy would fill the run-up to the Oscars with many events, including a dinner for the animation nominees that would include the animation Governors and other industry stars. This did not exist in 1988. John Lasseter and I knew each other, but we didn't know the other nominee, Cordell Barker, because he rarely left his home in Canada. We got in touch with him. He and his wife were coming into L.A. a few days early, so the six of us—me, John, Cordell, and our wives—went out to dinner. That was the big pre-Oscar Show nominee celebration.

Attending the Oscars at the Shrine Auditorium was a surreal experience. As I related earlier, we somehow got our hands on enough tickets to take the entire family to the Show. Needless to say, they were dumbstruck by the event. In those days, there were no ropes separating the regular crowd from the movie stars as they made their way toward the front doors. You would bump into someone, turn, and be inches away from Dustin Hoffman. It's funny to look at the photos from that day. My Dad, my Mom, and my brother Kenny all have polite smiles glued to their faces, but you can tell they are a bit overwhelmed by it all.

We were ushered to our seats. John, Cordell, and I were about eight rows back from the stage. The show began, and Rob Lowe and Snow White began their historically cheesy, infamous opening number. Did that have to happen my year?

It was about this time that I started to realize I might have to get up on that stage and give an acceptance speech. I knew John's film *Tin Toy* was a great little film and an audience favorite, but with the Academy voters, you never knew. I had spent the last few days writing down a speech. I didn't want to get up there and babble out the lame excuse "I wasn't really expecting this so I haven't prepared anything...".

I pretty much knew what I would say. I would thank Sue first and foremost for always being there and being the secret weapon behind the whole project. I'd thank the crew. I'd say something about how we hoped our film would expand the artform. As I sat there, I had those second thoughts about how lame I would sound. I wondered if every nominee had those thoughts. Surely not the actors. It was their business to stand up in public and express themselves. Animators do that vicariously through imaginary surrogate beings.

The show became a fog to me. I remember seeing Bob Hope and Lucille Ball and thinking that in future years, it might be cool to have seen them in person together. I don't remember anything else until the time came for our category. Carrie Fisher and Martin Short came on stage and made the traditional lame jokes about short things. They read our names as nominees. That was nice but terrifying. Then, Martin opened the envelope. *Tin Toy* won, and John crawled over my lap and into the history books.

Sue and I clutched hands, then applauded. Sue was always more philosophical about these things than I was. She didn't view the "loss" as a loss at all. She thought it was absolutely amazing and wonderful that this had happened at all. And, of course, she was, as she usually is, totally right.

We went to the Governors' Ball, the big party held right after the ceremony. It's a private party for the Academy members. We only got two tickets for ourselves. We had arranged a party for our family and friends at a restaurant, so we decided we would not stay too long at the Ball. We really didn't know anyone there personally. We knew all the movie stars, but at the time, I didn't feel it was right to approach them. I wasn't really part of that club—yet.

We went to the restaurant and had a joyous celebration, our own personal Ball. We had chosen our favorite French restaurant, a place called Chez Helene. It was owned by a magnificent French-Canadian chef named Mimi Hebert. She had started her restaurant as a tiny storefront in Venice just a few blocks from where we were making *Animalymics*. We used to eat at her place two or three times a week during that production. As I mentioned, Venice was a tough neighborhood in those days, and one evening, one of Mimi's customers was mugged—shot and killed—leaving her restaurant. The victim was the daughter of New York Senator Jacob Javits. Mimi immediately closed the place, but eventually relocated to a safer neighborhood: Beverly Hills. On Oscar night, she gave us her back room for the private party. The food was spectacular.

Other than LOSING the Oscar, there was only one downside to the night. We asked a friend to take the photos at the party because we knew we would be too distracted and preoccupied. He did that—and lost the film. So we have no pictures of our Oscar Ball.

30

Back to Commercials!

The Oscar experience was somewhat other-worldly. To me, I worried that losing the Oscar would be a business opportunity lost. I could not have been more wrong.

Most people have heard about the alleged "Oscar jinx", where the winners, especially actors, have a drought and can't get a good role again for years. The speculation is that they are either too fussy about the roles they are offered, believing they must maintain the "status of an Oscar-winner", or they are perceived as too successful and expensive. Perhaps that's true. What I do know is that as an "Oscar loser" my little company got a very different bump. We were perceived as certifiably good but affordable because we lost!

We started to get a variety of small jobs, and in all of them, we managed to find a way to set our company apart my using the mystical powers of computer graphics. We'd do a new CINEFEX logo by animating a retro-billboard and all the cars in the drive-in movie theater with our plotter system. We'd do a commercial for a seat belt company and create the entire airplane interior in CG.

It was not long before our three-room suite on Hollywood Boulevard was getting cramped. I moved our office to a clean, small office building on Olive Avenue

DOI: 10.1201/9781003558231-30

in Burbank, eight blocks from the Disney Studio and next door to the Valley's most iconic diner, the TALLY RAND.

I had always leaned on Sue to be our talent recruiter. We were ready to hire animators, and as usual, she came through with amazing results. The first two youngsters she brought in were animators Sue had met when she was animating on Brad Bird's AMAZING STORIES episode called *Family Dog*. Tony Fucile was a Cal Arts grad who was a natural draftsman and gifted character designer. He would become one of the industry's most famous designers, creating the line-ups for some of the most successful Disney and PIXAR features.

Ralph Eggleston was that young Cal Artian who had asked Roy Disney why *The Black Cauldron* "sucked so much". We hired Ralph as an animator, and he was a great animator. But it soon became obvious that his talents as a designer were something else entirely. From the first, there was something very special about Ralph Eggleston. He would end up as the lead designer on everything we did, and go on to a monumental career that literally transformed the animation industry, as I will explain later.

Ralph was from rural Louisiana. As a very non-athletic super-literate artist he had been a notable outcast in the ultra-fundamentalist Southern town he grew up in. When he moved to Southern California and the free-spirited creativity of Cal Arts, it was his grand escape and rebirth. With Sue and I, it seemed he had found the family that fit him.

With our computer process being our distinct advantage over other companies, it was natural to expand that operation. I bought two more Silicon Graphics IRIS machines. In those days, the processing unit, the size of a small refrigerator, expended a lot of heat and needed to be kept in a very cold room. At Olive Street, we had a storage closet that was against the outside wall of the building, so we got permission to cut through the wall and install an industrial-size air conditioner. Despite having three units cranking away 24/7, it stayed very cold in that room! Years later, when I visited computer studios in Germany and France, I saw that they stored their white wine and fresh produce in their computer cool rooms. That never occurred to me. We also hired and trained two new computer "Technical Directors" Mark Pompian and Brian Schindler.

It was exciting when we landed our first big "national" commercial, a spot for Kellogg's Frosted Flakes featuring that animation superstar Tony the Tiger. The young advertising executives had heard of our computer process and just wanted us to give them something "new and different". This was right in line with the traditional "original thinking" of all young account executives, who "want to do something no one has ever seen before" by "thinking outside the box" and "pushing the envelope".

We decided to design the spot in a 50s retro-style with the distinguishing, sensational new visual feature of a moving camera, courtesy of our computer system. We would build the 50s-style kitchen in our computer, and it could change perspective (as if the camera was moving) as the characters danced through the shot. Because Ralph was just starting to emerge as a designer we hired another of our friends whose resume satisfied the advertising execs. That was Mike Giaimo, who would later become famous for designing such films as *Pocahontas* and *Frozen*. The plan worked wonderfully and the scenes of the kitchen looked terrific.

This spot was one of my first experiences of working with "food wranglers". When you do a commercial that involves food, you have to hire people whose specialty it is to make the food look good. You can imagine the challenge of transforming those flat, colorless slabs of meat into the thick, juicy, lettuce-decked delights on hamburger commercials. Why would you need them for frosted flakes?

If you dump an entire box of Frosted Flakes on to a tabletop, you will discover that very few of those flakes are unbroken. The Food Team had two ladies that sat by a table and went through twenty-five (25!) boxes of Frosted Flakes and, using tweezers, carefully extracted only the perfectly intact flakes. They did that until they had fifteen cups of flakes, the number they felt was needed to shoot the fifteen camera takes they estimated we would need to shoot to get one "hero" take of perfect flakes being poured from a box into a bowl.

The photography was done on a live-action "insert" stage with a 35 mm camera. The background was chroma-key green, the box was green, and the bowl was green. That's so the only thing that would be visible in the final plate would be the flakes. They were shot at high speed so they would appear to fall in graceful slowmotion. We would supply the cartoon box and cartoon bowl, and it would all happen in our cartoon kitchen. That, too, worked as planned.

In animation, you prefer to have the soundtrack finished first so you can animate your motion precisely to the beat. The song for this commercial was called "Intermission" and the lyrics asked you to take a break and enjoy Frosted Flakes because they were "the no-cholesterol no-fat snack!" True, no cholesterol and no fat. But what about all that sugar!? It occurred to me that I had come a long way from warning kids about bad nutrition in *Annie's Sugar-Coated Nightmare*.

Soon after that commercial, another job came our way that would open an entirely new business opportunity for our process—feature film movie titles. We were asked to do the titles for the Shelley Long-starring vehicle *Troop Beverly Hills*. Somebody must have seen our Frosted Flakes spot and decided they wanted those unusual computer-ey moves in the animation. They also loved the retro look and wanted something similar for the titles. There was a very hot designer in town named John Kricfalusi, and the studio wanted him to design the spot.

John would later gain tremendous fame for creating the outrageous *Ren and Stimpy* series, but even at this early stage of his career, you could see his unusual and eccentric habits. Somewhat like Don Bluth's "Bluthies", John already had a small cadre of loyalists who formed his team. He insisted we use all of them on the show, but being a limited budget we got him to settle for just a handful. They were quite talented, and one of them, a background painter named Vicky Jensen, would later leave John's circle and become one of the key members of our company.

John hosted a party every Friday night at his house that he called "theory night". It was supposedly a chance for artists to gather and exchange theories about animation. I went the first Friday after he started working with us. As it turned out, the attendees were almost exclusively his cadre, and most of the theories were John's. His favorite topic was proving that the greatest actor who had ever appeared in live-action movies was Kirk Douglas. As an example of greatness, John explained that Kirk Douglas, when shirtless, could act with his back muscles only. One could not tell how seriously he believed these theories.

I always remembered the Kirk Douglas obsession, because years later, when John's fame and success were peaking, they did a story about him in a magazine. John staged a picture of him teaching his animation team about "art theory". In the photo, John wore a white lab coat, all his artists sat at easels wearing lab coats, and all of them had big drawing tablets with charcoal portraits of—who else—Kirk Douglas!

The title sequence for *Troop Beverly Hills* was a success, and the proof was the most definite result you can hope for. It brought us more work, and this time, from the world's most demanding client.

31

Honey, I Shrunk the World

It had been almost five years since Roy Disney, Jr. had rescued the Walt Disney Studios from a corporate raider by bringing in a new management team to revitalize the company. That team was headed by Michael Eisner, and the man he appointed to head Disney's film division was a young, dynamic, hyper-energetic executive named Jeffery Katzenberg.

As legend has it, after Eisner told Jeffrey that he was the new head of the film division, Jeffrey literally had one foot out the office door when Eisner called out to him remind him that this would also include supervision of the animation division. Jeffrey stopped in his tracks and reminded Eisner that he had absolutely no experience in animation. "You'll figure it out", Eisner retorted. This was the story I had heard, and I actually repeated it in these exact words when I once introduced Jeffery at an awards dinner. He did not correct me.

Jeffrey may have been small in stature, but he was very intense. The word was that he awoke at 5:00 AM every morning and started the day with one hundred inverted sit-ups. He drank twenty cans of diet-Pepsi every day. As an unrivaled testament to his self-discipline, when the Disney theme parks switched their soft drink sponsorship from Pepsi to Coca-Cola, on that day, he switched to drinking twenty cans of Diet Coke a day. Who else could do that?

DOI: 10.1201/9781003558231-31

For animation, Jeffrey was a quick learner. The first thing he did was try to repair the disasterous *The Black Cauldron* by cutting twelve minutes out of the film, apparently figuring that twelve minutes less terrible entertainment would be more palatable to the audience. It didn't work. He supposedly showed a bit of hesitancy in choosing the next animated film to greenlight, but finally approved a picture that would eventually be titled *Oliver & Company*. This project had originally had been pitched with the title *Cats in the City*, so some people jokingly suspected that Jeffrey sparked to it because it was thematically "Katz in Burg".

By 1989, he was feeling his oats. He already elevated the youngsters John Musker and Ron Clements to co-direct the movie that would change many things: *The Little Mermaid*. He seemed to be enjoying animation, so when producer Tom Smith approached him about doing an animated title sequence for the next big Disney family live-action film *Honey, I Shrunk the Kids*, Jeffry like the idea. He insisted that he supervise the title production. It was, after all, going to be looked at as "Disney animation".

This was years before Disney set up a TV or Special Projects animation division. Their sole animation resource was Walt Disney Feature Animation, and that crew was completely devoted to feature production. It was flattering to realize that somehow, Jeffrey had heard enough good things about our little group that he felt we could be trusted to produce animation with "Disney quality".

We got a call to submit a bid on the job. Disney liked our numbers, and that began my first working experience with Jeffrey Katzenberg. It was an unusual arrangement. We started the job as we always did, with preliminary design work and storyboards. As we completed a stage of work, I'd inform Jeffery's office that we had artwork to review. I was given a date to come in, and it was always at the same time: 7:00 AM.

I'd arrive at the Disney front gate about 6:30 AM to be sure I was in Jeffery's office before he arrived. It was nostalgic for me to walk through the very same gate I had passed through fourteen years earlier when, as a pony-tailed ignoramus from Chicago, I had come seeking employment with my manila envelope of greeting card art samples. Jeffrey's office was in our beloved animation building. By that time, all the animators had been kicked out and replaced by executives, but it was still nice to see it again.

I would sit in Jeffrey's outer office, artwork in my lap, and listen to his secretary plan his day. Jeffrey was on his car phone. His secretary made sure she was at her desk, computer fired up, when Jeffrey got into his car and dialed in. I could hear her repeating commands and setting and changing meetings as Jeffrey rattled nonstop on the entire ride. At precisely 6:54 AM, he would hang up, and six minutes later, at 7:00 AM on the dot, he would charge into the office. As he passed me he would motion me to follow him.

We'd have our meeting. I had the mini-version of the Katzenberg creative experience that my feature film friends would have. He was very sharp, remembered every revision we did, had precise and intelligent criticism and comments, and never dictated the exact way we needed to improve the project. He simply pointed out what wasn't working or what could be better and demanded it be improved. How? That was our creative challenge.

With the production of the *Honey* titles, I felt our little company was really hitting its stride. Jeffery loved and quickly approved the characters designed by Rich Moore, props by Bob Camp and Jim Smith and backgrounds by Ralph Eggleston. Mark and Brian built CG models for almost every shot; a typewriter, a phonograph, a vacuum cleaner, etc. The schedule was tight, so I spread the animation tasks among our small crew and a few freelance animators. We delivered on time and Disney was happy with the results.

So happy, in fact, that another Disney job quickly came or way. This would be a short film done for the *Pavillion of Life* at Walt Disney World in Orlando. It was not the topic we expected to see in a Disney film. It was to explain the basics of human reproduction. The title was *The Making of Me*, but we affectionately referred to it as "The Sperm Film".

In the film, the narrator, Martin Short (the presenter who had denied me my Oscar) explains that in order for a sperm to fertilize an egg, it must navigate a tremendously difficult journey. A little talking Sperm Guy would be the hero, and he would be surrounded by, and competing with, dozens of almost identical sperm guys. That detail of the imagery was perfect for our computer process because we could digitally copy and multiply the characters many times, and our computer could animate the crowd in a fraction of the time it would have taken to hand-draw them.

After being the only Sperm Guy to survive the hazardous journey through the fallopian tubes, our hero sees his goal: the beautiful fertile egg-girl sitting in her egg cup. She holds up a red target, and he gleefully plows into her, sending up billows of colored smoke years before the advent of gender-reveal parties. It was a very cute film and would play for years in the Florida park.

Our next job was one that told me we had truly won the trust of the Disney studio. We were asked to animate Mickey Mouse for the TV special *Mickey's 60th Birthday Party*. It had been sixty years since Mickey Mouse had become a worldwide sensation in the first sound cartoon, *Steamboat Willie*. Animating the most treasured and iconic cartoon character in the world was something Disney rarely trusted an outside studio to do, so it was an honor and a responsibility. The Disney marketing department made that point to me, but having what I liked to call a bit of "Disney DNA" in my blood, I didn't need to be educated about the history of the mouse, or the great artists that had done this before us.

In the special, we'd be animating Mickey in a live-action environment, interacting with a live person. The young comic actor Mark Linn-Baker would walk down a hallway with Mickey and chat about the classic cartoons that would appear in the special. Our Mickey would not just have been drawn perfectly "on model", but drawn with a perfect perspective that matched the camera angle and surfaces of the live shot. He also needed to appear to be truly looking at, and interacting with, the live actor.

I might point out that there was some irony in the fact that Mickey Mouse, the character whose popularity had created the greatest animation studio in the world, was the perfect anomaly of the illusion of 2D hand-drawn animation. I mentioned earlier that one of the greatest miracles of 2D was that the animator was free to draw anything as long as he could *get the audience to believe it*! You could "cheat" and caricature structure, motion, shape, etc., as long as the audience bought it.

Mickey Mouse was the ultimate example of that because the classic Mickey design could not possibly exist in three-dimensions. If you watch an old Mickey cartoon, you will notice that his ears are always round. When he's facing you head on, he has those two big round ears on each side of his head. But as he turns sideways, those ears don't appear flat as they would in real 3D. They "migrate" across his skull, always maintaining that perfectly round shape.

That's why Mickey costumes at Disneyland never look exactly like the Mickey you see in the movies. The ears don't migrate. We animated the ears in a classic way, and our animation was happily stamped by the Disney studio as "approved".

During the job, I recalled how the very first Disney animators had actually traced around coins to keep the perfectly circular shapes of the ears. I also knew that Mickey's design had gone through subtle alterations over the decades, with the black circular dot-eyes replaced by irises and pupils. I knew that Disney legend Freddy Moore had given Mickey his most famous "comeback" role in the appealing short film *Mickey and the Beanstalk*.

I made the suggestion to the Disney producers that it might be fun to have a segment of the anniversary special show some of these interesting stories about the history of drawing Mickey Mouse. After a few days, they got back to me with their response. They would *never* do a segment like that about Mickey Mouse!

The reason? The Disney folks told me that the central mythology of Mickey in the Disney empire was that Mickey was not a "created character". Mickey existed. When kids saw him, or met him, he was the real thing. He was the *living* symbol of Disney.

I thought that was a remarkable dollars-and-cents affirmation about the belief held by all animators: that animation had the power to create characters you believed in and cared about.

Because we were getting these profitable jobs that were also allowing us to do high quality work, I had not given any thought to becoming a "content creator". I remembered the unpleasant experience of trying to sell our ULTRACROSS show. One day, our good friend and former employee Rich Moore returned to us and pitched us an idea. Rich had an idea that he felt was a slam-dunk. He believed we were the only studio with the talent to do it right, and our growing reputation gave us the momentum and opportunity to sell it. He wanted to do an animated series starring one of Los Angeles' most enigmatic celebrities: Angelyne!

I describe Angelyne as a "celebrity" because there was no other term. Everybody in L.A. knew of Angelyne because her billboards were plastered all over town.

They showed the extremely buxom blonde bombshell in a skimpy outfit draped across the sign that was simply labeled "Angelyne". She was not known to have acted in any shows, or appeared in any ads, or have any notoriety other than the billboards. But Rich was convinced that she'd make a great cartoon character.

Rich had called the number on the billboard and spoken to her agent. Rich arranged a meeting with the agent, and when we went to his office on La Cienega Boulevard, he didn't strike us as much of a talent agent. He was an older guy, with Angleyne as his only client. We suspected that a better title for him might be "sugar daddy". Rich had done some pretty cool retro-style designs of the proposed character, which impressed the agent. He called a day later and told us that Angelyne would visit Kroyer Films and meet with us.

Sure enough, the day arrived and Angelyne's famous pink corvette stingray parked in front of our building and the starlet herself emerged. We gave her a tour of our company and she seemed impressed, but with Angelyne, it was hard to read any genuine reactions. She was always posing. You got the sense that playing this identity was all she did, and she did it *all the time*. There were characters in Hollywood who did similar things. There was a TV horror-film hostess named "Elvira, Mistress of the Dark", but everyone knew she was an actress named Cassandra Petersen. Angelyne had no other identity. In fact, we were to learn that she never, ever left her apartment without being Angelyne.

We pitched her the initial idea. With a bit of savvy that surprised us, she said she would need to read a few treatments of episode ideas before committing to any deal. We agreed to that. She mentioned that she had no experience with animation or animators but found our studio cute and fascinating. Rich mentioned that he was having a party that night, and if she wanted to meet more animators that would be a good chance to do it. She immediately accepted his invitation.

At that time Rich was sharing a small bungalow in Burbank with Tony Fucile and another Cal Arts graduate (and future Oscar-nominee for writing *Wall-E*) Jim Reardon. The place was the quintessential bachelor pad. When we'd come over, we'd always have to move some empty pizza boxes off the couch to make room to sit down. When we got there the place was already mobbed. It wasn't because anyone knew Angelyne was coming. They didn't. We had just gotten the time wrong. In those days, the animation community was still rather small, every Cal Arts grad knew every other grad, and every one of them felt invited to show up at any party on the radar.

A short time later we heard a knock on the door and sure enough, Angelyne had arrived. She was wearing a light tan leather bikini-type fringed outfit that barely contained her ample figure. I will never forget that moment. She walked into the living room, there was a hushed moment of recognition, and within seconds every animator had fled to the dining room or back yard. Sue, I, and Rich were left alone with her. Her raging sexuality was too much for the typical animator who was, as yet, only beginning to date girls.

That was the odd thing about Angelyne. She was externally overtly sexual, but to me, she had no genuine allure of femininity. She never responded in a way that seemed remotely genuine or personal. The posing was constant. I suspected that that was the reason that her fame came from still shots on billboards, and nothing else.

As it turned out, the Angelyne deal never happened. She wanted absolute total control and approval over everything. After the approval difficulties on *Troop Beverly Hills* I knew that would never work. We politely let her slip away back to her billboards. Just as well, because we got a new deal that would require all hands on deck.

32

Killing Santa

Warner Bros. had a big Christmas movie in the works. It was *National Lampoon's Christmas Vacation* starring Chevy Chase. Apparently, they had seen our *Honey* titles and felt an animated title sequence would be a great way to kick off their movie. The producers invited Sue, me, and Ralph to a screening of the rough cut of the movie. Chevy was there and politely met us, but that was the only time we would see him. We watched the film, and it was hilarious. The producers had no pre-conceived idea for the title sequence. We were to come up with that. They told us to come back as soon as we could to pitch our idea. Time was of the essence. The movie had a Christmas release date.

We went back to our studio and started to brainstorm. We soon discovered a big problem. The movie had already mentioned, parodied, made fun of, or lampooned every aspect of Christmas. No matter what situation we thought of—ugly outdoor lights, bad tree decor, lousy presents—the film already had mocked it. We started to worry. Here was our chance to get a big job on a major film and we were having brain freeze. What to do?

We did what most creative people did. We sought liquid inspiration. There was a pub just a few blocks from our office called The Buchanan Arms. It was the favorite watering hole of Burbank animators. I brought Sue, Ralph, Tony,

 DOI: 10.1201/9781003558231-32

Andrew, and Leslie Hinton, our production manager, and we ordered pitchers of beer and lamented our situation. As we did, things got looser and less proper. Finally, after a dozen lame, irreverent ideas had been tossed on the table and discarded, somebody made a desperate suggestion. "Why don't we just kill Santa?"

Kill Santa? That was pretty funny. Why not booby-trap the house so Santa had a hell of time trying to get in? Strangely, that sounded more and more like an actual good idea. We went back to the studio and started to brainstorm gags. We sketched a few on paper. Not bad!

That was the sequence we proposed to the Warner Bros. folks, and amazingly, they bought it. With this clear direction, the sequence unfolded pretty quickly. We created a storyboard that really worked. One of our new story artists, a kid right out of Cal Arts, had some great gag ideas. That "kid" was Andrew Stanton, who would later win Oscars for directing *Finding Nemo* and *Wall-E*. Ralph did small pastel thumbnail color sketches that defined all the designs, and our new background painter, Dennis Venizelos, starting turning out beautiful background paintings. We came up with clever way to use our computer process. It was perfect for the precision of the title lettering itself, but we also built CG models of Santa's sleigh and reindeer, the tree, the presents, etc. We had to animate things very quickly because the Christmas release date was approaching.

On both *Honey* and *The Making of Me* I had sent the ink & painting work to Steve Hahn's studio in Korea. Steve had given me a great price and the work was always completed very quickly. I called him about doing the *Christmas Vacation* job and he made me what was to be a fateful offer. He had just opened a new branch studio in Manila in the Philippines. He had good, experienced managers there and an eager young crew. If I sent the job there, he would give me a really low price and I would have the exclusive focus from the crew. They would finish the job with no risk of missing the deadline. I decided to try it.

We packaged up the work as we completed it and shipped it off. It was decided that because of the very tight deadline, the surest way to complete it in time was for me to fly to Manila and do the on-site approvals personally. Steve also had a full camera department, so they could shoot all the art and give me a completed film. That would eliminate the need to check and photograph the artwork in L.A. With that plan, I made my flight reservations to go to Manila.

The morning I was packing my bags to leave, Sue came in the bedroom and grabbed my hand. "You have to see this", she said. She dragged me to the living room. The TV had a news report live from Manila. There was an armed coup in progress There were tanks in the street. There were people firing guns at the Hilton Hotel—the Hotel I was booked to stay in!

"YOU ARE NOT GOING!" Sue said. Of course, she was right. I couldn't have gone if I had wanted to. The Manila airport was closed.

But what about our title sequence? Would Warner Bros. consider this a justifiable delay? I suspected that nothing justified missing the Christmas release of a hit movie. I was able to get on the phone with the manager of the Manila studio.

She said that our artwork had all arrived, and that the work was proceeding just fine, but because the airport was closed and there was no way to ship it back to us.

What a strange dilemma. You always expect something to go wrong on a job, but an armed revolt? That was a new one. I was at a loss as to what to do. We started to brainstorm ways to finish the job on time. We watched the news obsessively. Within just a few days, the government suppressed the revolt and the shooting stopped. We found out that the airport would re-open in a day or two. We did some calculations and realized that the best chance to deliver the job on time—maybe the only chance—was to stick with original idea and have me finish it all on-site.

We talked to the manager in Manila and she said the danger was over. Sue was not delighted with the idea, but I decided to leave the next day. I flew to Narita Airport in Tokyo where I was to make my connection to the flight to Manila. I was flying Business Class, and when I got on the plane, I wondered if I had rushed things. I was the only passenger in Business Class. I got that sick feeling that everybody knew something I didn't know.

Curious, I walked back to the curtain and peeked into the Economy section. It was packed! Apparently, the average guy just needed to get home.

A few hours later, we glided into the Manila airport at dusk. When I looked down at the tarmac, I was shocked to see that there were no aircraft anywhere. Apparently, the airlines had gotten all their equipment out during the fighting, and we were one of the very first to return. We landed, I whisked through customs with no problems and made my way to the terminal. When I got there, it was like a scene from *The Year of Living Dangerously*. The entrance hall was completely empty because it had been ringed with a ten-foot high chain link fence. Armed guards stood against the fence, and on the other side, in a continuous mash of faces, thousands of people crammed in, looking for their arriving relatives.

I looked around for some sign of welcome. I was hoping for one of those valet guys like at LAX with the MR. KROYER signs—but nothing. I made my way to the gate, and the guard opened it. What was I to do? I decided that I would just make my way to the curb, find a taxi, and ask to be taken to a big hotel. As I started to move, I heard people calling "Bill! Bill!" I turned and saw the Manila manager and her driver working her way toward me. There had been gunfire earlier, and all traffic had been stopped. They told me that no one was allowed to drive into the airport. That was why they were late. They had a van parked outside. They would take me to my hotel.

Thus began my first-hand introduction to third-world filmmaking.

33

Animation the Third World Way

My hotel in Manila had no other Americans in it because it was small, neighborhood place used by locals for visiting relatives. Downtown Manila was still recovering from the coup, so the barricades and military checkpoints made it difficult to stay at the big hotels. My hotel was in a nice neighborhood and just a mile walk from the studio. I usually walked because I liked the exercise, and I always liked observing the small details of foreign cities.

In the case of Manila in 1989, many of those details were not pleasant. The first half of my walk was through a gated neighborhood. Every house was inside a walled compound. These were not decorative walls. Each one was topped with broken glass or razor wire. There was a real problem with car crashes caused by speeding. Since no one paid any attention to traffic laws or traffic signs, the police took a more physical approach to slowing people down. They could not afford to install speed bumps, so they dug "speed ditches". Most residential streets had these trenches, and if you hit them going fast, you would break your axle. Of course, rich people and criminals solved this by riding in high-clearance Range Rovers.

When I got to the shopping district, there was a familiar sight: the golden arches of McDonalds. But this McDonalds was different from the U.S. version.

DOI: 10.1201/9781003558231-33

It had just one entrance, blocked by an armed guard who had complete discretion about who he let in the door.

I had to cross a drainage canal to get to the studio, and the contents of the canal were horrid. It was packed with every sort of trash, including some dead dogs and cats, whose carcasses were quickly nibbled way by rats. The building that housed the Hahn Animation Studio had a bank on the first floor. I got an immediate lesson in the trust the average business had in the local police. The bank had its own guards flanking the door, sitting on folding chairs. One held a shotgun, the other a machine gun. I got to know these two after a few days and took a photo with me holding a painted *Christmas Vacation* cel flanked by these gunmen.

It was a three-floor walk-up to the animation studio. The elevators, I was told, were very risky to take. The stairwell was quite dark, and as I walked up I heard crunching beneath my feet. When I went down for lunch and there was a bit more light I saw all the cockroaches I had crushed to death. They were the size of small pinecones.

When I reached the third-floor lobby, I headed for the studio door, I saw a uniformed guard, sitting at a folding table, punching animation paper with a paper punch. He had his automatic pistol resting on the table beside the punch. I was told that many businesses had their own armed guards. Because it irked Steve Hahn to have to pay a guy a full day's salary who just sat idly all day, he had moved a table out to the lobby so the guy could work. Manila thus became the only city I could name where armed men punched cels.

The studio itself was a lot like other animation studios. It was your basic dry-wall office building. The animators, inkers, and painters had cubicles in larger rooms. The few execs had their own offices. I noticed that there was a rather hefty Filipino gentleman sitting in the office at the end of the hall. He never seemed to do anything but read the paper. I was told that, indeed, he never did anything. He was the nephew of one of the big Filipino Army Generals. Having a relative like that on your payroll was the required form of payola to keep your business open and running without harassment in Manila.

Other than these oddities, the animation work was proceeding in the tradi-tional manner! By the time I arrived they had already copied all our artwork to cels and the painting and photography was moving along quickly. Using the Hahnho method, they worked fast and made mistakes, so being there in person and instantly calling out the corrections was, as we predicted, the only way to get the job done in time.

All the workers were very young, and most of them spoke English. I noticed that almost all of them had sleeping bags under their desks. As I got a bit more familiar and comfortable with them, I asked if they were forced to work really long hours when a visiting client like me was not around. No, they said, the stu-dio was quite fair about keeping a regular workday. Most of them kept sleep-ing bags because they much preferred to sleep at the studio than their homes. The studio had three things that most of their homes did not: air conditioning, indoor flush toilets, and safety. Some of them told me that their homes were so overcrowded that they were encouraged by their parents to sleep at the studio.

As we closed in on our deadline, I took the entire crew out to lunch at a nice restaurant as a way of thanking them for their work. I was clearly the first client who had ever done this. I also got the sense that most of them rarely set foot in a restaurant with tablecloths.

There was one other American in the studio, Adam Kuhlman, who had married a Filipino girl and was the in-house animation director. He said he generally liked living in Manila. The one thing he had trouble getting used to was remembering to check the toilet before he sat down. Apparently he had had a few incidents with snakes crawling in through the plumbing.

The Hahnho studio had one feature that was universally true in the world of overseas outsourced production. Salaries were cheap. These youngsters did not have a lot of training or experience, but for most of the tasks in post-production, like xeroxing, painting within the lines, and checking for color pops, they could do as well as anyone. Even if they were a bit slower and sloppier than American workers, their pay was so low that it made the business profitable. Even though the pay was low by our standards, these jobs were some of the best-paying jobs in the area, with working conditions that were safer and more physically comfortable than most professions. I found those conditions to be similar to the other off-shore studios I visited in Korea, Thailand, and India.

Pay Day in Manila was Friday, and I was surprised to hear from the studio manager, Chris, that the only way to pay people in Manila was in cash. Nobody trusted banks to handle transactions like credit cards or checking accounts. She told me that her routine was to walk to the bank just after lunch, take out the entire studio payroll in cash, stuff it in her purse, and walk back. She said that this technique was so unobtrusive that she had never had any trouble.

I went with her to the bank that Friday just to see some more of the town. She withdrew a giant wad of cash and jammed the roll into her wallet, then stuck it in her handbag. I don't know if it was the fact that I was with her, perhaps being the foreigner that draws attention, but we were not half a block from the bank when three young guys slammed into us. They jostled us, then ran up the block, paused, and took off in three different directions.

"I've been hit", Chris said. She looked down at her handbag. It had been slit open with a razor. They had grabbed the case in her purse and were gone before we knew—literally—what hit us. Thankfully, neither of us had been hurt. Then Chris dug into her bag and drew out the wad of cash! "They got my prescription sunglass case!" she said happily!

My week in Manila drew to a close. It looked like we would finish on time. As a reminder how close we were getting to Christmas, when I walked home through my walled neighborhood, I saw a group of young kids singing Christmas carols. The Philippines, after all, was a Catholic country. They could have been right out of a Disney film. Every little kid was dressed in white, and they held votive candles. They went from gate to gate and sang beautifully. As I walked past them, I heard the bolt slide and the large iron gate swing open. I watched as a uniformed guard, with a machine gun slung over his shoulder, handed out candy to the carolers.

I had gotten some advice from a friend that when eating at restaurants in Manila I should never eat chicken, beef, or pork because those animals often scrounge in dumps and eat all kinds of questionable things. The safest thing was to eat only seafood. For the eight days I was there, I stuck to this rule. On my last night, the studio managers took me out to dinner to a very special place. It was a restaurant called "The Crystal Palm Room" and it was in the most famous hotel in town, the historic Manila Hotel, where General Douglas MacArthur stayed during WW2.

The restaurant was grand, and got its name from a giant crystal palm tree sculpture in the center of the room. China plates, crystal goblets, white table-cloths, and waiters in tuxedos added to the atmosphere. Here at last, I thought, is a restaurant where it would be safe to order beef for dinner! I ordered a N.Y. steak.

A while later, our meals were served, and my steak looked and tasted, delicious. Our waiter came by and asked if everything was to our liking.

"How is your steak?" he asked me.

"It's great", I replied.

"You know", he said, " we fly those in every day from L.A.!"

How exotic, I thought. I'm in the Philippines and I'm probably eating a steak from the Safeway in El Segundo.

34

Fairy Tales Will Come True!

National Lampoon's Christmas Vacation hit the theaters on time in December and was a big hit. Our titles were well-received. It was not a surprise when we got the call to do another title sequence. This would be for *The Jetson's Movie*, a theatrical feature based on the popular TV series. We wouldn't have to produce the entire sequence. Hanna-Barbera, the big TV animation company that did the series and was now doing the movie, would be providing all the character animation. They were hiring us to do what they could not do: computer-animated spaceships.

The spaceships were easy to build, and I would be doing all the animation myself. This was especially fun because I would be working with one of the old-time legends of animation, the "H" of H&B, Bill Hanna. Bill was almost eighty years old but still a vibrant character. There wasn't that much animation to do, so we just had a few sessions together. I'd go to his office at H&B, and he'd describe what he wanted. When I had animation to show him, he'd come to our office, sit with me, and I'd do the tweaks on the spot with him sitting beside me at the computer.

What was fun and unusual about Bill was that he would *sing his comments* to describe the speed and rhythm of the movement he was looking

DOI: 10.1201/9781003558231-34

for. He'd say, "Right now it's going wah-wah-wah, and I want it to be more wumpity-wumpity-wumpity". Strangely I knew exactly what he meant, and the job went like butter.

I also had the privilege of being invited to lunch a few times at Bill's booth at The Smoke House Restaurant. This was one of the oldest eateries in Burbank, right across from the Warner Bros. Studio, and Bill always had the corner booth in the main dining room. He would order his luncheon martini and hold court with whoever stopped by. It was a real blast-from-the-past experience, one of the last holdovers from the Greatest Generation of cocktail lovers.

Our next job was a change of pace from our feature film title business. It was a job for Mattel Toys. Instead of having a toy line connected to a TV series, Mattel decided to connect a TV series to a toy line. They were already well into production on a line of toys called *Computer Warriors*. These were like mini-transformers. They were miniature cartoon warriors that hid out in average desktop items like soda cans or pencil sharpeners. The idea was to have the mundane object on your desk suddenly fold inside out and become the flying vehicle of a small robotic warrior. We weren't going to do a series. We would just be producing a half-hour special, with a slightly better-than-series budget.

It seemed like a fun project. Although we were definitely not the typical TV series production house, like Hanna-Barbera, we were the studio of choice because of our computer capability. We could build the transforming objects in CG and fly them in exciting action sequences. Mark and Brian got to work on the CG models while the rest of us applied ourselves to layouts and animation.

Fast-moving animated objects had to move "on 1's" so they would not appear to jitter, so that mean twenty-four painted cels for each second of screen time. This job was going to require a lot of ink and paint. I considered a return to the Philippines, but I got a strong recommendation from some colleagues to consider a studio in West Germany. The Berlin Wall had fallen and businesses were starting to locate to East Berlin. Apparently wages and rents were very cheap there, and a young German producer coincidentally also named Hahn—Gerhard Hahn— had just opened a shop. He was offering great deals to get his studio established.

I talked to Gerhard on the phone and he was persuasive. I agreed to send him some work. We sent a few test scenes and they did a good job, so we decided to use his studio for the painting.

It was quite hectic around our small, crowded office as we went into full production mode on *Computer Warriors*. We didn't have a lot of visitors, so I was surprised one day when two gentlemen with distinctly Australian accents asked to see me. We sat down in my office to chat and I quickly learned that they were the guys behind what was at the time the biggest hit film in Hollywood, *Crocodile Dundee*. Peter Faiman had been a very successful TV director in Australia when he had been tapped to do the film, and he had obviously hit it out of the park. Wayne Young was one of the producers of the film, and it was he who had come up with the idea for the project they were now developing.

Peter and Wayne wanted to make an animated feature film. Because of the fantastic success and popularity of *Dundee* they had already secured financing from an Australian company. They had come to Los Angeles to secure a distribution deal and find a studio to produce the animation. They had quickly learned that Jeffrey Katzenberg and Disney had no interest at all in doing an outside project. As they began to check around, they were distressed to learn that the other big animation studios in town were all TV-focused, and the quality was far below the "Disney quality" that Aussies were aspiring to achieve.

It should be noted that at this time in 1989, the only legitimate feature film studios with any track record were Disney and Don Bluth. Bluth had done pretty well working with Spielberg on *American Tail* and *The Land before Time*, but now he was on his own with an original idea called *All Dogs Go to Heaven*. And his studio was in Ireland.

How had they found us? Peter and Wayne had already hired a writer to do the screenplay, and he was "the best animation writer in town" by virtue of having writing credits on the last three Disney features. His name was Jim Cox, and he happened to be married to Penney Finkelman Cox, the producer of that hit Disney family film *Honey, I Shrunk the Kids*. Jim had recommended us because of our work on the titles, and when the Aussies checked our credits, they decided that we were the only studio in town doing the kind of Disney-quality animation they were looking for.

"That is flattering", I told them. "But you do realize that I only have twelve employees"

"You can staff up!" they said gleefully! I suspect they thought you just hired a film crew like a live-action film would do. They had that easy-going "g'day mate" kind of bravado, and they started to make me think I should seriously consider this. It was then that my wife Sue asked what story they wanted to make.

"It's about faeries in the rainforest", they said.

I glanced at Sue and saw that kind of neutral smile that I knew meant "are you kidding me?" Just a few days before we had been talking about what kind of cool, original story we might come up with to move animation away from the cliche of fairy tales. And now, of all things, an actual *fairy* tale?

Wayne Young's wife, Diana Young, had written a series of children stories about faeries in the Australian rainforest. We weren't aware that Australia even had a rainforest. It wasn't like she had written books that were Best Sellers with a built-in audience. The stories were unpublished. But Wayne had convinced an Australian company that this was the next big thing, and that the makers of *Crocodile Dundee* would strike gold again. The stories were called *The Ferngully Mob*.

We chatted for a few minutes more. I started to describe the daunting logistics of making an animated feature film, and having to build from scratch a production team to do it. Wayne and Peter were undaunted. They told me to think about it and call them tomorrow.

When they left, we had a company meeting and talked about this remarkable offer. No one was particularly excited about the topic. But there was *that one thing*. When would we ever again have someone walk into our office and give us the chance to make a feature film? Could this be real?

In the end, we weren't stupid enough to turn it down. I called Wayne and Peter and we started talking about the deal.

The company in Australia that had agreed to finance the film was called FAI. "FAI" stood for FIRE and ACCIDENT INSURANCE. It had been founded a generation ago and was one of Australia's largest and most successful insurance companies. The founder had just retired and handed over the reigns of power to his relatively young and inexperienced twenty-eight year old son Rodney Adler. Rodney was looking for ways to both innovate and diversify the company, and prove to his elderly Board of Directors that he deserved to run the show. It was in that fortuitous moment that Wayne and Peter waltzed into his office and told him that the best way to set himself apart in the insurance business was to fund an animated feature film.

Forget that FAI had no experience at all in film production, or that Wayne and Peter had no experience in animation. It may have been a good example of the Dunning-Krueger phenomenon, where complete lack of knowledge in a subject produces a feeling of complete assurance and confidence. Rodney agreed to fund the picture.

When Wayne and Peter came to Hollywood I suspected that they were having problems adjusting to the way deals were made. I don't know how things went down in Australia, but despite their recent success they discovered that it was tough to get meetings with the people they needed to meet. They finally met two young, aggressive producers who they sparked to, Jamie Willett and Jeff Dowd. Willett and Dowd had had a bit of success, and they were L.A. natives and natural networkers.

When I met them, it was apparent to me that Jeff Dowd was rather a unique character. He had a laid-back but somewhat outrageous personality. His immediate enthusiasm for *Ferngully* would prove to be the kick-starter, but little did I know that he would unwittingly affect the career of another of my Hollywood acquaintances, Jeff Bridges. The Cohn Brothers modeled their character Jeff Lebowski, the star of their film *The Big Lebowski,* To this day Jeff Dowd calls himself "The Dude".

Willett and Dowd got the Aussies one step up the ladder to meet with Hollywood big shots Bob Cort and Ted Field, who liked the project, and who in turn got the meeting with Joe Roth, the head of Fox Studios. So when then deal started to come together, *FernGully* already had seven producers. It would add two more Australian producers later when these seven proved problematic, and eventually a tenth producer—the one who actually worked.

The Aussies benefited from some very lucky timing. They were meeting with Joe Roth just weeks after Disney's film *The Little Mermaid* hit the theaters. *Mermaid*, directed by my close friends John Musker and Ron Clements, would have a monstrous impact on the animation industry. After the modest performance of their last picture, *Oliver & Company*, Disney had actually started to question whether they should keep the animation division going. Roy Disney, Jr. had been adamant that they keep it alive, and it was quite possible that the existence of the legendary department rested on the performance of *Mermaid*.

So it was that Disney, Hollywood, and everyone else was shocked and delighted when *The Little Mermaid* did huge box office. What was very noticeable and groundbreaking was that this picture broke through the traditional limitation of the "family audience" demographic and became a "date movie". Rarely before had childless teenagers and young adults gone to an animated movie.

I went to see the movie on opening weekend desperately hoping it would be a good picture. Needless to say, it knocked my socks off. After I got choked up watching Glen Keane's phenomenal animated performance of Ariel in "Part of Your World" I knew the movie would be a smash. In a typical Hollywood backstory, the "suits", in this case, Katzenberg, had originally wanted to cut this song because it supposedly bored little kids. Instead, it became legendary.

With *Mermaid* and the solid box office the previous year of *Who Framed Roger Rabbit,* there was a buzz that a new age in animation was beginning. It would, indeed, be labeled the "Second Golden Age" and flow seamlessly into the seismic shift of computer animation. With that sentiment being discussed around town, it was natural that Joe Roth and Fox were interested in testing the waters of feature animation—especially if an Australian company was footing the bill.

Wayne and Peter started to come to our office daily to get things rolling. I told them I wanted something in writing and some money before we started to work on the film. They boasted than in Australia a "man's word is his bond" and things got going as soon as you shook hands. Ironically, this was actually the way some deals happened in Hollywood. When a man the stature of Joe Roth told you that you had a deal, you could literally take that to the bank before all the contracts were executed. Funny enough, when Joe Roth did agree to distribute the film, it was the Aussies who balked at sending us money until they had a signed agreement with Fox.

My contract on *FernGully* was as thick as a phone book. Part of the complexity came from the fact that not only would I be directing the picture, but my company would be the production entity. That contract would not be completed and signed for months, but we executed a "deal memo" and the money started flowing.

After some discussion, we decided that the very first thing we needed to do was a research trip. This idea of what might be mis-labeled as a "location scout" was a relatively new thing in the business of animation. No Disney development artists had ever gone on a trip to Bavaria to research *Snow White*, but this idea of visiting actual locations was catching on. Disney had sent its animation team to Australia to prep for *The Rescuers Down Under*, and research trips would be the norm in feature animation for the next decade.

Our movie would take place in one location, the Australian rainforest, and because of massive deforestation there weren't many locations to choose from. We would be spending most of our time in Lamington National Park in North Queensland, in mountains so remote that it had proven uneconomical to log them out. We'd fly to Sydney, take a plane up to Byron Bay, and drive to the mountains.

We would take just a small crew on this trip. It would be me, Sue, Ralph Eggleston, Tony Fucile, Mark Pompian, Vicky Jensen, Dennis Venizelos, our Producer Tom Klein, and a freelance designer I had worked with named Jean Perrimon. We would go in January. Everyone would fly direct from L.A. except me. I had a commitment to stop in East Berlin and approve the last of the work being done at Gerhard's studio, so I would fly from Germany and meet everyone in Sydney.

Berlin in January had some of that gray bleakness that seemed so recognizable from WW2 films. West Berlin was quite lively, but when my cab driver took me through the Brandenburg Gate to East Berlin it was truly another world. While the West had rebuilt West Berlin as a glittering showcase of capitalism, the Soviets seemed to have wanted to punish the Germans by leaving the East in ruins. Construction cranes were starting to pop up, but many buildings looked untouched since the war.

Leave it to Gerhard to have gotten into a building the second they allowed him to move. He had a huge warehouse loft and he was paying next to nothing in rent, literally a fraction of what he paid in the West. No wonder he could deliver on a small budget. The building still had bullet holes in the exterior, but it did have electricity. I remember going to lunch at what was jokingly referred to as a cafe. It was a small shop with wooden tables, heated by an old iron stove with a pipe going through the roof. Very retro.

I went to the flea market at the Brandenburg Gate on Sunday morning and bought some unusual souvenirs, including Soviet army gear. Gerhard gave me a tour of the city. He showed me the areas where the Soviet troops had billeted for the forty-five years they had occupied the city. When they left, they took everything, even stripping out the plumbing and door handles.

Gerhard's company had finished the painting on *Computer Warriors* so I was off to Australia. I would fly West to East, and it was not direct. The flight from Frankfurt to my stopover in Singapore was the longest nonstop flight in the world at that time. Because I like to visit exotic places, I schedule a two-day layover in Singapore because I thought it would be exotic.

It was anything but. Singapore was the cleanest, most sterile place I had ever been. Having visited Hong Kong, Seoul, and Manila it was almost suburban in its cleanliness and order. I sought out the famous Raffles Hotel and found it to be far from notorious.

The one significant impact the stopover had on the production came from my experience at breakfast in my hotel. I was reading the local English-language newspaper and came across a remarkable article about a new, modern, extremely expensive skyscraper that was about to be demolished because of something called FENG SHUI.

I had never heard of Feng Shui, but apparently it was a traditional Chinese practice that sought to harmonize natural forces with the environment. The building in question had been built by a Western firm that considered the location to be prime real estate. The local Singapore Feng Shui practitioners had deemed the sight to have horrible energy. Despite those warnings the building had gone up—and remained completely vacant for five years. No Chinese company would touch it. Having failed to get any tenants, they were tearing it down.

I had the thought that there might be something to this idea of Feng Shui. Months later, when we asked our devoutly Christian real estate agent in Los Angeles to consult a Feng Shui practitioner about the energy of any proposed location for our studio, we had a hard time convincing her we were serious.

35

Raindrops Falling in Our Heads

If you look at a map of Australia, it's easy to spot the town of Byron Bay. It's the Easternmost point of the continent, a little bump sticking out of the coast that happens to be where the South Pacific and Antarctic currents meet. That makes it a fantastic place to snorkel and scuba dive. It has become a world-class vacation and surfing spot, but its origins are quite different. The town was founded to support one industry: logging.

To the West, the landscape rises into the mountains of the McPherson Range, once lush with a rainforest filled with valuable, majestic cedar trees. The Aussies started to log these in the 1800s, cutting them and sliding them down the hillsides in what became known as "shoots". The business slowed as it became more difficult to transport the logs. A local guy named Romeo Lahey began efforts to preserve what was left of the virgin forest, but by the time the government actually passed laws to do that, an Irish clan called the O'Reilly's had already been squatting in the mountains for decades. Rather than try to evict mountain people (like Americans did with the Tennessee Valley Authority) the Australians took a more practical approach. The O'Reilly clan could stay—and run the Park headquarters and Guest-house.

DOI: 10.1201/9781003558231-35

After a few days of recovering from jet lag in Byron Bay, our animation team boarded some vans and headed to the O'Reilly Hotel in Lamington National Park. The first few hours of the trip were through coastal plains with cattle farms. As we climbed in elevation, the land was still open but brushy. We were surprised to learn that this had been rainforest when the white settlers arrived. As in America, it had not taken long to strip the land.

I recalled visiting the famous Concord Bridge in Massachusetts years before. The bridge sits among tall, shaded trees, but when you look at historic woodcuts of the famous "shot heard 'round' the world" battle in 1775, the landscape is wide open and almost treeless. Then you realize that in 1775, Massachusetts had been occupied since the 1650s, so in that hundred years, the settlers had cut down every tree for fuel and building materials. A similar thing happened here, with apparently a bit of intentional rainforest-burning on top of it.

Once we reached the high elevation, the landscape changed to lush forest. This is what we had come to see. Our theory had been that we would do a much better film if we could experience and understand the land we were portraying. That theory turned out to be true, but became even more meaningful. We were about to see wonders that we could not have imagined or invented. What's more, we would end up with a philosophical principle that we felt was critically important. We decided to only use real flora and fauna in our movie. We wanted to show that *FernGully* was not a paradise that existed only in fantasy, but existed in reality. If people realized that, perhaps they would be more motivated to preserve and protect it.

The first thing we noticed about O'Reilly's Hotel was that almost everyone was named O'Reilly. And looked Irish. Surely they must have married outside the clan at some point? Maybe it was too long a walk down the mountain.

The Hotel was very woody, nestled in the forest, and comfortable but not cruise-ship extravagant. We threw our bags in our rooms and gathered on an outside terrace for a welcoming drink. As you may have heard, Australians like to imbibe, and it is unsociable to refuse. We got our beer and cocktails and arranged some wicker chairs in a circle and started to talk about our plans for the next few days.

As we did, a rather large brown snake scooted out of the underbrush and crawled right past our chairs, actually gliding over the bare feet of our writer, Jim Cox. It happened so fast that no one even had time to jump, or express surprise. Jim cracked a joke about "the welcoming committee" but we noticed that our hotel hosts were uncharacteristically rigid. After a moment, one commented that the snake "looked like a brown snake". We all agreed it was brown. It turned out that is the actual name of the snake—the Eastern brown snake, and it is one of the most venomous snakes on earth.

"No worries", our hosts said. "Never seen that happen here. Not likely to happen again!" But we moved the meeting inside to the lounge anyway. It turns out that Australia is loaded with poisonous things, a few of which would encounter later. Ironically, the two islands of New Zealand, which many people mistakenly think are similar to Australia, do not have a single poisonous creature of any species. Australia just got lucky.

For our trips into the forest, our producers had engaged the services of a guide. His name was Glenn Threlfro, and he was one of the country's most famous nature photographers. Glenn had already published several best-selling photographic essays about Australian wildlife. He was known to have sat motionless for hours in the bush to get a shot of some rare bird or beast. He was a tall, very thin, very funny self-deprecating character.

When you think of these wildlife adventurers like the "Crocodile Hunter" you imagine them decked out in safari outfits with expensive camping gear. Not Glenn Threlfro. He showed up in what we learned was his usual "bush attire": ragged short shorts, a T-shirt, and old tennis shoes. He did have one other piece of outdoor gear. If the rain came down heavy he would pull a plastic baggie from his back pocket and tuck it over his head.

Glenn drove an old mail truck that had been fitted with extra seats. It was his version of a tour bus. We climbed in and started a very bumpy ride to a clearing he knew where we would have some wildlife encounters. As we bounced along, I noticed that there was a large canvas bag tucked under the driver's seat. Like everything else in the truck, it jostled as we drove, but on closer observation it seemed to me to be moving on its own.

I finally asked, "Glenn, is there something in that bag under your seat?"

Glenn smiled at me, and a few moments later we jerked to a stop near a large clearing. After we were all out of the truck, Glenn grabbed the canvas bag, reached inside, and drew out a six-foot long boa constrictor! The snake was called a "carpet boa" because of the pattern on its back. Glenn said he had seen the snake crossing the road on his way to our hotel and he thought we would like to meet it. We all got a chance to handle the snake. It was our first hands-on experience with a rainforest inhabitant, and it made such an expression that we included it in the movie.

That process would continue throughout the visit. The sights we saw would completely shape the contents of the film.

Glenn showed us two of the most distinctive floral features of the forest. The first was the tree called the strangler fig. This tree starts as a seed on a living tree and eventually engulfs the tree with its roots, killing the host and leaving a huge lattice-like tree with a hollow center. We featured this tree in the film as the place where Crysta meets the escaped lab bat, Batty Koda.

Another signature feature was the "fairy ring", a circle of trees growing in a ring. This usually resulted from the roots of a fallen tree sprouting a new generation of trees in a perfect circle. The aborigines thought this was a magical place, so of course it became an important location in our story.

We saw a large bird that Glenn identified as a "rainforest turkey". We asked if it was good to eat. Glenn said that the recipe for rainforest turkey was widely known. You plucked the bird, cleaned it, seasoned it, and put in a pot along with a large brick. You boiled it for six hours. Then you threw out the bird and ate the brick.

We had a picnic lunch in a nearby clearing. As we ate, we were startled when a half-dozen huge lizards emerged from the undergrowth and walked toward us. Glenn identified these as goannas (the Australian version of an iguana), who were quite harmless and often quite brazen when it came to a free snack. We were eating roasted chicken parts for our lunch, so we started tossing whole chicken breasts to the goannas. We watched, fascinated, as they cradled the entire breast in the pouch of their neck, walked to a rock, and began to slam the breast against the rock until they broke up the bone. Then they swallowed it whole.

Of course, we had to put that in the movie. We replaced the chicken breast with our human hero, Zak, who gets shrunk down to chicken breast-size..

After dinner one night Glenn led us on a nighttime excursion that was one of the most remarkable and magical of the trip. The Australian rainforest is full of phosphorescent plants that glow in the dark. He showed us a grotto whose walls were covered with hundreds of tiny mushrooms that made the cave look like a star-filled planetarium. He led us to a stand of trees that had large, stair-step fungus attached to the trunk. These looked like small glowing platforms. We never would have imagined such things existed if we hadn't seen them. Of course, both of these phenomenal locations are in the movie.

During the next week we took hikes deep into the rainforest. It rained a lot, but we had rain gear, and although we were in the mountains the hiking was not difficult. There was, however, one natural feature that caused some consternation: leeches!

Leeches are ever-present in the rainforest, and we were warned here was no way to avoid them. On our very first hike we ran into two visitors who had ventured into the forest in shorts. Their bare legs were so covered in the small, cylindrical little creatures that they looked like hair. It took them a half hour to pick them off, often stinging them with a lit cigarette butt.

We were told we could not prevent them from invading our clothing, but we could prevent them from biting and attaching themselves to our skin by rubbing on a repellant called "RID". We applied that in abundance and it did the trick. My wife Sue, however, tried to keep them from crawling up her legs with a creative solution. She wound a roll of sticky gaffer's tape around her boot tops with the sticky side out. After about a mile of walking, she tugged up her pants to see if it was working. Sure enough, the tape was covered in leeches, wiggling and waving on the tape like waving grass. It so disgusted her that she opted out of that day's hike and went back to the hotel to shed the evidence.

I remember on that hike that when we stopped for lunch, I briefly set my sandwich down on a rock so I could open my canteen. When I picked up the sandwich there were three black leeches on the white bread! How could they move so fast? Needless to say, we had to include them in the movie.

On one hike, Glenn stopped at an embankment and pointed out a series of small, silky discs pressed against the wall of mud. He took a stick and gently lifted one, which hinged up like a tiny doorway. This, he said, was the nest of a unique insect called a "trap door spider". They built their nests into hillsides with the trap door entrance. The spider could easily exit but predators could not enter. The spider lined the tunnel with a silky web.

After Glenn walked away, I lifted the little door to inspect the tunnel. I put my finger in and felt the incredibly smooth surface of the tunnel. Somebody filmed me doing that, and later that evening, when we watched the day's videos as we always did, Glenn almost choked. He told me that the trap door spider was one of the most venomous insects in the world, and if I had been bitten, we were too far from help for me to have survived the bite. Maybe it was selective memory, but that creature did not make it into the movie.

We ended our visit with a sense of vibrant inspiration and over a thousand photographs of every detail of the forest. We returned to Byron Bay to do some development work before we headed back to the states.

36

I Do Live in a Tree!

Our lodgings in Byron Bay were idyllic. We shared a small compound of visitor guest cabins in a forest right against the beach. It was just a short walk through the narrow wooded pathways to the shore, and this journey had only one inconvenience. We discovered that after dark, when you could barely see where you were stepping, the pathway became filled with toads. And not just large, slimey toads. These were "cane toads", an invasive species not native to Australia that had overrun the local forest.

It wasn't simply the fact that it was kind of gross to step on a wet toad. Cane toads were technically poisonous, with a toxic slime on their skin. You were advised to wash your feet the second you reached the beach, or your cabin. What was even more bizarre about this situation is that we were told that the toxin on the toad's back was hallucinogenic. People were known to have licked the toads to get a psychedelic experience. We wondered who the first person was to think of doing that.

While Ralph, Tony, Vicky and Dennis started drawing and painting designs while the inspiration was fresh in their minds, Sue, Tom and I sketched out the basics of how the production would proceed once we got back to the states. We had only been at it for a few days when Wayne and Peter informed me that when we returned to Sydney, I would have to make a presentation to the Board of Directors of FAI, the financing company.

"I'm sure they'll love seeing what we're doing with the project", I chirped. There was an awkward pause. Wayne and Peter somewhat reluctantly admitted that it was more than "just an update'. I had to sell the project.

I thought the film was a done deal. Not exactly, they confessed. It was a pretty sure thing, but the Board had never liked the risk that the young company President had gotten them into. They had insisted on final approval.

So, instead of doing some free-wheeling visual development, we switched gears and customized our artwork for a hard sales pitch. We bought poster board and rubber cement and made presentation boards for the character designs, locations, and even a few action sketches of proposed scenes in the story. When we got to Sydney, I loaded all of these into a huge portfolio and trundled off to the FAI headquarters.

I don't have to tell you that Insurance executives are not the world's most jovial creative minds. I gave what I thought was a killer pitch, and got barely a twinge of response from the men in suits. I left the room to let the *Crocodile Dundee* guys make their final plea. I went back to the hotel and our whole crew retired to the bar to await the verdict. As you know by virtue of the fact that we did make the movie, the Board did not stop the deal. But they were never crazy about it, as I would learn later.

We were back in Burbank in early February and began the immense task of not just making the movie, but of creating the company to make the movie. There were a hundred things that had to happen, but a priority was simply finding a building big enough to house the 130-plus employees we expected to hire. The first two buildings we found that seemed suitable were in Burbank. We put in offers for both, and immediately lost the rental contracts to, guess who—Disney! Whether it was intentional or not, they were not helping their competition.

We finally found a location that was odd, but strangely perfect. It was the old Stroh's Brewery in Van Nuys. The building with the fermentation vats was derelict, but the administration building was in good shape. It was a large, one story midcentury design, and all the offices had floor-to-ceiling windows that provided abundant natural light. Better still, it sat in its own private, 40-acre park-like setting and had 300 parking spaces. We hired a small crew to prepare it for production, which included constructing a projection booth to turn the main conference room into a theater.

Back in our small Burbank office we went to work on that phase called "pre-production development". As I mentioned before, everything in an animated film must be designed. With Ralph Eggleston leading the way on production design and Tony Fucile doing character design it was like opening a salon in Italy and having your first two apprentices be Michelangelo and Leonardo Da Vinci.

Almost immediately, Tony did a series of drawings for our main character, Crysta, that we absolutely loved. After decades in the industry Sue and I felt we had a frame of reference that informed our judgment, and we sensed that Tony had created the character we wanted. Our producers, however, could not believe that we could make a final decision so quickly. They made us hire other freelance designers and reviewed at least forty more designs. It was a bit frustrating to listen to their endless comments and be made to address the dreaded, inevitable "notes". The one positive of the ordeal was that, in the end, we ended up using Tony's original design!

Diana Young, the writer of those original stories, had hired an Australian illustrator to do some character designs for her soon-to-be-published book. The producers sent us those designs, but they were incredibly detailed drawings that looked like Aubrey Beardsley woodcuts. They had dense amounts of "pencil mileage" that could never have been used in a hand-drawn in film. When we got our Crysta design approved, it was a much easier matter to have Tony work his way through the rest of the cast using a similar simplified style.

Deciding on a design style for the backgrounds and props was not as hard. We did a lot of experimentation with different styles, but in the end decided that a slightly stylized but faithfully detailed approach would be the right one. We wanted to dramatically portray and preserve the true details of the rainforest that had inspired us.

While the visual development moved forward, the all-important story work began in earnest. Since *Snow White* the stories for animated films had been created primarily by the storyboard artists. When Jeffrey Katzenberg took over Disney animation, he thought it was a good idea to bring in traditional screenwriters to shape the films. The problem was, of course, was that most screenwriters do not think visually. They work first on structure, which is needed, but since dialogue is much more interesting to read than descriptions, they rely heavily on dialogue to tell the story. Storyboard artists by nature seek to tell the story through pictures.

The basic structure for *FernGully* was established soon after we returned from Australia. It would be the story of a young boy working for a predatory logging company who would accidentally meet a young girl who was a member of the "indigenous tribe" that inhabited the rainforest his company was invading. The boy would be magically transformed into a form where he experienced the wonders of the rainforest with the tribe, and by doing so be converted into a defender of the forest. When the massive logging machine showed up to destroy the faeries' home and mystical tree, he would lead the charge and protect the forest.

That basic idea seemed good to us. Coincidentally, it would serve, without much editing, as the description of another movie made two decades later: *Avatar.*

Jim Cox wrote an outline and began writing the script. Our story crew started to visually develop certain action sequences from the outline. Casting voices for an animated film is a critical step in the process. At this stage of the industry, the pattern of creating an all-star cast of famous actors for your film, as Jeffery Katzenberg would insist on in his future productions, was not yet the norm. Every animator knew that you should seek two qualities in the voice chosen for an animated character.

First, the voice should have distinctive qualities or "timber" that would provide accents and intonations that you could connect to gestures and actions. Many actors rely heavily on their appearance to convey their performance. Take away the picture and just listen to the voice and even some of the most famous stars sound rather bland.

Second, that voice had to *fit the personality* of the character. It had to appear to come from within the character. The main problem with a famous celebrity voice is that it can be so identified with the live actor that you cannot help but picture that actor when you hear the voice. You never believe that the animated character is a unique individual. The worst example of this would come a few year's later in the movie *Shark Tale*, when all the celebs overwhelmed the character designs.

In the very best casting, the voice was so perfect for the character that even if it was a famous actor, it disappeared into the cartoon. Tom Hanks doing Woody in *Toy Story* is the perfect example of that.

For *FernGully* we hired a well-known casting director to help us. Her name was Marci Liroff, and she had cast terrific films like *Footloose* and *Pretty in Pink*. Marci started to arrange casting sessions, but we were all surprised when Peter and Wayne announced that they had already decided who they thought should be the star of our movie. There was one person ideal to play Crysta: the Irish singer Sinead O'Connor.

Wayne had told us from the beginning that the character of Crysta would win the hearts of girls all over the world just by "flitting around free in the rainforest". We responded by suggesting that Crysta would probably need some character development beyond her flying abilities. Now Wayne and Peter decided that all the spunk and rebellious spirit they imagined in Crysta was contained in the rebellious Irish singer.

We were cautious on hearing this idea. "But can she act?" we asked. Even Marci was dubious. Wayne and Peter had the solution. They would personally fly to Ireland and give Sinead an acting audition. This was a pricey idea, but because they held the purse strings, it was soon arranged.

A week later they returned with the audition tape. We all gathered in the Burbank office to listen to it. It was terrible. Peter would feed her a line, like "Logging is only bad if you live in a tree" and Sinead would shriek (shrieking is an accurate description) "I DO LIVE IN A TREE!!" Sue, me, Marci, and Ralph all raised our eyebrows. I finally offered my take on the situation.

"Well, I guess that proves that she can't do it". Our group nodded in agreement.

But not Peter and Wayne. "We think she can do it", they said. We could not believe they still thought that! We had a spirited disagreement, but Peter was sure that with an acting coach, Sinead could be our Crysta. As luck would have it, when they got back to Sinead she refused to work with a coach, so we finally were able to cross her off the list. The next year, when we were in the final stages of production, Sinead O'Connor tore up a picture of the Pope on *Saturday Night Live* and became the target of international outrage. We dodged that disaster. We chose not to mention that whenever we saw Peter and Wayne.

The most inspired casting on the film was choosing Robin Williams to play the role of Batty Koda. We weren't sure who had this idea first, but Robin was so ideal for the character that it is hard to imagine anyone else being considered for it. We certainly never discussed any other choice. Batty Koda had to be lovable, sympathetic, but deeply troubled. He had escaped a human lab and had wires sticking out of his head that, when twitched, caused him to assume multiple personalities. Who could do that better than Robin?

Robin Williams had never done a voice for an animated character when Marci called him. He agreed to meet with us at a nondescript location, the Marriott Hotel in Larkspur, near his home Marin County. Sitting on twin beds in a hotel room, Peter, Wayne, and I described the project to him. I talked about our visit to the rainforest, how we intended to bring the genuine beauty of the place to the screen, and our hopes it would have an effect on the audience. I like to think that he recognized the sincerity we were bringing to the project. To our immense delight, Robin quickly signed on. In a move that was so "Robin" he used his celebrity to drive an incredible deal with Fox. His salary would be points *off the gross* (no chance for creative bookkeeping to disguise the revenue) and every cent would go to Sting's non-profit Rainforest Fund. His deal would eventually generate millions of dollars to that fund.

We hired more character and prop designers to create the multitude of designs needed for the show. Dan Jeup did most of the rainforest animals. We were going to need a lot of faeries, so I had the idea to hire one of the most prolific and talented designers I knew, Phil Mendez.

At the time, Phil was one of the few black first-tier animation designers. When he first started at Hanna-Barbera years before, he told me he had felt slighted when all his fellow designers were moved into private offices while he labored in the bullpen. As a protest, he moved his desk into the men's bathroom. The creative touch he applied was the sign on the door. After the word "MEN" he taped the letters "DEZ". He soon got his own office.

I knew that Phil got intensely excited about freelance projects, but could lose enthusiasm quickly. Our producers were surprised when I gave him just a two-week contract. Sure enough, Phil cranked out fifty incredibly charming character designs in just ten days - then went on to another project.

In any commercial job you do, you must deal with the process of approvals. The approvals almost always come from the person who controls the money. Sometimes, that can mean layers of executives, who traditionally are reluctant to make a decision because it has the potential of bringing blame on their heads if the project tanks. On *FernGully* we were lucky in this regard because Fox Studios did not ask for input. They allowed the money, i.e., FAI, to take responsibility.

FAI in turn transferred all that authority to Peter Faiman, director of *Crocodile Dundee* and a man who made decisions decisively. Or so we were told. It turned out that Peter, who had been one of Australia's most successful directors of live broadcasts, had that dynamic confidence to make a creative call on the spot in a live situation. What he did not understand at first was that decisions in animation, once made, are difficult and expensive to change on the spot at a later date. There is an old saying in animation: "You tell a joke and you wait two years to see if anybody laughs". When we would show Peter designs like Phil's faeries, he would like them but be hesitant to sign off. Sometimes he would give an approval and change his mind later.

Those are not unusual occurrences in the creative process, but the problem with our production was that our finite budget could barely accommodate do-overs. When I finally got Peter to appreciate the logistics, he reluctantly agreed to sign-off by literally signing off. I would place a stack of designs in front of him, and with a wry and slightly sarcastic smile he would scribble his initials on each one.

As we prepared to move our operations into the Brewery building, I felt a bit nostalgic about leaving the Burbank office. In addition to being the place where our company had grown and prospered, it had added immeasurably to my personal life. The neighborhood that adjoined our office had tree-lined streets with sidewalks, exactly like the streets I grew up in Chicago. Burbank, being its own city and not under Los Angeles law, had a small-town vibe very unique for L.A. When I took walks in the neighborhood to clear my head or get a bit of exercise, I would always walk past a white two-story farmhouse surrounded by huge, majestic pine trees. In my mind I would always say, "That's my dream house".

I have been very blessed in life's major decisions. Just when I came of working age, I found my vocation—animation—and never looked back. When it came to love, at Disney I found the girl of my dreams, married her, and never looked back. In May of 1990, I received my first big paycheck as the director of an animated feature film, and on that very day, when I drove past my "dream house", there was a FOR SALE sign on the front lawn. It turned out that Sue had also been in love with the house. We knocked on the door, met the owners, and by 9:30 AM the next morning, had closed the deal to buy it. We never "comparison shopped" any other houses or even negotiated the price. I plunked down my advance as the down payment and we lived happily in that house for the rest of our Los Angeles' lives.

37

Building an Airplane—In Flight

When I look back at it now, I can't imagine how we did it.

We had rented a building of 20,000 square feet that had nothing in it. We had to get desk, chairs, light tables, drawing boards, shelves, storyboards, editorial equipment, computer cabling, and office supplies like pencils, paint brushes, staplers, push pins, rulers, etc.—as well as several hundred thousand sheets of animation paper and acetate cels. And then find the 130 skilled people who would use it all. And do all this while we were in full production on a movie.

What I find remarkable is how most of this happened without me being very much involved. While I was immersed in casting, story issues, and voice recording women were building the company.

We had hired Kendra Haaland as a Production Manager. Kendra was an advertising executive from Minneapolis whom we had met when she came to L.A. to visit her brother Brett, an animator friend of ours. We were so blown away by her intelligence and energy that we hired her even though she had zero animation experience. Kendra was the ultimate go-getter and problem solver. Working with another of our friends, Libby Simon, they helped make our facility come together quickly. After *FernGully* Kendra would become a successful producer at Disney.

DOI: 10.1201/9781003558231-37

Sue Kroyer was our one-person recruiting and H.R. department. Although Sue would later be a key creative contributor on the movie (as both an animator and a Sequence Director!), the indispensable task she did was hiring almost all the artists. Sue has always been the greatest networker, but her eye for talent really served us well. She had no doubt that Ralph Eggleston was ready to design a feature film. She chose all the lead animators and let industry word-of-mouth work for us. We attracted an amazing collection of talent. During production, it was Sue that kept her eye on the crew and morale sky high. We had crew barbeques every Friday after work, and great holiday parties. She was my secret weapon that everyone knew about.

Sue assembled an animation team that had some of the greatest animators of our generation, including Tony Fucile, Doug Frankel, Kathy Zielinski, Bob Scott, Crystal Klabunde, and Dan Jeup. But to do A-list animation they had to work at a Disney-style pace, which meant doing only six to ten seconds of animation per week. A quick calculation told us that we needed about ten more animators than we could find in Los Angeles. Remember, this was 1990, five years before the first CG feature. In the hand-drawn era the pool of skilled 2D animators was very small.

We knew where we could find those extra hands—in Canada! Canada has always been a hotbed of animation. It had produced three Oscar-winning mega-stars of animation: Richard Williams, Norman McClaren, and Frederic Back. (A side-note: I consider Back's *The Man Who Planted Trees* to be one of the greatest films ever made. Not just animated films. Greatest of ALL films.)

Along with Cal Arts, Canada had the other world-class school for 2D animation: Sheridan College. Canada had THE NATIONAL FILM BOARD that supported Canadian artists like my Oscar competitor, Cordell Barker. We knew some of the great animators working in Toronto, and after a few phone calls we became convinced we could attract them to our project. In a fortuitous twist, Sue's sister Karen wanted to open a branch office in Toronto, so we just piggy-backed on to her effort. Karen did all the management, we hired the artists, and we ended up doing one fourth of the animation there, using Canadian A-listers like Darlie Brewster, Wendy Perdue, Charlie Bonifacio, Chuck Gammage, and Anne Marie Bardwell.

As the production went on, it became apparent that even the Canadian crew was not enough to finish on time, so we really went offshore - to Denmark! There was a terrific studio named A-Film in Copenhagen, and we got terrific work from their crew, including artists like Stefan Feldmark and Hans Perk.

Unlike big studios with big budgets, or multiple projects where a crew can be shifted to match the workload, Kroyer Films had just enough people and just enough money to make one movie. We could not afford to have people sitting around doing nothing. Because of that, the two years of production were a constant scramble to get story sequences in decent enough shape to shove into the production pipeline. Every department, from story to layout to animation to assistant to ink and paint, was always jamming to "feed the beast".

I was at the top of that pyramid, working very hard to stay ahead of the stampede. I worked eighty-hour weeks for months doing all the final approvals on story sequences, designs, and final artwork for layouts and backgrounds. I recall having the realization that, toward the end of the movie, I knew every one of the 1,100+ scenes by name. Not only by name: I could literally remember how many levels of artwork were in each and every shot. Oddly, I forgot most of this detail within months after wrapping the movie.

On top of that, I actually did almost all of the computer animation myself. I would arrive at the studio at 6:30 AM every morning and animate until the crew arrived at 8:00 PM. It had been just ten years since I did TRON, but the process of animating by computer had evolved quickly. Unlike the old days, when each CG company had to create their own software, there were commercially available software packages for purchase.

We bought one of the first designed specifically for motion, WAVEFRONT PREVIEW. I no longer had to hand-write frame values, or dial them in and hit "save" as I did at Digital Productions. Now I had a mouse that allowed me to move the character, or parts of the character, in real time, by sliding the mouse and watching the pose change. I still hit "save" for each key frame, but now I had various ways for the computer to make in-betweens.

I could adjust the speed and length of "ease-ins" or "ease-outs", and I could easily shift keys and change speed. At that time, it was still not possible to move colored (shaded) models in real time, so I animated using "wireframe" models that were basically white-line outlines of the final model.

A feature that I used a lot was "streaking". In WAVEFRONT PREVIEW, after you had created all of your frames, you could type "-s" and it would playback all of your frames in order, but on top of one another. This created a mesh of overlapping white lines that clearly showed the arcs and spacing of all the poses. You could instantly spot a glitch, or a bump, or bad spacing.

If you have ever seen Norman McClaren's classic animated short film *Pas de Deux*, it looked just like that (I recommend watching that film on YOUTUBE!).

The computer-animated images added great production value to the movie. We made logging machines, falling trees, bird flocks, and dimensional environments like the glowing fungus trees. We even used a simple model of Batty to animate his flying sequences. That simple wireframe that looked similar to the wireframe owl in *Labyrinth* provided a guide that made Batty's animation much easier to do. We ended up using 40,000 frames of CG animation in *FernGully*.

Recording voices for an animated film is done early in the schedule. You must choose those final takes so your animators have a performance to animate to. We did most of our recording in Hollywood. When we could, we'd have actors do their recording together if the scene called for it. We had cast Cheech Marin and Tommy Chong as two rambunctious rainforest bikers called the "Beetle Boys". They did a hilarious recording session, and would you believe it, when the session ended they flopped down on a big cushy couch in the studio and lit up a gigantic joint! They took a toke and offered it to me. Sharing a joint with Cheech and

Chong? This was like being offered a martini from Dean Martin. No way would I pass that up!

Robin Williams preferred to record his work near home, so we made the journey up North to George Lucas' Skywalker Ranch in Marin County. I had never been to Skywalker. It was George's fantasy studio. We had lunch in the big white house that serves as the studio HQ. While we were eating George Lucas himself stopped by the table to say hi. It was very cursory "hi" to all of us. George was totally focused on Robin. From the gist of the conversation we sensed that George was after Robin to do a future project. After the meet-and-greet I learned that our writer Jim was a bit disappointed that George seemed to have completely forgotten they had ever met. They had had a meeting on another project just the week before.

Robin Williams was exactly the genius we knew he would be. In fact, one my most difficult tasks on the movie was trying to decide which Robin Williams' take to use on a scene. Robin would listen to our description of the scene, study the storyboards I had brought, and absorb the moment. He'd record a few versions of the dialogue from the script but then start to improvise. Every take seemed to be funnier than the last. Much of what you hear in the movie are lines Robin invented.

Months later, when we had to record a few re-takes, or new lines that had emerged in the story process, we did those recording sessions in L.A. Unlike sessions with the other voices, like Tim Curry or Tone Loc, which usually were just me, a producer, and "the talent", when Robin recorded it was a mob scene. It seemed like every studio executive, talent agent, and manager had to be there to "support" Robin. It got so bad that we had evict everyone from the recording studio except the engineers and our little *FernGully* group. Even with that, when it was over, Robin came into the booth and chatted and joked with our crew for ten minutes, just being a nice guy.

I had an odd incident recording Tim Curry. When Tim was cast as our villain Hexxus he toured our studio. We introduced him to Kathy Zielinski, who was both the designer and the lead animator on Hexxus. Kathy is one of animation's most brilliant artists. She had just finished designing and animating another villainous character, the tentacled sea-witch Ursula in *The Little Mermaid*. Tim was very impressed with Kathy and sent over a sculpture of his own face that he thought she might find helpful for inspiration.

Months later I'm recording a few pick-up lines with Tim. We projected some of Kathy's animation on screen so he could "loop' his line of dialogue to match the animation she had done. Tim looked at the animation, dropped his script, and stalked out of the room. He went into an office and would not come out. Minutes later the phone rings, and Tim's agent is telling us that Tim is upset because we are using his likeness—and his contract did not pay for that. After a few apologies, my producer promised Tim we would alter the design. Tim returned and finished the session. If you have seen the movie you will probably agree that Tim's performance, especially the song *Toxic Love*, is brilliant.

When Tim left I turned to our producer and reminded him that it was going to really impact our schedule to change the design of Hexxus who was, in the scene Tim had seen, a noxious tower of smoke created with complex FX.

"We're not changing anything", he said. "It's a frikkin' cloud. Let him sue us!" Apparently when Tim saw the scene in color it didn't bother him, because he never mentioned it again.

It was remarkable that in a few months we had the Brewery building fully staffed, fully equipped, and humming along like a real studio. The word got around that seemingly out of nowhere an entire feature production had popped up in L.A. Everyone wanted to visit. It was exciting for me when Frank Thomas and Ollie Johnson came by. They loved what we were doing, and gave a wonderful talk to the crew. We felt quite privileged to have that historic connection to animation history.

To my surprise I started getting calls from Hollywood celebrities. Everyone seemed to have an idea for an animated movie. Warren Beatty and Robert Towne came by to talk about their proposed "whale movie". Warren and his wife Annette Bening took Sue and me out for dinner several times to explore the potential of making the project. I admit I had trouble getting around the problem that whales have eyes on the side of their heads and therefore would be hard to make facial expressions. I don't think that was the project-killer, but we did not proceed and the project never got off the ground elsewhere.

Will Smith, who had just hit it big with *The Fresh Prince of Bel-Air* came over one night after work. Will came by himself and just wanted a tour. He seemed fascinated with the complexity of the production. Sally Jessie Raphael pitched us a project that I can't remember, and we didn't spark to it. She did leave me an autographed copy of her latest book.

My greatest thrill was receiving a visit from one of my idols, Julie Andrews. She was absolutely as charming and classy as I had dreamt she would be. She had an idea for a movie based on Noah's Ark, but with a twist of adding another dimension. I gave her a deluxe tour of the studio. I wanted to give our staff a chance to meet her. I took her to the alcove where Tony Fucile was working. The back of his desk faced out, so we couldn't see him. I said, "Hey Tone. Can you come out here? I want you to meet someone".

There was a mumbled grunt that sounded like, "Can't come out". I asked again for him to just step out for a moment. Again, just a grunt. Perplexed, I squeezed through the gap between the desk and the wall to see what he was doing. He sheepishly pointed down to his legs. Tony had wrapped gaffers's tape around his legs, taping himself to his chair! I turned to see Julie right behind me. She stared at Tony, then at me. I could see that thought going through her head. "Is this the way you treat your workers?"

Tony quickly explained that he was missing his deadlines because he was always getting up and getting distracted, so this was his solution! It took Julie a moment to process this idea, but I sensed that she bought it. Animation was a different business! We had to politely decline to work on her project until we finished our film. Hers was another project that vanished into the ether.

You know who didn't visit our studio? Fox executives. It was a standard thing for film execs to visit a director on the soundstage during production, with a chance to mingle with the actors. It was not nearly as glamorous to visit a glorified warehouse by the railroad tracks and see a bunch of animation nerds bent over their drawing boards. I did not feel slighted by not being visited. One less tour to take up my time. I did get invited once in two years to a "catch-up" lunch at the Fox Studio, where I got to sit near Darryl Hannah. I am sure my exec wished he was lunching with her instead.

We never went to the expense of setting up our own camera department but used outside services for the production. Each day, I would sit with our editor, Gillian Hutshing, and view the film tests on a KEM moviola and give notes. On Fridays, Gillian would assemble all that week's animation pencil tests and we would have a screening for the entire crew before we stepped outside to our big front lawn for our Friday night ritual of beer and hamburgers on the grill.

To me, the most magical thing in the building was happening in Ralph Eggleston's cubicle. Even at the young age of twenty-five Ralph already knew more about film design than most veterans. He worshipped William Cameron Menzies, the legendary designer of *Gone with the Wind*, the man for whom the term "production designer" was invented. Ralph was revitalizing some of Menzie's techniques, the most important being an idea called "the color script".

The Color Script was a series of small thumbnail sketches that contained the color palette of each separate, distinct sequence in the film. The detail of the objects pictured in each panel was somewhat abstract, with the essential element being the combination of colors. Ralph created strips that had thirty-two sequential rectangles representing the thirty-two sequences in our movie. With one sweeping glance you could watch the progression of color, and the mood they conveyed, of the whole film.

Ralph was one of the first to reintroduce this technique to animation filmmaking. He would continue to use this on the films he designed at PIXAR, like *Finding Nemo*, *The Incredibles*, and *Inside Out*. Because of Ralph, color scripts would become a standard component in animated feature productions.

After he had determined the color in each sequence (which I almost always automatically approved—even I recognized a genius at work), Ralph would proceed to create small color pastel paintings of every shot. These were usually just 5×7 inch pictures, but they had every nuance of color and shading. He did over 2,000 of these for the picture. They were like miniature Monet paintings, and were the unquestioned guides for the color work in each scene.

Our background painters, Dennis Venizelos, Jeff Richards, and Vicky Jensen, would follow those pastel guides and paint all the backgrounds for *FernGully* on site in our building. *FernGully* was going to have over 100,000 painted cels, and those would be done overseas, most of them at Hahnho in Seoul. I would also visit, and then hire, James' Wong's studio Cuckoo's Nest in Taiwan to do a chunk of work when Hahnho reached its production limit.

Because of these other studios, *FernGully* had become an international production. This was before the internet and ZOOM conferencing, so I had the challenge of directing animators a thousand miles away. I came up with an effective solution. I would stand in front of a video camera and record my "handout instructions" on each scene. Speaking into camera, I could go into all the verbal detail I needed, but I could also act out specific physical actions. I could hold up layouts, storyboards, and thumbnail sketches to explain exactly what I wanted. This method had several advantages I had not thought of. For one thing, the animator could play the tape over and over to make sure he/she understood exactly what I wanted. If that scene had been set aside for some reason and the animator was picking it up a week later, the tape made it possible to get a fresh review of my direction. Finally, and this was handy for me, the animator could no longer say, "You didn't say that", or "I thought you wanted something else". I had proof!

The videotape handouts proved to be so effective that I started doing them for our animators within our own building. That saved me valuable time. I could record those at home a night rather than make the rounds and stop and handout scenes in person at the studio.

It was important for me to visit these off-shore studios to keep morale high and momentum moving. It was always fun to go to Toronto and visit with those Canadian superstars like Darlie Brewster, Roger Chiasson, and Wendy Perdue. In the middle of production I found myself popping up to Canada and over to Korea on a regular basis. The travel became almost as mundane as a trip to Santa Barbara. One Friday night I headed to LAX with my carry-on bag for a quick weekend trip to Seoul. We were in the middle of the Pacific Ocean when I realized that I had failed to pack my passport. I told the flight attendant. A few minutes later, the co-pilot was leaning over my seat to tell me that he had called ahead and informed Korean immigration, as he was *required* to do.

I asked if I could have a copy of my passport faxed over. He said that was up to the Koreans. When we landed, there were two Korean policemen waiting for me at the jetway. I was taken into custody and placed in holding cel. Again, I tried to ask if there was some alternative solution to confirm I had a legal passport. The Koreans were very tough. There was one plan of action in this kind of situation. I would be held in this room and then placed on the very first flight out of Seoul going non-stop to a United States destination. It did not matter which U.S. destination. I might be on the next flight to Boston! They would not even let me out to use a phone (this was before cell phones).

After an hour I was escorted through the airport to a departure gate. I looked at the departure screen. The flight was to Honolulu. I noticed that there was a payphone just a few feet away against the wall. As my guards explained the situation to the gate agent, I casually slipped over to the phone and was able to place a call to Sue at home. Thankfully she answered. I told her the situation and asked her to get my passport on a flight to Honolulu ASAP. I barely had time to confirm the plan when the guards stuck me on the plane.

It was odd to arrive in Honolulu without a passport to re-enter the country. I sat in a waiting area. The only door was blocked by a podium, manned by an armed guard. Behind the podium was the Great Seal of the United States. I felt like a man without a country; an outsider looking in.

After an hour a representative of the airline came in and had a lengthy talk with the Immigration Guard. I was told I would be allowed into the terminal, but I was not to leave the terminal. The airline rep told me that my passport was, indeed, on its way. I could use a facility in the terminal to shower and take a nap. The airline would cover those costs, as well as fly me to L.A. or back to Seoul, no charge. That all seemed so nice of them. I later found out that they were in rather deep trouble for letting me board that flight at LAX without checking if I had a passport.

Six hours later, showered and refreshed, I was on a flight to Tokyo, where I would switch to a flight to Seoul. I would end up arriving almost exactly twenty-four hours later than expected. That included an additional sixteen hours of flying, almost all of which I slept through. Since I had been chronically sleep-deprived because of my brutal production schedule, the passport fiasco ended up giving me some needed rest.

38

The Traditional Crash and Burn

The "crash and burn" is a proud animation tradition that seems to happen on every animated feature. It's that moment well into production where you have a realization that despite all your planning, and your confidence that the story is terrific, the film is just not working.

The fact that this seems to happen all the time, even on the movies that go on to be the biggest and most popular and successful ones, doesn't provide comfort when it happens on your movie.

To be honest, we didn't have a super-serious crash and burn with the story itself. No matter what you think about the story of *FernGully*, we did make some valuable adjustments that we felt helped it, but we never abandoned or even seriously altered the outline we started with.

Our crash and burn was a crisis of confidence in the production itself. A little over a year into things, FAI started to get nervous that we would never be able to make the movie for the money they had committed. Part of that panic came from an ignorance of how animated productions worked. There was a progressive ramp-up where things start slowly but gain momentum as you go. If you gauged the level of production by how much work you completed in early months, you would expect a shortfall. We knew those numbers would improve.

DOI: 10.1201/9781003558231-38

Apparently there were other things at work that I was not aware of. I was surprised to find out that I was about to get *two more producers* on the movie, and they would now supersede Wayne and Peter as the authorized representatives of FAI. Their names were Brian Rosen and Richard Harper. They had a successful production company in Sydney called Rosen/Harper Entertainment, and the FAI Board had turned to them to "get a rein on the production".

Along with them came a representative from the Bond Company. It is typical for a financer to engage a Bond Company as insurance that the movie will be made for the approved budget. If there are irregularities or any reason to believe the production is out of control the Bond Company can take over the production.

I was very surprised and, I must admit, somewhat insulted that they suspected we were doing a bad job. We had been killing ourselves making the picture, often asking a lot more of our crew than they were being paid to do.

Brian Rosen was the producer that personally moved into our building to manage this inspection. Working with the rep from the Bond Company they did a minute review of our operation. Brian had never worked on an animated film before (how's that for a choice by FAI!) but he was very eager to learn. After a thorough review both Brian and the Bond rep concluded that we were doing an exceptional job. In fact, they both became our staunchest allies in the final push to complete the production. The problems that were bothering FAI lay elsewhere.

I have never found out the details about the "above the line" expenses of *FernGully*. These are dollars that are spent by the producers for everything other than our animation production. I got a sense of that problem from one incident uncovered by Brian Rosen. When reviewing the costs, Brian learned that Wayne Young had been living all this time at the Mondrian Hotel, one of the fanciest, hippest, and most expenses hotels on the Sunset Strip. Brian considered this to be an excessive expense. He told Wayne that he must move out of the hotel immediately. To soften the blow, Brian managed to find a rental house just up the hill from Mondrian that was far less expensive. Wayne was not happy about it but he moved out of the hotel and into the rental house.

That was why it was surprising the next month to get a big bill from the Mondrian Hotel. Brian called the Hotel to ask about the bill. Surely, there must be a mistake. Wayne had moved out. Yes, he had moved out, the Hotel reported. But he had continued to order room service, and the bellboys were running the meals up the hill every day!

Perhaps that was a clue of why FAI had asked Rosen to "rein things in". Wayne stayed around the production, but one could sense a bit of tension between him and Brian. I think Peter might have also clashed with Brian, but he had left us because he got a directing gig on an American movie called *Dutch*. It starred Ed O'Neill from the *Married with Children* hit show and was expected to be another big hit. No matter what problems FAI had with Wayne and Peter, I got along with them, and they liked what we were doing with the animation. I never forgot that they were the ones that believed that a studio with twelve employees could make the movie. To echo General Patton's thought: "I may have a lot of faults, but ingratitude isn't one of them".

At the conclusion of the bond inspection a Vice President of FAI came to Los Angeles to meet with Brian and review the situation. Brian told me that my company had nothing to worry about, but, having gained an understanding of our process and become aware of our struggles to make a great film within the budget, he actually suggested I make a pitch for more money! I did that. I gave the VP a tour of the studio, and really laid it on thick about what an amazing thing we were creating: a timeless classic that could save the rainforest!

When it was over, Brian met with the VP and conveyed to me his response. The VP was impressed with our company. He thought the animation looked great. But FAI had never liked the project, so they would supply the money they had already committed—but not one cent more.

We had weathered the bond crisis, but new issues kept cropping up. One day I got a phone call from a representative of the company that owned our building. Apparently, the Walt Disney Studios had expressed serious interest in buying the entire Brewery property. He informed me that some Disney execs were coming that very afternoon to tour the place: Michael Eisner and Jeffrey Katzenberg!

I told him that could not happen. We were producing a film in direct competition with Disney, and all of our proprietary artwork was on display. We couldn't have the Disney people seeing that. The rep's response: "Too bad. You're just a renter, and this is real money. They're coming".

I did the only thing I could think of. I got on our public address system and told the crew that some Disney execs might be walking through our building in the next few hours. I asked everyone to remove all their drawings, model sheets, designs, and sketches from their walls and bulletin boards. I went outside to the parking lot to wait for the "delegation" to arrive. I thought perhaps I could steer them away from walking through our building.

Within an hour two black SUV's cruised into our lot. They drove past the old grain elevators, past the vat building, and finally past our building. The windows were tinted so I could not see who was inside. Without even stopping, they cruised right back out the gate. Perhaps they could tell without inspecting it that the Brewery property was not what they were looking for.

Very relieved, I went back inside to tell the crew. I was stunned by what I saw. All the walls of the hallway, the alcoves, and the main corridor were plastered with xeroxed pictures of the same photo: songstress Peggy Lee! Ms. Lee had just won a very contentious legal battle with the Disney studio over her royalties for her songs used in the classic film *Lady and the Tramp*. After years of fighting she had won millions of dollars from Disney. Our animation crew, with that animators' sense of humor, thought Michael Eisner might enjoy seeing Peggy Lee's face again. And again. And again! As much as I admired their quick thinking, I was happy he skipped that tour.

FernGully, like *Tech Threat* before it, was on that cusp of changing technologies. While most of our film was traditionally inked and painted, we were one of the first films to have digitally painted 2D animation. About a year into production I was approached by my friends Steve Sidley and Steve Wright to view a test from their computer graphics company. They were developing their own digital ink & paint system. They showed me a 2D pencil test, then the same footage colorized using their new system. It looked pretty good!!

Sidley-Wright and Associates were very anxious to get their system noticed, and the perfect way to do that was to do a sequence in a major theatrical film. Since Disney and Bluth weren't interested, *FernGully* offered their best opportunity. I was reluctant, having had years of experience listening to overly-optimistic computer programmers. My reluctance had the effect of them lowering their bid to a cost so low that it was an offer I couldn't refuse. Having Sidley-Wright colorize an entire sequence would not only help our budget—it would take a lot pressure off of our traditional painting pipeline.

We decided that the best approach would be to give them one "modular" sequence, a few minutes of the movie that was almost a "stand alone" bit. A song would be perfect for that, and one we chose was the hilarious tour de force of Robin Williams called *The Batty Rap*. We gave them all the artwork and they did their thing. In the end, the sequence looked pretty good. The average viewer might not notice it, but we were a bit disappointed that the outlines of the characters, so crisp and sharp when xeroxed, were slightly soft when scanned digitally.

We were xeroxing all of our cels, just as animation had been done since the process was introduced in the 60s. Because acetate is never 100% transparent, when you placed one cel on top of another cel, the color on the one on the bottom would be slightly grayed-out. You had to mix a slightly different color to make up for that change. Toward the end of *FernGully*, I was visited in my office by two engineers from Germany. They claimed to have invented an acetate sheet that was 99.6% transparent. They showed me a sample of the cels, and sure enough, they were magically clear. I regretted to inform them that while brilliant, their invention was seventy years too late. Cels would shortly be obsolete because the process of colorizing animation was about to go digital.

And it did. Disney's system CAPS (Computer Animation Production System) was used to colorize their film *Rescuers Down Under* and every subsequent film. Although Disney would hand-animate for a few more films (through *Princess and the Frog*) all the films would be painted digitally. Dreamworks would do the same with their own system. Even CAPS would be phased out when films became all-CG animated.

FernGully was still in the traditional mode, and our Ink & Paint Department had the distinction of being the most colorful room in the studio. The walls were lined with color models, there were shelves and shelves of paint bottles, and every desk had stacks of artwork in process. Although most of the actual painting would be done overseas, our department had to create color models for every character, prop, and painted effect. Those models would be shipped with the scenes and act as guides for foreign painters.

It is deceptive how complicated this can be. The audience would not notice it, but a simple character can have many color areas. The falcon that chases Crysta in the first sequence is just a bird, but when you note feathers, fluff, claws, eyeballs, eye whites, pupil highlights, etc., it takes twenty different colors to paint one cel.

Many of the characters and FX in *FernGully* have hand-inked or "self-colored" lines. Since we used gray xerox lines, any line that needed to be colored line had to be hand-inked by an artist. That included a lot of fire and smoke effects, as well as lips, eyebrows, etc.

The biggest task of this department was "checking" and prepping all the artwork that came back from Korea and Taiwan before it was sent to camera for final photography. Every single cel had to be hand-checked. Errors had to be corrected. Paint that had chipped had to be repaired. Every cel had to be literally polished with a special cloth to remove any smudges or fingerprints.

When I watched our Ink & Paint ladies (yes, all female) handle all this artwork with such conscientious, loving care I could not help but feel that some of that love and care must somehow come across to an audience watching the film. It is almost a spiritual connection. The physical beauty of painted cels has been one of the greatest losses of the digital era. If you ever hold a genuine *FernGully* cel, you will feel like the movie is in your hands. They are just gorgeous.

Our I&P department used four tons of paint on the movie. You read that right—four tons, eight thousand pounds. The painted cels weighed sixteen tons. We know that because we weighed the boxes when FAI made us give them to an art gallery when the movie was over.

As we approached the end of production, there was one more unexpected disaster. I was in a meeting when our producer Kendra Haaland tapped me on the shoulder and motioned for me to follow her. Once in the hallway she told me something I could barely believe. She had just received a call from Airport Security at LAX. Apparently two unidentified men had somehow entered the secure U.S. Customs holding area and stolen two of our packages! These were boxes from Hahnho in Korea that contained over 4,000 painted cels. It wasn't just the number of cels. These were some of the most detailed and complex shots in the movie. They had been in the works for months. That's why they were coming this late in the schedule.

How could this have happened? Airport Security had videotape of the thieves carrying off the boxes, but their faces were obscured and the license plate of the car they drove had been altered. Remarkably, we had been alerted by the Customs people a few months earlier that drug smugglers had been hiding drugs in foreign shipments as a way to get them into the U.S. We never suspected this could apply to our shipments, but apparently this was the likely explanation. If it was drugs, we thought, perhaps the thieves will discard the artwork once they retrieved their drugs. That was a desperate hope. We soon came to the horrible conclusion that our artwork was gone for good.

What now? We had a movie to deliver, and only a few months left to do it. Our policy was always to make Xeroxed copies of all the artwork before we shipped it overseas, so we had copies of the original pencil art. But it had taken months to paint it. Some of the shots were among the most ambitious in the movie, like the big LEVELLER machine chomping through the forest. Sadly, tragically, we had to simplify some of these shots just to finish the film. Some of the most dramatic scenes became just "serviceable" shots.

We finished on time. The last phase, the final sound mix, went well. It was incredibly fun to hear all the sound effects for the film, and hear the picture enhanced by Allen Silvestri's score. I thought our music supervisor, Tim Sexton, had done a good job giving us some great songs by some very big artists, like Raffi and Elton John. I had a chance to preview these songs during production, and didn't have many notes.

I did have a note on the song, *If I'm Gonna Eat Somebody* that was to be sung by Tone Loc. That tune had been written by Jimmy Buffet. Jimmy came to the studio for a tour and played us the song for the first time. He had that quintessential laid-back "Margaritaville" persona that would make him a mega-mogul. I suggested to him that since a goanna would probably not be familiar with human-style foods like "a sandwich" or "a stew" maybe he could find different lyrics. Jimmy smiled and said he'd think about it. Of course, he never changed a word! I don't think billionaires typically take notes from animators.

39

Is There Life after
FernGully?

FernGully hit the theaters in February 1992, almost two years to the day from when we returned from our research trip to Australia. It was nothing short of miraculous that we had made a movie in that short a time while building a studio. It did good, not great box office, but its home-video sales were spectacular.

We paid some attention to the revenue, even though we weren't going to share in any profits. I suppose as artists we were just as anxious to have the work appreciated. Jeffrey Katzenberg was the first industry person to call me. He phoned me at home the morning after the release to congratulate me. He particularly enjoyed Ralph's production design. My secret reaction was, "Wow, for an executive he really does have a good eye!"

We got good reviews in the press, and we were especially happy that Siskel and Ebert, the premiere critics of that time, gave us their valued "two thumbs up" approval. We found out that we were about to be given a special honor. *FernGully* would be the first film ever to be shown to the United Nations in the U.N. General Assembly Hall—on Earth Day!

We made plans to go to New York City and invited any of the crew who wanted to come along. We ended up with a contingent of about twenty. We were surprised to find out that FAI, our Australian funder, actually owned a Hotel in New

York. Sue and I would be provided a suite, and our crew would get discounted rooms. The Hotel was an old one on Central Park South. Our room overlooked the park, but the Hotel looked like it had not been renovated in fifty years. No worries—we loved the location.

The United Nations screening was very memorable. Dudley Moore, one of my favorite comic actors, started the show by waxing poetic about saving the rainforest. He introduced the next speaker, and who better could FAI have hoped for than Australia's most famous export, Olivia Newton-John. She said nice things about the film, then introduced the man of the moment, FAI's young President Rodney Adler.

I had only met Rodney once, very briefly in Sydney, and I had no communication with him at all during the production. In a bit like the rarely-seen owners of a professional sports team accepting the trophy, Rodney seemed very proud and delighted to have this moment in front of the Assembly. And why not? His crazy faith in the venture had made it all possible.

A few years later Rodney would be caught up in some shady business dealings in Australia. He would spend some time in prison, and FAI would declare bankruptcy. That would have disastrous consequences for *FernGully*, because the rights, wholly owned by FAI, would go into receivership for decades and prevent any further development of the property. But on this day in New York City, no one suspected that was coming.

Our little crew had a lot of fun in New York. We did some standard tourist stuff, but the highlight for us was partying one night at a club called the LIMELIGHT. It was in an old gothic church, and to say it was a departure from proper religious piety would be the understatement of the century. The music was electric and blaring, and the crowd was multi-everything. There were drugs everywhere, illicit behavior in the bathrooms, and glass booths with naked go-go dancers whom you could fondle by placing your hands through rubber gloves in the glass wall. For us animators, it was a big change from watching Road Runner cartoons.

Back in Los Angeles, I had the very sorrowful task of releasing most of the crew that had worked on the movie. They all knew they were "project hires" and would not stay after the film was done. We had had a very tight crew, and had such a wonderful experience together that it was difficult to let them go. Sue and I held an anniversary reunion five years later and almost everyone showed up. We have continued to have those reunions every five years, and even thirty years later we still filled the backyard with *FernGully* veterans. It is not unusual even today to see FACEBOOK posts where our crew members name *FernGully* as the best experience of their careers.

Sue deserves most of the credit for that employee loyalty. She once said that she learned her philosophy of handling employees from her first supervisor, Karen Marjoribanks. That guiding idea was that "people do their best work when they are happy and feel appreciated". Being surrounded by such people, supremely talented people who are also friends, was our greatest work experience too.

Thinning the staff did not mean the end of Kroyer Films. We were determined to keep our doors open and do another movie. I was offered a chance to bid on doing the production for several TV series but I just did not feel that was our sensibility. Other than *Ultracross* I had never considered working in limited animation and I did not want to start now. We engaged a very high-end business agent to search for another feature deal. While he was setting meetings around town, a very different and unique opportunity came our way.

Joel Silver, Hollywood's hottest producer of such action franchises like *Die Hard* and *Lethal Weapon* called me asked for a meeting. He was interested in doing an animated action movie. This was a thrilling idea for us. It was exactly the kind of genre-expanding idea we wanted to be part of, and who else in the world better to push it than Joel Silver? Joel already had the story outline. It was about a zombie-hunting tough guy detective in New Orleans. The title was also the main character: *Arrow*!

Joel wanted to create one of his signature teaser-trailers, but in animation. The money he offered was not excessive but enough to do a good job. We designed the world and the diverse characters, including Arrow, his blues-singing girlfriend, a voodoo queen, the wicked sorcerer-villain, and a lot of zombies.

For voice casting, Joel Silver went his usual route, getting big stars. Imagine our surprise and excitement when we learned that Arrow was to be voiced by one of the world's biggest stars, Mel Gibson! This would be Mel's first experience at voicing an animated character. I didn't get a chance to meet Mel, because Joel recorded him in New York, but his vocal performance was perfect for the character.

We did a storyboard that Joel liked. He had a few notes and we did the revisions. Working at this level of the Hollywood hierarchy was a different experience. We were in Joel's office showing him designs one day when I looked up to see Sylvester Stallone in the doorway watching us. I briefly wondered if we might draft him into the cast!

We did our first pass of animation. Joel's writer had written the script for the trailer, so I hired an actor to narrate a "temporary scratch track" to play with the visuals. We assembled in Joel's editing room and played him the pencil test. He liked our work and just had a few notes on the animation—but he hated the voice-over. "You have to use my guy", he said. "His guy" was Don LaFontaine, who had done all of Joel's trailers. Nicknamed "The Voice of God", Don became identified with his signature opening phrase, "In a world...".

I immediately contacted Joel's producer and he said he would arrange for Don to record the narration in New York. We went back to work, made all the tweaks in the animation, added the special effects, and three weeks later were back in the editing room to get Joel's final approval. I had not yet received the new voiceover of Don LaFontaine, so I left the old one on the film.

The editor hit the start button, and my temp narrator's voice said the opening line "Sometimes an unusual case takes an unusual private eye". Joel Silver reached over and hit the STOP button. He stood up, clearly agitated. "Bill", he said, "my movies have grossed over two billion dollars in box office, so when I tell you to get another narrator, I expect you to LISTEN TO ME!!"

"Joel" I responded quickly. "We recorded Don. We just haven't received the tape yet!" Joel cooled down, but he still seemed agitated. He approved the shots and left the room. I asked the editor if he thought Joel would stay upset with me.

"Nah", he said dismissively. "He's been using that same line on people since his movies grossed five hundred thousand dollars".

We finished the *Arrow* trailer and thought it was exciting. Arrow came across as a really tough guy. His girlfriend was very sexy, the voodoo stuff was creepy, and we had zombies getting their heads split open and arms ripped off! Fireworks in the French Quarter!!

Joel set up the screening for the Warner chieftans Bob Daly and Terry Semel. They were polite in their response at the screening, but we got the bad news from Joel two days later that Warner Bros. had "passed" on the project. They didn't think *Arrow* fit the family demographic for animation. Worse for us, Joel decided to shelve the project. His deal with Warner was exclusive and lucrative and he didn't want to shop the project elsewhere. Arrow died. The trailer, never released publicly, has become something of an industry collectable.

That rejection also left Kroyer Films without a big project. I had put more money into the Arrow trailer than Joel had paid us, and I had also kept a number of "key employees" on payroll. I was spending my meager profits from *FernGully* to keep our feature film hopes alive. I had that gigantic 20,000 square foot facility, fully equipped for film production, sitting 90% empty. That was very depressing.

I took out a line of credit to pay expenses, but we could not land a feature deal. We had some good ideas we were pitching, but the mood of the big studios was shifting. The rumor in Hollywood was that Steven Spielberg, Jeffrey Katzenberg, and David Geffen were going to open their own animation studio to compete directly with Disney. We found that the other studios were not interested in funding an outside, independent animation studio like ours. They were examining the possibilities of starting their own in-house animation divisions.

If that situation wasn't grim enough, mother nature hit us in the gut in the form of the devastating Northridge earthquake. Our building was not far from the epicenter and was badly damaged. Every one of the floor-to-ceiling windows was smashed. Broken glass was everywhere. It was uninhabitable. Sue and I decided to vacate the Brewery building.

In a moment of inspired generosity, we gave almost all the animation desks, supporting furniture, and supplies to the Cal Arts animation department. They were experiencing a period of budget-tightening, and we were told for years afterward by the department manager Martha Baxton that we had saved the department with our support. I don't know if that's true, but it was nice of her to say it.

Closing the building was a somber event, and word got around that we were scaling down. One afternoon I got a call from my old friend John Lasseter. His company, PIXAR, was gearing up to make their first feature film. John felt that Ralph Eggleston would be a valuable addition to his crew, and he wanted to know if it would be OK if he called Ralph to discuss that. Ralph had been with us for years and he was like a brother to us, but I knew that the PIXAR gig could be a great opportunity for him. I thanked John for extending me the courtesy of asking permission to call him. Yes, give Ralph that chance I said. Ralph went to PIXAR to begin what would be one of the greatest careers in animation history.

Kroyer Films moved into smaller offices and immediately got a new, very interesting assignment. I had not paid much attention to the video game world since *Tron*, but it was growing rapidly. No company was growing faster than one called ACTIVISION, and they contacted us about doing character animation for one of their most popular games, *Pitfall Harry*.

At that time, Activision was still small enough that we dealt directly with the owners and founders of the company, Bobby Kotick and Howard Marx. While sitting at our dining room table, Howard told us the story of how they started this soon-to-be-billion-dollar company.

Bobby and Howard were roommates in Manhattan. They were novice gamers, developing their idea for a company and supporting themselves by staging "rave clubs", a sort of "pop-up party" where they would rent a space for the night and make a club.

Bobby flew to Dallas to a computer gaming convention in search of backers. He had no luck. He was having breakfast in the hotel cafe when he literally backed into the chair of a well-dressed gentleman. As they chatted briefly the man asked Bobby why he was visiting. When Bobby explained that he was looking for backers for a computer gaming company, it sparked the man's interest.

"My name's Steve Wynn", the man said. "That sounds interesting". Yes, Steve Wynn, that casino magnate! When Bobby said he was returning to New York City, Steve Wynn suggested Bobby join him on his private jet. On the flight back Bobby pitched the idea for Activision. Steve told him he'd think about. He told Bobby to wait for a call the next morning, and be sure his partner Howard was with him.

Sure enough, the next morning Bobby and Howard sat waiting in their apartment. The phone rang. Steve's voice said: "Go down to the front door".

At the curb they found a limousine waiting. They climbed in and were driven to the East River heliport. A helicopter whisked them down to the Wynn Casino in Atlantic City. Already they knew they were out of their element. They were escorted to a luxury office where Steve Wynn was waiting for them.

"I thought it over", Howard remembers him saying, "and I'd like to be in business with you. Let's keep it simple. I'll supply all the money, you do all the work, and we'll split the company 50/50".

Howard and Bobby exchanged glances. Could this be true? Full financing—from a partner with connections? "YES!" they stammered. Bobby said they'd start drafting a contract right away.

"No", said Wynn. "Here's the contract". He held out his hand. Bobby, Howard, and Steve shook hands, and that's how Steve Wynn became half-owner of a billion dollar gaming company.

The original *Pitfall Harry* had been a low-resolution "scroller game" where the character was made up of just a few pixelated squares. For the new version, called *Pitfall Harry: The Mayan Adventure*, Activision wanted us to create full 2D character animation. We did a new character design that they loved. They had come up with a large "menu" of the modular bits of action that the character had to do. That included running, jumping, dodging, swinging from vines, etc. We started animating some of the actions and they were happy with the movement. But that was not the challenging part.

To make the "gameplay" work, Harry had to seamlessly transition from any one of these modular movements to any other modular movement. That meant that we had to create "hook up poses" at the start and end of each modular action. It was challenging to do that, but we understood why it was important.

The Activision producers let us sit in on game testing sessions so we could understand how this game would work. They had a room full of thirteen year-olds sitting at consoles and playing "beta versions" of the game. I remarked on how young the testers were. Howard told me that some of these kids were veterans with six years of testing experience!

In gaming, he explained, it's all about the game play. We animators put great stock in the story, and the designs, and the characters' personalities. In a game, those things are nice to have, and you'd like them to be appealing, but in the end, it's the "hook" of the gameplay—the pure act of playing—that keeps kids addicted to the game. That's why Pitfall Harry's animated movements had to flow seamlessly from one action to the next, so there would be no break in the flow of action.

I always remembered that principle. I wondered how games could have the lamest backstories and most pitiful story concepts and still be successful. It was because the action was fun to play.

We worked on *Pitfall Harry* for months. We became pretty clever at linking the actions. We didn't know it, but we were perfecting a technique that years later would form the basis of software programs like MASSIVE, where hundreds of separate motion-captured actions would be unified to create crowds with hundreds of character performances.

It didn't take long for the Activision programmers to plug our "animated modules" into the game engine they had created. We got a call from Bobby Kotick that he wanted Sue and I to fly to Las Vegas with him to see the finished game on display at CES, the Consumer Electronics Show. CES was the big yearly convention featuring all the new tech equipment for film and gaming.

The night we arrived we were invited to a small party at Steve Wynn's hotel, the Mirage. We had learned that Steve suffered from an eye condition called retinitis pigmentosa, causing him to have limited "pin hole" vision. He had a spectacular art collection in his suite. We wondered if he could even view his paintings in their full scope. Steve was a most gracious host. Sue thought of Steve as the Walt Disney of Vegas because of the way he had transformed the town. We had never met Walt, so it was a thrill to meet Steve Wynn.

The next day we went to the convention to see our game. Activision had a booth playing *Pitfall Harry*. At the booth right next to it, a rival company was premiering their game. They had the volume up so loud that it was impossible to hear any of the music or sound effects on *Pitfall*. Bobby had asked them to lower the volume but they ignored him.

While we were there, Steve Wynn arrived. He was accompanied, as he usually was in public, by two very large guys. Steve commented on the loud music, and Bobby told him of the problem they had getting their "neighbors" to lower the volume. Steve turned and whispered something to his "associates", and the men went to the next booth. I never knew what Steve's associates said to those folks, but one minute later the volume in that booth went down to nothing. You had to strain to hear any sound. And it stayed that way for the rest of the convention. I guess they made them an offer they couldn't refuse.

Pitfall Harry was a big success for Activision In an interesting sidenote, Bobby Kotick told me that their initial business plan for the company was to develop original games and develop them into movies. He quickly discovered that his plan needed to be reversed. He would become wildly successful make games out of existing movies. Today Activision/Blizzard is worth billions.

After *Pitfall Harry* delivered we did a few small jobs, but nothing exciting. We wondered if we would ever get in the feature film game again. We were surprised when the very situation that had kept us from getting financing created a new opportunity. Apparently it was true that other studios were interested in starting their own animation divisions. To do that, they wanted filmmakers with experience. Sue and I were suddenly in demand!

40

Warner Bros. and the Failed Quest

I had racked up considerable debt trying to hang on to our staff and develop new projects, so it was something of a godsend when several different studios started courting Sue and I for our services. A small bidding war had the wonderful result of providing us with a very lucrative deal. We signed a contract to help start a new feature animation division at the very company that had rejected *Arrow*: Warner Bros. The new division was to be called Warner Bros. Feature Animation.

My signing bonus alone paid off my debts, and Sue and I would both receive great salaries with bonuses based on performance. One of the first things we did was something they hired us specifically to do. We attracted talent to the studio. Many of our old employees quickly signed on. Chief among them was Steve Pilcher, our "Ralph replacement". Steve was an illustrator who was living in Toronto when Sue saw his work in some children's books. Recognizing a special talent, she invited him to work with us in L.A. We just did one project with him before the Warner deal brought us both into the studio.

Once again Sue's eye for talent was flawless. Steve would eventually move to PIXAR and be Production Designer on their big movies. In fact, it's an odd bit of trivia that half of Pixar's first twelve films were designed by artists that Sue "discovered"; Ralph Eggleston and Steve Pilcher.

DOI: 10.1201/9781003558231-40

To head the division, Warner's hired people who had been junior executives at other companies. They did have experience in animation production, but not in key creative positions, so they were anxious to show they could step into leadership roles. That aggressive attitude was to cause me problems.

The execs made a quick evaluation that we would never be able to find enough talent in Los Angeles to fully staff a feature crew. Their idea was to tap into the European talent pool, and to do that, they intended to open a London office. I could not believe their first move. They wanted me to fly to London for a long weekend and "spread the word". In the 90s, the animation community in London largely revolved around a pub called THE STAR AND GARTER. If you were a London animator looking for work, you went to the pub and asked around. If you had a production and needed artists, you went to the pub and asked around.

Warners sent me to London on a Business-class ticket and arranged no meetings with people, no tours of buildings, no studio visits. I was literally just to go to the STAR AND GARTER every night, buy pints of beer, and let everybody know Warner's was coming to town. I still can't believe I did that, but it ended up being one of the few imaginative and productive ideas our execs came up with.

Sue and I were immediately tasked with coming up with ideas for a feature film. We pitched several, but the one our new bosses sparked to was *King Tut*, an adventure based on the famous boy-king of ancient Egypt. We met with some writers and got an outline started, and our artists began cranking out pictures for visual development. Steve Pilcher did some incredible images that got people excited about the project.

Unlike my own company, I was a cog in this studio, and a lot of things would be happening that I wasn't aware of. One of them was the hiring of a music supervisor whom I had not met. Another was hiring a producer that was to supervise my film - hired without even consulting me. I was not happy with that, but trying to be a team player, I soldiered on.

To my pleasant surprise, the Music Supervisor did something exciting. She announced that Sting might be interested in doing songs for our movie. Since Elton John and Phil Collins had done great things at Disney, I could see why Sting might be open to the idea. She announced that Sue and I would be flying to London with a number of execs to meet with Sting. That was a nice bonus.

In London, they put us up at a fancy hotel right near the BAFTA headquarters. I had a chance to grab dinner with one of my idols, the legendary Ray Harryhausen. Ray was the godfather of stop-motion animation. His skeleton fight in *Jason and the Argonauts* is classic cinema.

We were to meet with Sting at our hotel the next afternoon. Around mid-day, we got a phone call from him. He wasn't keen on making the trip into town. Would we consider coming to his home instead? Twist my arm! We heard that rock-n-roll royalty like George Harrison, Keith Richards, and Sting lived in grand old English manor houses - because they were the only people in England who could afford them.

Sting's estate was near Stonehenge. We arrived at dusk at his walled compound. The huge wooden gate automatically swung open and we drove up the driveway to (as expected!) a real English manor house. The great musician met as at the door. We were escorted through the grand front hall, complete with tapestries, a large fireplace, and the unbelievable touch of several large hounds lounging on the carpet. We had a wonderful supper in the dining room. Sting himself walked around and personally served each of us the main course. He really seemed to enjoy the role of Lord of the Manor. Sue sat beside him, and when she told him she was born in in Wisconsin, his immediate question was musical. "Isn't there a song about that place?"

Sue proceed to sing the old tavern song "My name is John Johnson I come from Wisconsin I work in a lumber yard there..." Sting got a real kick out of that.

After dinner we pitched the concept of the movie, and he seemed to like it. We thanked him profusely for his hospitality and returned to the real world. A few weeks late I was in my office at Warner's when my assistant told me that Sting was on the phone! He had written a demo song and played it for me. It sounded terrific. I asked him if he could send us a copy, and he said he wanted to tweak some things first.

In one of the great examples of ironically bad timing, the official announcement was made of the event that we had all been expecting. Jeffrey Katzenberg, Steven Spielberg, and David Geffen had founded their new studio, DREAMWORKS. It would have a feature animation division headed by Jeffrey. Soon another important detail about the company emerged. The first film of the new company would be an animated feature about ancient Egypt. It would be called *The Prince of Egypt*!

It did not take long for Warner Bros. to decide that they would not go head-to-head against Dreamworks with competing Egyptian projects. *King Tut* was dead. I mean our movie, of course. We knew about the mummy.

I had barely absorbed that new reality when the Warner execs told me they had another feature film idea ready to develop. It was a movie about Knights and Damsels based roughly on the King Arthur era, with songs already composed by the Broadway songwriting team of Ahrens and Flaherty. I was not a big fan of their music, and when I heard a few of the demo songs they had recorded all I could do was compare them to the Sting demo. It was a disappointing comparison.

The decision had been made, however, and the medieval movie was a "go". That was just the first of a series of decision that I found questionable. The execs had decided that I must take on a "co-Director". Co-Directors on animated movies were not new. Ever since Musker and Clements had succeeded so well on *The Little Mermaid* multiple directors had become the thing to do. The Dreamworks Egyptian movie was to have *three* co-Directors!

In my case, I was asked to team with a development artist with no directing experience at all. He was a persuasive guy whom the execs felt would be a quick learner. We started the process of developing the picture, and soon had a working title: *The Quest for Camelot*. In keeping with the traditions of a real animation studio we took a research trip to England for a few weeks. Steve Pilcher was inspired by the old castles and rune stones we visited and started doing some terrific visual development paintings.

The execs had hired several writers to work on a script, and in a departure from what I considered to be the normal process, they were writing apart from me and the story crew. They produced a first draft that followed our basic outline, and the execs decided that they wanted to cast the voices of the characters based on that draft. That in itself is not unheard of, but the first actor they chose was a shock to me: Christopher Reeve.

Christopher Reeve, if you will recall, had gained fame playing *Superman* and had a fantastic career ahead of him when he had a horrendous accident. He was thrown from a horse and permanently paralyzed from the neck down. He was living in his country home outside of New York with his wife and a full-time medical team.

The suggestion had been that he read for the part of an old wizard. I questioned whether Chris could even do this, considering the severity of his condition. Somehow, our execs had the idea that an animated voice-over performance was the perfect way for him to do some acting again. I do not where the idea came from, or how enthused Chris and his people were about it, but I was sent off to his country home to direct the audition.

When I arrived, I was met by his wife Dana and escorted to the den, where a sound team had set up a portable recording booth. After a few minutes Chris was rolled into the room in his wheel chair. It was disturbing to see him in his condition. The one part of him that was the old Christopher Reeve was his face, because directly below his chin a foam ring supported his neck. Below that, he was immobilized in the chair with a series of tubes for life support. I said hello and did my very best to make this entire recording process seem perfectly normal.

Chris explained to me that he expected to have some limitations because he could not breath on his own. A machine did that for him. Because breath control is so vital in a vocal performance, he wanted me to know that before I started asking him for adjustments in his recordings.

I mentioned earlier that there are certain qualities that animators find useful in a vocal performance for an animated character. Unfortunately, Chris no longer had the timber or range that made his voice interesting and textural. He had good timing, and you could sense his great talent for creating a character as he delivered the lines, but his "vocal machinery" held him back. As I watched him try to conquer these challenges, I knew that this was what his life would be like from now on, and I could hardly imagine the courage it took for him to face this new life he must live.

When we wrapped the session he thanked me and the sound crew. He was a complete gentleman, and he never complained to anyone about whether this had been a strain for him. I left the session feeling very down about the whole experience. I was very doubtful that his vocal performance, when heard by itself, would be considered usable. Ultimately, it was not used.

Back at Warner Bros., I had a chance to view some superstars in an unexpected way. Michael Jordan was filming the live action/animated feature film *Space Jam*. As part of his contract he had gotten Warners to construct a full-size indoor basketball court inside a tent on the back lot. A friend of mine working on the film told me to meet him after dinner, where he would "sneak me in" to the hottest show in town.

The show was a pick-up game that Michael would arrange with some friends to "stay sharp". His "friends" were basketball superstars like Magic Johnson, Scottie Pippin, and Dennis Rodman. Michael and Magic would be opposing captains and choose teams, half of which were NBA pros and half were regular crew guys from the film. It was a remarkable chance to see two of the greatest players of all time match skills in what you might describe as a schoolyard setting.

The gist of it was that Michael Jordan was obviously the most skilled individual player on the court, but Magic was truly magical in the way he enabled his teammates to shine. One of his crew was a Warner production assistant who was only 5′ 8″ inches tall and looked like a midget compared to the pros, but he was hyper-active, always working hard to get open. Magic would feed him the ball with those spectacular "no look" passes that were legendary and the P.A. would score an easy basket. It was a metaphorical lesson for every director: make ever crew member succeed.

On the QUEST production, we finally got the first rough cut of the storyboards up on reels. This is always a moment of tension, because it is the first time you get a semblance of the story you are trying to tell. Typically you will have dozens of these reviews in the production of the picture, and revisions are expected. As I expected, the picture had a lot of problems to address. My co-Director and I had split the duties into supervising separate sequences. As we watched the film, I thought (and I believe I am being fair) that my sequences were far more cohesive and effective than his sequences.

When it came time to get the studio's notes, I was stunned. The changes that they were asking me to make were just terrible ideas. They made little sense, and they were nothing like the movie we thought we were making. I tried to argue about the notes, trying to be the team player, trying to at least get some explanation of the logic or intent behind these bizarre requests.

I was called into a meeting that was to be one of the more fateful of my career. I was told that the "process" of Warner Bros. Feature Animation was that the notes from the execs were to be treated as instructions, not suggestions. Most of them had been in positions in their previous jobs that had not allowed them to give notes, and following in the footsteps of Jeffrey Katzenberg, it was their time to have an impact on the films. I was told that my co-director had agreed to implement all their notes into his sequences.

I don't think my decision on this situation was as immediate as walking out of the meeting, but I do know that within a few days, I decided that I couldn't work the way they were requesting. I made the point that I had been hired with the expectation that I would be directing a movie, and my contract specified that.

It was assumed I would respond to notes, but there would be a point where I would cease to be directing and instead become simply an implementer of the exec's directions. I did not want to function that way.

There was a brief, awkward period where this conflict paralyzed my participation in the project. I asked to either be given the decision-making authority I felt I was entitled to or released from my contract. Finally, Warner Bros. decided they preferred their "process" and told Sue and me our services were no longer required. Because I had legitimate grounds for seeking the authority described in my contract, our termination deal was quite lucrative.

We walked away from the production with good financial compensation, but the emotional disappointment was deep. We were abandoning many of the artists we had brought into the company, and I would have that bad taste of not being able to finish a production I had started. Since I only had one feature film credit to my name, and that had been a wonderful working experience, this was tough for me to deal with. At the time there were two things I did not know that might have softened my sense of despair.

First, being taken off an animated feature would prove to the rule, not the exception. It would happen on half the future PIXAR films. Sometimes the person was just not the right fit for the project. In the case of *Quest for Camelot*, I was certainly not the best fit for their process.

Second, that "process" they tried to impose on me ended up creating a film that was, statistically, one of the worst films ever made. I have never seen *Quest for Camelot*, but measured by critical response and box office receipts, it scores at the bottom of both standards.

Perhaps the most damning evidence of its failure was that after that one film, Warner Bros; decide to terminate the animated feature film division! When they realized that they had signed multi-year guaranteed contracts with many of the artists, they decided to "burn off" those contracts by making one last film. They decided to produce Brad Bird's idea called *The Iron Giant*. Brad had to make the movie on a very tight budget and schedule to accommodate the contracts of the artists. He agreed to make the movie with one unusual condition. He would report directly to the studio brass, and would not be required to take notes from, or report to, the "execs" that I had dealt with.

Brad made *The Iron Giant* on a shoestring budget. When it was finished, Warner Bros. released it with minimal publicity and promotional support because they were closing the animation division. In spite of that, the film has gained a cult following and is considered by audiences and critics alike to be a wonderful movie.

As for me, I was sitting at home wondering if I would ever direct again.

41

Time to Go Digital

While I was pondering my next move, the animation industry was at a cross-roads. A few years earlier, Disney's *The Lion King* had become the highest-grossing animated feature of all time. It was primarily a 2D hand-drawn film with some computer effects like the famous wildebeest stampede. That had been followed the next year by PIXAR's *Toy Story*, the film that marked the true water-shed in animated feature entertainment. Just as *Snow White* had proven that an audience would sit through a feature-length cartoon, *Toy Story* proved that such a cartoon could be made completely in CGI.

Although Disney would make a few more hand-animated features, the writing seemed to be on the wall. Audiences loved CG movies, and producers dis-covered that it would be far, far easier to find animators who could manipulate computer models than animators who could draw characters. Dreamworks first three features were hand-drawn but it was clear that Jeffrey Katzenberg also con-sidered CG to be the future.

After the Warner Bros. debacle I was hesitant to dive back into a major studio's animation department. I visited PIXAR to check in with John Lasseter and my friend Ralph Eggleston. PIXAR was doing *A Bug's Life*. It was great to view the preproduction art, especially the character designs.

 DOI: 10.1201/9781003558231-41

I went across the bay to visit my old computer compadre Carl Rosendahl. Carl had founded Pacific Data Images years before and built it into such a CG powerhouse that it had caught the eye of Jeffrey Katzenberg. Jeffery wanted Dreamworks to get into CG to compete with PIXAR and decided the quickest way to do that was to acquire an existing studio.

As Carl led me around the studio and showed me the preproduction art of their current project, I was stunned. The characters were bugs! They were making a movie called *Antz*. An untrained artist would have had a hard time telling the PIXAR bugs from the PDI bugs!

We all knew Jeffrey wanted to compete with PIXAR, but this seemed a bit too close. That said, both movies were made, and did OK. The ultimate fallout was somewhat predictable. Within a few years Jeffrey would dominate PDI and Carl would be out the door. Jeffrey's move would pay off when the first Oscar awarded to an animated feature went to the CG-made Dreamworks/PDI movie *Shrek*.

I could see at the time that PIXAR and Dreamworks had solid line-ups of directors for their upcoming movies. I wasn't sure where or if I could fit in. As it turned out I didn't have to make an immediate decision, because a directing job came along that seemed to be the perfect short-term panacea.

After that famous 1986 CG-industry melt-down I described earlier as *DOA* (dead on arrival), one of the many start-up CG companies that rose from the ashes was Rhythm & Hues. Founded by my friends John Hughes, Pauline Tso, Keith Goldfarb, and Charlie Gibson, R&H (its nickname) had great success doing commercials. I often visited their offices in Hollywood to see what amazing new CG imagery they had created. In 1998, they moved to a much larger facility in Marina Del Rey. They were growing fast, and following on the tail of PIXAR were actively pursuing a reputation for high-quality CG-character animation.

I got a call from Charlie Gibson. He said he heard I had come free from Warner's and wondered if I could direct a commercial at R&H. It had CG characters and they wanted a "Disney quality" performance. I was happy to do that, if nothing else than to get out of the house and "back on the horse". I was truly arriving at a formative time for the company. The entire second floor of the new building was still just open wood framing. Only the offices of the directors and managers had been dry-walled. They put me in the corner of one of those offices and I went to work.

It was a commercial for Mucinex, the congestion drug, and it featured blobby, gooey characters. My initial task was to simply direct the performance, so I would do an initial description of how I felt each shot should play, then sit with the animators at their workstations and refine the motion. At that time, I had not had hands-on experience with any animation software other than what we had used at Kroyer Films. It was fascinating, and somewhat daunting, to watch the machinations my animators had to do to achieve a performance using the R&H software.

Like most CG animation companies, R&H had their own proprietary software. Their animation software was called "Voodoo", and it seemed appropriately named because it seemed intentionally mysterious. The late 1990s was the first time that commercially "off-the-shelf" software for CG production became available, and that would have the effect of allowing new companies to compete because they could simply buy their production systems. The biggest companies like PIXAR, Dream-works, Pacific Data Images (PDI) in San Francisco, and R&H had all taken the approach of writing their own systems since no commercial packages had been available when they entered the CG fray.

It was remarkable how different these software programs were, especially if you were an animator. It was not an automatic thing to switch from animating at PIXAR to Dreamworks to PDI to R&H. The interface for each company was different. Some allowed you to use a mouse or a dial box as I had used at Digital Productions. Some systems, like PDI, were almost completely "scripted", meaning you typed in most of your values to see an object move. For this reason R&H included a mandatory two-week training program for every new employee to learn the software.

I asked John Hughes why he did not switch to one of the new commercial packages like WAVEFRONT. John said that R&H had unique advantages maintaining their own system. They could de-bug any problems on site because the creators still worked there. They could create new customized add-ons at will. Most important, when they had to gear up a production and add twenty new workers, they didn't have to pay an outside company for twenty new software licenses, with support. Those were all free. I got the feeling from his passionate explanation that John had a fatherly pride in his own software.

I was only at the studio for a few days when they asked me to helm a second commercial. I was happy to do it. It was fun to work at R&H. I could already sense what time would confirm. R&H was going to be on the cutting edge of every advancement in CG-filmmaking for the next decade. Just before I arrived they had enjoyed their first huge dose of fame and success by winning an Oscar for Best Visual Effects on the international hit film *Babe*.

Babe, the charming crowd-pleaser and box office hit, owed its very existence to a supremely innovative technique invented by Rhythm & Hues they called "2 1/2-D animation". If 2D was hand-drawn, and 3D was how people thought of dimensional CG animation, then 2 1/2-D was in the middle. It started with a 2D image and manipulated it with 3D tools.

This technique was used to make real animals appear to talk and act. On *Babe*, real farm animals were filmed in real locations. The director knew exactly what the animal was supposed to be saying in each shot, so, working with animal trainers, they did what it took to get the animal to physically move as the performance dictated. The animal would walk, sit, turn, or even move its head in motions that later would appear to be gestures.

When a "plate", or performance clip, had been chosen by the director and played against the vocal performance, that film was turned over to R&H. R&H had already created 3D-CG models of each animal's head. Those computer models had all the "controllers" installed to animate that face, including moving the jaw, lips, cheeks, eye lids, eyebrows, etc. Workers called "trackers" would pains-takingly manipulate a wire-frame image of the CG head to match and fit per-fectly over the filmed live action picture of the animal's head.

Once every frame of the shot had been tracked and the CG head moved seam-lessly on top of the real head, the animator would animate the CG features to speak the dialogue and make expressions. Then the live action imagery of the fur, hair, lips, etc. of the original image would be "mapped on to" the imaginary surface of the CG model. That's how real animals were made to appear to talk.

Because they invented and owned this proprietary technique, Rhythm & Hues became the studio of choice for any film that needed talking animals.

There were no companies in Hollywood quite like Rhythm & Hues, and from my forty years of experience, few have ever been like R&H. Most companies take their personalities from the leadership, and this was certainly true at R&H. For starters, it was not owned by a large parent corporation or major studio. It was owned by its four founders. If you wandered through the building you would have a very hard time figuring out who those four people were based on their workspace. John, Pauline, Keith and Charlie worked in small offices of identical size and decor to those of all the other managers and commercial directors.

The first week I was there it was suggested to me that I might want to attend the "Company Meeting" on Friday. At 5:00 PM I gathered with most of the employees in the company screening room. The meeting consisted of John Hughes address-ing the group, and using a projected Keynote presentation, reviewing all the jobs in-house at the time and the status of the future work they were bidding on. What was absolutely mind-blowing to me was that at the end of the talk John shared the company's *financials!* He showed the money in the bank, the projected revenue, and the projected profits or deficits! Given the long-standing joke about how art-ists in Hollywood were treated (like mushrooms—kept in the dark and fed sh*t) this kind of openness was unbelievable.

Many a week John would project a troubling deficit in the company's bank account, but somehow, new work always came in to save the day. John and the founders viewed R&H as more of an artistic communal effort than a business. They wanted the employees to feel like they had a stake in the company. Rhythm & Hues did not have a union because as some union organizers learned to their chagrin, the R&H employee benefits were better than those that any union was offering. That included full health care and very generous vacation time.

Most important to me, the respect and consideration shown to the artists was not just heartwarming; it was genuine. It reminded me of our vibe at Kroyer Films. Because of the leadership, there was no chance of a subculture of abusive middle-management popping up. Everybody at R&H was nice, right down to the mailroom. In the next decade, this would stand in stark contrast to what was happening in some of the major studios' animation divisions. After my experi-ence at Warner's it was like finding refuge in a storm. My motivation to dive back into the Hollywood jungle dropped off considerably. I could not imagine finding a better work environment. The fact that the projects at R&H were at the cutting edge of CG animation was especially alluring.

I hoped they would consider me a positive asset. The Art Department manager, Stacy Burstin, gave me a desk in the corner of a large office. I would work at that desk for the next twelve years.

42

Talking Animals "R US"

As the twentieth century drew to a close computer graphics had come a long way from the build-as-you-go approach we used on TRON twenty years earlier. Fantastic advances had been made in animation software, lighting, and modeling. Photo-real images were possible, with limitations. Rhythm & Hues made industry headlines when they created one of the very first visual effects shot in a live-action movie that had only "photo-real" objects. There were no fantasy beasts or locations. It was for a Morgan Freeman movie called *Along Came a Spider*, and it was a car crashing through a bridge railing and being suspended over a waterfall. Although totally CG, it was supposed to fit seamlessly into the live-action scenes around it. It succeeded—barely. Viewed today, it seems very rough, but it was a milestone.

Many of the CG tools necessary to simulate reality, like water, fur, smoke, fire, etc., had to be created using custom software. Every studio was in competition to create their own tools to grab a bigger share of the market. Soon after I arrived, R&H felt they were ready to debut a new piece of code that they had developed—a "fur program". They felt they had the perfect project to do it.

One of the most visible R&H achievements at that time was their series of commercials featuring the Coca Cola Polar Bears. They had done a half dozen

DOI: 10.1201/9781003558231-42

of these spots, and the Christmas editions had become something of a holiday tradition. People just loved seeing a family of polar bears sitting on an iceberg, chugging big bottles of Coke. The bears were slightly stylized, but they were still recognizable as big, furry, white bears. If you looked closely, they weren't furry at all.

When the first spot was awarded, there was no way to create fur in CG. R&H had won the job by using a clever visual trick. It was possible to add texture to a surface, so the R&H lighters had added a rough texture to the bear's skin that looked something like cottage cheese. Then they carefully placed spikey little uneven needles on the contours of the bear's silhouettes. To an audience not paying close attention, it gave the impression of fur. It helped that these spots were for TV, and this was years before hi-def TV.

Now, however, R&H believed they could make a polar bear with actual fur, and they asked me to direct that commercial. They paired me with an experienced producer named Bert Terrari. Bert had done previous Coke spots. He was clearly not the kind of guy who suffered fools, so the client trusted him. He had been a helicopter pilot in Vietnam, flying into combat zones to support or evacuate troops, and he had taken some hits. He still had pieces of shrapnel in his legs from the war.

When he returned home to L.A. he had started a career as a private helicopter pilot for executives. He was picking up some passengers on one of those landing pads on top of a skyscraper in downtown L.A. Just as he lifted off, he passed out, falling forward on the joystick and luckily causing the bird to immediately settle back down on the pad. It turned out that some of that shrapnel had shifted and blocked an artery. That incident ended his career as a chopper pilot. Through a circuitous series of events, he ended up as a commercial producer.

We had our first meetings with the Coke people and they showed us their idea for the spot. It was very cute. A mama bear sits on an ice flow holding a coke. Her baby bear is just a few yards away but on another ice flow, separated by water. Mom encourages the baby to swim over by patting the water. The baby finally dives in and swims to Mom to enjoy his Coke.

This was a fun concept, and we left the meeting projecting nothing but positivity. When we got back to the studio, we hit the panic button. We had a new fur program—but what about the water? Like every other studio in town, we had yet to write many good tools to simulate water, a.k.a. "fluid dynamics". It was going to be especially challenging to have our new fur move in waves as the little bear swam underwater. But what about the surface of the water when he dives in and climbs out? We had no way to do that!

I addressed the problem in the age-old, time-honored way we addressed all difficult problems in animation. I suggested we cheat! I did a storyboard that showed the little bear leaping off the ice and toward the water, but I had the camera dive below the surface of the water before the bear hit the surface. That way we didn't have to see the splash. We just added lots of bubbles to the bear under the water to suggest turbulence. And his exit from the water? I simply had him swim up and out of frame! The next time we saw him, he was already sitting beside Mama Bear, drinking his Coke! No exit splashing!

The client loved the scenario. They didn't seem to notice how it conveniently eliminated any splashing because it felt like a natural way to view the action. We went to work and soon had a rough test of the animation. Again, they loved it. But there was one little piece of the action that they still wanted to see, and that was the shot where Mama Bear pats the water to entice the baby to jump in.

A paw (or hand) slapping water and making it splash would be possible to do in a few years, but at this moment in CG history, there was no way to pull it off. We had gotten this far with cheating, but we couldn't avoid this shot. Then I had an idea that none of the "CGI purists" in the building would ever have thought of. I suggested we simply animate the splash using 2D hand-drawn animation. I called Kathy Quaife, one of my FX animators from *FernGully*, and she animated a splash that looked totally real. We scanned that into the computer and digitally composited it with the CG bear and CG water surface. It worked perfectly. It's in the final version.

It had been over twelve years since *Technological Threat*, and my invention of that system for combining CG-animation with hand-drawn animation had been motivated by the fact that neither of the two mediums could do it all. I appreciated the irony that the same principle had proved true on this job. However, this would be one of the last times that the two mediums would be combined this way. CG was developing too fast.

Two departments at R&H could have been used as examples of "the canary in the coal mine" for the way they changed over the decade. When I moved into the building in the Marina, R&H had a huge editorial department. There were six editing benches equipped with the viewers and splicers necessary to handle the thousands of feet of 35 mm film. At that time, movies were still shot on celluloid film, so the footage we got from the studios was real film stock. There were racks and racks of metal film cans holding reels of films. Since all the imagery we created at R&H was digital, we had to convert all that 35 mm film into digital files to work on them. In other words, every frame had to be scanned on our digital scanners.

Digital pictures use a lot of data. Since hard drives were not yet big enough to hold the terabytes of data we were dealing with, files were stored on tape drives, and the tape drives were stored on a robototic tape rack. This robot was the futuristic child of the old record jukebox. When you wanted a specific shot, the robot located the tape that shot was stored on. It rotated the stacks of tapes until your tape faced the robotic arm, then the robotic arm plucked out the tape and placed it in the tapereader so the data could be transferred temporarily into a network hard drive.

A programming feature that hinted at what later might be called Artificial Intelligence, the robot kept track of which tapes were being requested most often (usually the jobs in process) and placed that tape in a stack closest to the arm for faster retrieval. Even when it wasn't retrieving tapes for data transfer, the arm was constantly sorting the tapes into a more efficient arrangement.

Ten years later, most movies were being shot digitally and all the footage we got from the studios was already digital. Data storage capacity would be enormous. The tape robot would disappear, as would the shelves of film cans and editing tables. The R&H editorial; department would be just a few offices with computers and big display monitors.

The second department that evolved to extinction was the tracking department. When those 35mm film frames were scanned, they displayed a 2D "flat" image. R&H would be producing dimensional 3D effects and characters that were supposed to fit into that 2D world. The "trackers" were technical artists who sat at computer monitors and painstakingly fit new 3D models of the objects in the frame on to the 2D objects in the frame. As I described earlier, a digital pig's head would have to be scaled, rotated, and manipulated by the artist to perfectly fit over the 2D picture of the pig in the frame. The same was true for the environment, props, and even human characters. If any surface was to interact with a digital effect, it had to be tracked.

Since a huge amount of R&H's business was digital talking animals, the tracking department took up an entire soundstage with more than fifty desks. Because this task was labor-intensive but not critically creative, most of this work was eventually transferred to R&H's office in Mumbai, India, where it could be done for one-fourth of the cost due to the salary gap. This did eliminate a lot of entry-level positions from the L.A. office, but it was necessary to stay financially competitive.

As the decade rolled by, "smart software" that was the precursor of artificial intelligence would continually automate this task. By the time the editorial department had vanished, the job of tracker had all but been replaced by A.I. Even the Indian workers were unnecessary. Today, your smartphone does this same tracking automatically in real time.

After my Coca Cola Polar Bear hit the airwaves, the popularity of R&H's fur program brought in a lot of work. One of the first jobs was for a Tom Hanks' film called *The Green Mile*. Set in a Southern prison, Hanks stars as a sympathetic prison guard. One of his inmates has a pet mouse, and R&H was hired to animate the "digital double" of the real mouse they had trained to do some work on set. They couldn't train a real mouse to duck and dodge a pursuer, so we did that. They certainly did not want to have a real mouse get crushed to death under the boot of a sadistic guard, as the script called for. Our fur program made our digital mouse match the real mouse perfectly, even in close shots. We did such a convincing job that, to this day, people think they killed the little guy. Thanks to CG, no (live) mice were harmed.

With our patented *Babe* talking animal technique and our new fur program, a lot of work was coming our way. I was about to do a string of major feature films. I wouldn't direct the films—just the animals.

43

Dinosaurs, Dogs, and Cats

Ironically, the next animal character I did in a feature film had no fur at all. R&H got the assignment to do the dinosaurs in the live-action film titled *The Flintstones, Viva Rock Vegas*! This was a sequel to a previous *Flintstones* film, both produced by the animation studio Hanna-Barbera. This new film would be more extravagant than the original. It would have digital dinosaurs.

H&B had already decided to use puppets for many of the close-up shots, and for that, they hired the premiere puppetry masters, the Henson Creature Shop. We had the odd assignment of building CG models of the dinosaurs that were precise duplicates of the Henson puppets. Since the Henson dinosaurs, like the pet DINO, had rubbery skin, that was the texture and color we matched.

Puppets do not have a great range of motion, and puppet faces rarely have more flexibility of expression than a working jaw and some tilting eyebrows. For that reason, it was a bit frustrating for us to have to limit our animation to the simplicity of a puppet. The close-ups were agonizing to do, but we did have a lot more freedom in the wider action shots.

It's a well-known, time-honored principle that animated characters will always upstage live characters in a scene. Since animal characters are unreal, fantastical, and move in impossible ways, they always draw your eye and attract

DOI: 10.1201/9781003558231-43

attention. The most famous example of this is Gene Kelly dancing with Jerry the Mouse in the film *Anchors Aweigh*. Even though Gene Kelly is the greatest dancer of all time, and Jerry (by virtue of his animator) is simply copying the exact dance moves of Kelly, you can't keep your eyes off the mouse.

The *Flintstones* director Brian Levant was quite conscious of this. He loved us going broad and wild with the motion when the dinos were the main characters in the shot, but if they shared a scene with the live actors, we toned them down. We couldn't do any Chevy Chase-like mugging in the background.

The *Flintstones* was a fun movie to work on because the sets were so silly. We shot the *Bedrock* exterior scenes at a California state park called Vasquez Rocks. All the interiors were shot on the Universal lot on soundstages. Every room was a cave. The most memorable sequence in the movie for me was the big banquet scene. There was a long slab of fake granite that served as the banquet table. I would eventually be animating digital Dino as he ran down this table and destroyed the banquet.

Before the shot I was hanging out in the shadows when I noticed one of the stars, Joan Collins, standing near me. Joan had been a glamorous Hollywood star who was adding a bit of name recognition to the younger, lesser-known cast. She was doing what could only be described as facial calisthenics. She apparently had had a bit of work on her face that made her facial muscles stiff, and she needed this rehearsal to loosen things up. This was my first exposure to the substance called Botox.

As I was trying hard not to notice, a girl stepped beside me, holding a tray of neatly arranged objects. If you have ever been on a movie shoot, there is a group of workers called "craft services" that is the catering crew. Between serving the full meals at lunch or dinner they often walk the set with trays of snacks. As I looked down at the tray beside me, the "objects" appeared to be huge candy bugs. My first thought was, "How creative! They made some prehistoric snacks for us!" I was just about to grab one and pop it into my mouth when the girl abruptly sprang forward and gave the tray to the propmaster. He proceeded to place each bug in one of the soup bowels on the table. Thank God I had not eaten a prop!

As Animation Director, I work under the supervision of the Visual Effects Supervisor, and on the *Flintstones* I had one of the best in Hollywood, Douglas Smith. Doug had won the Oscar for Visual Effects for his work on *Independence Day*. One of the smartest and most skilled VFX Supervisors in town, I was always amazed that he never, ever, lost his cool or raised his voice, no matter what hysteria happened in a shoot. I noticed that despite his unusually quiet, low-key demeanor the Director paid close attention to every word he said.

Doug and I were completely in sync on the animated performances, and the animation on the *Flintstones* went smoothly. It wasn't long after we delivered the final shots that I was assigned to my next film. Once again, R&H would be paired with the Henson Creature Shop and tasked with matching their puppet animals. The film was called *Cats and Dogs*.

The director was a very young guy named Larry Guterman. Larry's student film had gotten the attention of Steven Spielberg, and the word was that it was that endorsement that had landed him this plumb assignment. When I read the screenplay of the movie I thought it was the funniest script I had ever read. If Larry did a decent job it could be a huge hit!

I thought our animation on *The Flintstones* had been pretty good, but the challenges we were facing on *Cats and Dogs* were in another league entirely. For one thing, nobody knew how dinosaurs really moved—especially Muppet dinosaurs—so we had a lot of leeway on how we animated those characters. Everyone in the world knew how cats and dogs moved. And these were not going to be cartoony cats and dogs. They were supposed to be identical digital doubles to real trained cats and dogs.

For this movie, we would be doing a huge amount of that "2 1/2-D" facial animation, where we manipulated the live footage of real animals to make them speak and act. We would also, for the first time, be doing full CG character animation of the entire animal. It would not just have to look real. It would have to be indistinguishable from the real dog or cat it was doubling for.

Fortunately, Rhythm & Hues was constantly improving their toolsets. Not only had our fur program been refined to be completely realistic, but we now had a "bone-and-muscle-system" that was mind-blowing. Up to this film, most computer animals had just been a polygonal mesh whose shape was distorted to bend and squash like a body. Now, R&H built the characters from the inside out. They literally modeled and built a real dog skeleton that was "rigged" so it walked exactly like a dog. Then, they applied muscles to the bones, and then they applied skin over the muscles. When the animator moved the skeleton, the muscles and skin reacted to create a very realistic-looking dog.

We started doing animation tests using these new tools, and people were absolutely amazed. We did a shot of the star dog, a beagle, walking in a circle. He looked so real that everyone looking at the computer screen thought we had simply photographed the real dog walking. Then, we stripped away his skin and he still walked in the circle. Then his muscles vanished and his bones walked in the circle. Mind-blowing!

The Visual Effects Supervisor on this film was Bill Westenhoffer. I had not worked with him before this film. Bill would go on to be one of the Oscar-winning elite VFX Supervisors of all time, and I could certainly sense that intensity and attention to detail in the way he ran the show. He didn't miss a detail.

Cats and Dogs was to be shot in Vancouver. Bill Westenhoffer had to live there during the whole shoot. He could answer every technical question, and many of the performance requests were ones that he would clarify with the director and then convey to me. I would only fly up for certain sequences that were particularly precise.

On my first trip, I got a sense of the scope of the task we were dealing with. Right after I arrived at the set Bill escorted me to some large circus-like tents that were a good fifty yards away from the set. When I stepped inside, it was like being in a dog show. There were over thirty individual fenced kennels lined up in a row, each with a bed, water bowl, food dish—and dog! There must have been twenty-five different breeds. The production had hired Boone Narr, one of Hollywood's premiere animal trainers, to do the movie. The plan was to try to get as much of the performance as possible from the real dogs. What they couldn't do, we would do in CG.

When I arrived at the soundstage, I had a reunion with Dave Barclay, the head Henson puppetmaster. We had worked together on *The Flintstones* and Dave was heading the puppet team. The first thing I noticed as I watched the live filming was the limited movement of the Henson puppets. *The Flintstones* had been a rather cartoony movie, with cartoony, stylized sets, over-the-top performances, and dinosaur characters that did not attempt to appear real. *Cats and Dogs*, however, was supposed to be a movie about real animals, and the Henson puppets did just not look real. Having skilled puppeteers on the set was very entertaining, in the moment, and having puppets for the actors to act with in real space gave the shots a good energy. But those puppets were going to end up being a problem for the movie.

Sure enough, a few months after principle photography had finished, we got a call from Warner Bros. that our shot list was expanding. When they watched the film in dailies they realized that on the big screen, the puppet faces did not hold up. Compared to our CG animals, who looked very real, the Henson puppets looked like, well, puppets!

In addition to tracking and replacing the faces of the real cats and dogs, we would now use exactly the same process to track and replace the faces on the puppet cats and dogs!

As animation progressed, I had an interesting disagreement with Bill Westenhoffer about animating the dialogue of the animals. In traditional 2D animation, we never "over-articulated" the shapes of the mouth when a character was speaking. In reality, most people do not over-articulate. If you turn off the sound on most movies, it's hard for anyone but an experienced lip reader to tell what people are saying. In fact, lip reading is a very inexact science because people naturally speak with "lazy mouths".

In 2D animation, we animated "by phrases". We would always hit the "hard" sounds, like "b" in boy or the "p's" in paper, but generally we kept it much looser. Watch any old animated film and you will see how true this is. Look carefully at *Pinnochio* and you will be rather shocked at how his mouth bears little connection to the words he is speaking. That's one reason why 2D animation was so easy to dub into other languages. If you watch *Lady and the Tramp* dubbed into French, you would swear that the animators animated those mouths in that language.

Bill Westenhoffer, coming from a Visual Effects mindset, had the natural inclination to be as precise and realistic as possible. He insisted that we articulate every sound that the dog or cat was speaking. He would sit in dailies and suggest minute adjustments to tongue placement or lip compression. He was not wrong asking for these precise manipulations, and it certainly did not hurt the film, but to me, it was choosing literalness over artistic interpretation, and I was always for the artistic view.

Whenever I watch a live-action movie and see an actor barely move his mouth as he speaks, I think of the precision of pronunciation in *Cats and Dogs*.

There was a very fun sequence in the movie where two Siamese cats use karate to beat up Lou the Beagle. I had taken karate classes for years (witness the accuracy of Bruce Kwakimoto's ducky kata in *Animalympics*!), and this was a perfect chance to apply genuine Shotokan technique to a movie fight scene. If you watch the sequence, you'll see great balance in those cat kicks, and the spinning round-house kick that sends the dog flying has real overlap and physics that makes it feel believable.

In the end, *Cats and Dogs* was a hit. Our animation was highly praised. R&H was now considered the premiere "animal house" of CG studios.

The next movie to come our way featured one of the world's most famous animal stars: *Scooby Doo!* I was excited to work on this film because I thought the famous Scooby design would be a kick to bring to life with CG animation.

The first task we had to do was get an approval on the final look of Scooby. I was able to get a maquette from Hanna-Barbera. A maquette is a plaster sculpture used by animators to view the character from all angles. Sometimes, in the case of the illogically-eared Mickey Mouse or very "flat" characters like the *Peanuts* gang, a sculpture can be inaccurate, misleading, or even useless. But the Scooby sculpt was very cartoony and representative of the 2D design.

We took photos of the sculpture, and then I had our Photoshop artists simply apply photo-real fur texture and eye glint so he looked like he belonged in a live-action film. We showed that to the folks at Warner Bros. and they hated it!

"We are not making a cartoon", they said. They wanted a "real" Scooby. Surely, they did not mean an actual Great Dane, we asked. In a typical studio response, they said they could not tell us what they wanted, but they would know it when we showed it to them.

I had an idea to narrow down the decision. There was a 2D program we used called a "morph". You could take two different flat images, connect key points on the images that corresponded, and the computer would gradually change one image into the other. You might remember that this was first notably used to change one animal into another in the George Lucas' film *Willow*.

I took a picture of a real Great Dane dog and lined up a picture of our photo-shopped cartoony Scooby design, so they were in the very same pose. Then I "morphed" the image between the two, so Picture #1 was a real dog and each successive picture got more cartoony until Picture #12, our cartoony dog. We showed that to Warner Bros. and asked them to choose a number between #1 and #12, with #1 being the most real.

We were disappointed when they chose #3. It seemed that we would be doing a very real Scooby Doo. I will admit that we secretly pushed the design to be a bit more cartoony than they had chosen. But we never showed the client a still frame of our version. There is an important principle in animation: "A design is not a character until it moves". We waited until we had some animation, and when we presented our first motion tests on "cartoony" Scooby, the client decided that he looked just fine.

I had a large crew to supervise on Scooby. Like *Cats and Dogs*, I had about thirty-six animators working full-time. Unlike 2D animation, CG animation did not require teams of different artists. In hand-drawing, you would have your lead animator whose drawings were always "rough" but contained enough information to define the performance. The Lead Animator had an Assistant Animator who would do the rough in-betweens so the complete motion could be viewed, including overlapping actions, drapery, etc. Once the rough animation was approved a Key Assistant would do a selected range of "clean-ups", that is, the final, beautiful clean drawings that you would actually see on screen. The Key Assistant was followed by the in-betweeners who would do the remaining clean drawings, working over the roughs and following the cleaned-up guide drawings.

In CG animation, you just had one artist: the animator. There was no need for a rough assistant because the computer filled in all the action. There was no need for a Key Assistant or clean-up artists because there were no drawings. You were animating a computer model.

R&H had their own custom animation software (VooDoo), but the tools it offered were similar to the many commercial packages available. Unlike the early days, the animator had a large "toolset" to choose from. The "workspace" on the screen started to look like a control panel from Starship Enterprise. It was a far cry from the simple tools I had been using as recently as *FernGully*.

The animator could have multiple windows that showed his scene (and character) from top, front, side, and the camera perspective view. Another window showed the curve editor, another the timeline, another the rig controls, and custom windows could display lines of code if the animator wished to "customize" the workspace.

As you might guess, the old, traditional, essential skill of drawing had been replaced by a necessity for technical competence. Some, but not all, great 2D animators were able to make the transition to CG. That's why our crews changed dramatically.

From my "historical vantage point", two things stood out to me at this time as monumental shifts in the animation.

First—women animators were making huge strides. In the days of hand-drawn animation, women animators were almost non-existent. If you looked at Annie Leibowitz' famous *Vanity Fair* photo of the Cal Arts Animation class of the 70s, it featured seventeen men and two women. Remarkably, that was a relatively accurate ratio of working male vs. female animators at a that time.

By the mid-80s at R&H, half my animation staff was women! This was not due to any affirmative action programs. R&H couldn't afford to hire on any basis other than pure talent and ability. The fact was that women animators were just as good. When we reviewed sample reels we did so without reference to race, gender, or anything other than the work we were viewing.

What changed? I have read scientific studies that say that the female brain processes dimensional perception differently from the male brain. In other words, it's harder for a woman to mentally visualize and reproduce an object dimensionally. In 2D, you had to be able to draw a character turning in any direction. Whether you debate this theory or not, the fact was that we saw very few sample reels from 2D women animators that featured this ability.

Computer animation, however, completely replaced this requirement because the computer rotated the model in space for you. All the animator had to do now was manipulate the model to do the right actions. It turned out that women could do this just as well as men. This is evidenced not just by the increase in women animators but the seismic shift in female enrollment in animation schools.

The second major shift I noticed was the more technical approach to performance. In the days of hand-drawn animation, it was so much work to animate a scene that you didn't just sit down and start drawing. Old animators used to give us this advice: "no matter how long they give you to do a shot, spend half of that time thinking about it and planning it".

That's why we would think about every aspect of the shot, mull over possibilities of performance, and do little tiny "thumbnail" sketches that showed every main pose and action—before we started to animate. It was too much work to be wrong. You were so sure about what you were drawing that when you were done, you sent the shot to camera just to validate your vision—and to make those minor adjustments that were usually needed.

With the advent of the computer, I noticed changes in the animator's approach. Very often they started animating just minutes after the handout. Very few took the time to draw thumbnails. In some cases, this was because they weren't good draftsmen at all—hence their choice of being computer animators.

The approach was to quickly throw in a few poses and let the computer do the work. The computer in-betweened the shot instantly and you could at least see basic action. Then, the animator adjusted the action. It was not executing a pre-thought vision. It was more of an exploratory "hunt and peck" process of creating a performance.

Even more odd (to me), the introduction of an important tool called "the curve editor" produced another new technique. The curve editor was a graph that had a collection of lines (like a heart monitor) that displayed the "pathways" or curves of the values of the settings in the shot.

If the arm was bending at the elbow as it waved goodbye, a curve would display a wave that arced up and down to mimic the numerical value change. With a curve editor, you could play the action in real time and, by dragging points on the curve and changing the curve, change the action of the character.

What was to me conceptually odd, and somewhat antiseptic about this technique, was that animators began massaging and adjusting their curves as their mental process of refining the shot rather than simply watching *the character itself move.*

With all these changes, at the end of the day, you still had your animation Director (me) requiring that the shot be effective entertainment.

With a large animation crew like we had on these big animal movies I spent most of my day in "dailies", the session where we screened the work and made comments or gave approvals. It was helpful to the animators to hear the comments made about other animators' shots because it established a unified approach to the acting. After all, we were asking thirty-six actors to give one performance—Scooby's!

It wasn't effective to have thirty-six animators in a dailies session because it took up too much of their time. I split the team into three groups of twelve. They still got that experience of team-thinking without spending hours away from their workstations. I appointed the most experienced animators as Supervising Animators, and I delegated a lot of the responsibility to them for following up on the smaller details of fixes and notes.

If you watch *Scooby Doo*, and you are very picky, you will notice some odd liberties with took with the character's anatomy. Scooby did a lot of things a dog would never do, so we had to bend and stretch his joints and limbs in ways you would never do to a real animal. It sometimes looks pretty fake, and in later films we would get more obsessive about rigging the character model to maintain more believability when doing extreme actions.

A few months after the film wrapped I was invited to be a judge at a very popular animation film festival. The festival was called CARTOONS BY THE BAY, and it was easy to see why it was popular. It was held in one of the world's most beautiful places, the town of Positano on the Amalfi Coast of Italy. Positano is built on a steep cliff that slopes down to the Mediterranean Sea, so there are no streets (and therefore no cars) in the town itself. You carry your luggage down steps to your hotel. Or, to be more precise, you have one of the young men hanging around the parking lot carry it for you.

Sue and I were lodged in a very romantic hotel, the Palazzo Murat, once owned by Napoleon's brother-in-law. It had a terrace shaded by 200-year old vines that overlooked the sea. We would eat breakfast there every day and chat with the other members of our jury, some of whom were animation legends. John Coates had produced some of the most famous cartoons ever made in Britain, including the seasonal classic *The Snowman*. He was a jovial hale fellow who had a hundred stories. His sister Anne Coates, whom I knew at the Academy, was the editor on *Lawrence of Arabia* and had edited perhaps the most famous scene-cut in film history: Lawrence's puff of the match flame that cuts to the rising desert sun.

This terrace is where Sue and I met the couple that we would come to view as our animation role models. Bob Balser and his wife Cima were already in their seventies but had lost none of the vigor that had made them so influential in the animation world. They had owned a studio in Spain for decades, but Bob was most famous for being the Animation Supervisor of the classic film *The Yellow Submarine*.

His stories about that film were captivating. He told us that the Beatles hated the idea of the film because they had already been burned by another animation production using their songs; a British TV series done on the cheap. They refused to have anything to do with the feature. The filmmakers used replacement voices, and had to rush the production because the producer's right to include the Beatles' songs expired after one year. When the film was almost finished, they screened it for the Fab Four, and the Beatles flipped! They LOVED it! They loved it so much that they wanted to replace the "replacement voices" with their own voices. Bob had to explain to them that they couldn't afford to do that, so the Beatles simply recorded that short live action scene at the end of the film.

A few days into the festival, the Director informed me that they had planned a tribute to the great Warner Bros. animation director Chuck Jones. Chuck had passed just a few weeks before. The organizer asked me if I had known Chuck personally, and if so, would I introduce a screening of his films? I didn't go into the full review of how important Chuck had been to my life and career or how he had given me the confidence to even attempt a career in Hollywood. I simply said I would be honored to say a few words.

The next night, they used the biggest theater to screen Chuck's cartoons. In a wonderful and inspired gesture, the festival had put up posters around town that the screening would be open to everyone for free. As I stood off stage waiting to be introduced, the doors swung open and the crowd surged in. Within moments, every seat in the theater was taken. I suppose it was a result of the somewhat looser fire codes in Italy, but all the aisles were jammed with kids sitting on the floor. You could not see a square foot of carpet.

I got up and said something, which had to be translated into Italian, because few in the audience, especially the kids, spoke English. I took a seat offstage as the films began. The first film was Chuck's classic *What's Opera Doc?* Of course, I thought: good choice. Italians love opera!

I watched the audience as the film ran. It was like a moment from *Sullivan's Travels* or *Cinema Paradiso*. Every face was riveted the screen, and everyone—especially the little kids—was laughing hysterically. They were completely immersed in a cartoon film that was made over fifty years ago, done in a language they could not understand. I recalled that Chuck was the philosopher who had coined the famous test of visual humor. He said: "If you can turn the picture off and understand the story, it's radio. If you can turn the sound off and understand the story, it's animation".

I had the thought that this was the perfect tribute that Chuck himself would have loved; that his work could reach across time, across cultures, across language barriers, to bring laughter to an audience. Yes, Chuck. That's animation.

44

The Academy and the Second Golden Age

As the twenty-first century dawned the term "The Second Golden Age" was already being used to describe the resurgence in the theatrical animated feature. The First Golden Age had been the run of Disney classics from *Snow White* to *Jungle Book*. Starting with *The Little Mermaid* in 1989 Disney had a string of hits including *Aladdin*, *The Lion King*, and *Tarzan*. Dreamworks animation was thriving and PIXAR started with three hits in a row.

A trend was emerging. Animated feature films were among the highest-grossing, most popular, best-reviewed films being made and were being ignored during awards season. *Beauty and the Beast* had broken through to get an Oscar nod for Best Picture, but that was an anomaly. It was Jeffrey Katzenberg's relentless PR campaign that had badgered Academy voters into including it in the nominations.

I had joined the Academy right after I had been nominated for *Technological Threat* back in 1989. I was a member of the Short Films & Feature Animation Branch, one of the Academy's seventeen branches. Soon after I joined I was elected to the Branch Executive Committee, a group of about thirty members (it varied year to year) who managed whatever business the Academy's Board of Governors delegated to them.

DOI: 10.1201/9781003558231-44

Each Branch had three Governors. Our three were true "old timers"; animator Bill Littlejohn, famous voice actor June Foray, and former Disney assistant Carl Bell. It was tough to unseat an incumbent in those days, so those three were solidly in place for years.

I suppose it is my nature, but I soon became quite outspoken on matters related to our branch. Even though I was not directing fully animated feature films, it irked me tremendously that they were being ignored by the Academy. The reason was not hard to understand. Ninety-five percent of the Academy's members made their livings working on live-action films. In their minds, live-action films were "real films". In their careers, they barely knew anyone, or had any contact with anyone, who worked in animation.

As the popularity and success of the animated feature film grew, we made it a campaign to point out that these films could no longer be ignored. Finally, the Board of Governors agreed to consider a new Oscar category: Best Animated Feature. In our branch, we actually debated whether this was the best solution. If we did create such a category, some felt it might be the death knell of any animated feature ever being honored as Best Picture of the Year. The new category would "ghettoize" animation into its own niche.

The counterargument to this fear was right in front of us. No film since *Beauty* had even been considered for a nomination, and we saw no indication from the other sixteen branches that they had any motivation to suddenly become animation enthusiasts. Also, getting our own category did not technically prevent an animated film from being nominated for Best Picture. A picture nominated for Best Foreign Film could also be nominated for Best Picture.

The Board of Governors told our Executive Committee to write a proposal for the new Oscar category. I was appointed to the subcommittee that would draft the rules. An interesting and perplexing question came up quickly.

Exactly what qualifies as an animated feature film?

There had been an Oscar for Best Animated Short Film almost since the Oscars were invented. They started the category at the fifth Academy Awards back in 1931, and there had never really been any question or controversy on what an animated film was. *It was a cartoon!* Distinguishing Mickey Mouse, Daffy Duck, or Bugs Bunny from Clark Gable was not difficult.

One of the reasons I was appointed to the Rules Committee was my reputation as a "computer guy" who also grew up in traditional animation. And to the dismay of my fellow committee members, I immediately gave them the bad news that we could NOT identify an animated film by how it looked. Having done a pseudo-photo-real owl five years earlier for *Labyrinth* it was obvious to me that photo-reality was right around the corner. That meant that an artist could choose to make a film using the exact same techniques and technology that would produce a cartoon, but in a design style indistinguishable from a live action film.

At the time that notion was greeted with skepticism, but Tim Burton's remake of *Planet of the Apes* was in production and those apes looked pretty darn real.

We decided that *the look* of the film would be not a relevant factor in branding it as an animated film. What would? We decided that it must *be animated*. To be more precise, we decided that an animated film was one in which *the performance* of the main characters was created using animation techniques. Animation had to be present in 75% of the movie. Our principle goal in using this definition was to preserve the art of animation. More precisely, we wanted to recognize and protect the role of the animator as the actor.

We further defined the acceptable "animation techniques" as basically frame-by-frame animation. This was admittedly an old-school definition but again, we were trying to protect the animator-as-actor. The fact that computer animators were already using "scripts" to facilitate movement was not addressed. What was precisely addressed was disqualifying motion that was created using "real-time" techniques such as motion capture and puppetry. Those techniques were not "original motion that was created", as we always defined animation. They used real motion that was captured or copied.

These definitions would cause a lot of controversy in the years to come. They still do to this day.

There was one other peculiar rule applied to the category that was unique in the Oscar rules. Because there was concern from the live-action members that there were not enough animated features being made each year to merit an Oscar, we had to verify that a certain minimum number of films qualified in the category in order to "trigger" the award. We'd submit our list to the Board of Governors and only then would they approve the category. After a few years, this rather insulting process was eliminated because the number of animated films being produced increased dramatically.

The final result of our committee's efforts was the creation of the new Oscar for Best Animated Feature Film. The first Oscar was awarded in 2001, and in a symbolic coup that must have made Jeffrey Katzenberg dance on his desk, the Dreamworks' film *Shrek* took the prize! After seventy years of unquestioned dominance in the world of animation, Disney Animation was denied this historic moment. In fact, Disney Animation didn't even get a nomination that first year. The other nominees were *Jimmy Neutron: Boy Genius* and the PIXAR film *Monsters, Inc.*

A technicality in our rules allowed the film's producers to define the nominees, and that had the unfortunate result of denying the Oscar to the *Shrek* co-Directors. The statue went to one person, a producer. This rule was changed the next year to assure that a film's director (or co-directors) were never again denied the Oscar. I have always regretted that Andrew Adamson and my good friend and *FernGully* designer Vicky Jenson, the co-directors of *Shrek*, didn't get that coveted statue and the title that forever precedes your introduction: Oscar-winner.

The ability to name the nominee was not the only imperfect rule. There was frequent debate about what films met the definition of "animated". When *Stuart Little 2,* it became a test case for qualification. The movie as shot in live action, but many of its main characters were animated. It literally came down to a person with a stopwatch counting seconds of animation to see if animation figured into 75% of the film.

The next year, we disqualified *Team America World Police* because it was a puppet film. Puppetry was real-time filmmaking. The cameras rolled at film speed as puppeteers worked the strings. It was not frame-by-frame animation. This was clear, but already the problem was emerging. *Team America* was clearly not going to be accepted as live-action film. In the future, where would films like this fit?

A more publicized debate arose when Robert Zemeckis, one of Hollywood's most successful directors, became enamored with the technology of motion capture and started to make movies using this technique. Here was a case where *The Polar Express* and *Beowulf* clearly did not look like live action movies, but our committee was prepared to reject them as animation because they were created using mo-cap. Zemeckis protested vehemently and said that they were animated.

When our Rules Committee discussed this, it was decided that the only way to determine if the Zemeckis' film was "an animated film" was to closely examine the production techniques. Since I was the committee member deemed most experienced in CG animation, they sent me to SONY studios to do the examination.

I sat at the workstations with the *Polar Express* animators and viewed the "raw footage" they had received from the motion capture sessions. They explained what they had to do to refine that imagery for final approval. It turned out that most of the mo-cap required serious fixing to smooth the action, to prevent glitching, or even attaching the character's feet to the floor. Most remarkably, since the motion capture did a very poor job at capturing the actor's facial movements, 95% of facial movement in the film was pure old-fashioned original key-frame animation.

Although Zemeckis and the studio were selling the film as a revolutionary breakthrough in performance capture, it depended a lot on animators. In fact, I discovered that the total number of animator-hours racked up on *The Polar Express* was actually more than the animator-hours spent on the most recent fully-animated SONY CG animated feature film *Surf's Up*. No matter how the studio viewed the role of the animators, the fact that they had done so much work on almost every frame clearly—technically—satisfied our definition of an animated film.

This "dirty little secret" was true of most mo-cap films. They still relied on animators. The next year Peter Jackson would push for an Oscar nomination for Andy Serkis for Andy's mo-cap portrayal as Gollum in *The Lord of the Rings*. When I got a chance to see the ultra-confidential side-by-side footage of Andy's performance compared to the final Gollum performance, it was apparent that most of the nuanced motion of the Gollum's face was absent in Andy's performance. That should have been expected. It was almost impossible for real human features to move with the exaggerated degree of motion necessary to drive the more extreme features of the fantasy character.

This same controversy would arise again years later in the first *Avatar*. Although James Cameron would claim his film was expressly NOT an animated film, and in fact prohibit it from being entered in the category of Best Animated Feature, it would have qualified because ALL the facial acting of the characters had been created by animators. It was revealing that the animation crew on *Avatar* was not lower-priced foreign workers doing simply "digital clean-up", but A-List American character animators whose credits included traditionally animated films.

One notable difference that I appreciated was the contrast between the Zemeckis animation direction and the Cameron animation direction. Since both productions filmed their actors' faces in addition to the mo-cap, the animators had that live footage as reference. Zemeckis had his animators copy the live-action exactly. They were not allowed to exaggerate or take liberties with the motion because Zemeckis felt he must preserve the performance of his stars. For that reason, the motion of those films has been criticized for its stiffness and lack of expressiveness.

Cameron, on the other hand, did not ask the animators to copy the motion. He asked them to study the "intent" of the performance and then manipulate the exaggerated features of the fantasy characters to reproduce the same feeling. Richie Baneham, the Animation Director (and why would a fully mo-capped film need an Animation Director?) came up with a name for this kind of animation. He called it "empathetic animation".

I asked Richie if his animators missed the chance to create an original performance and instead had to follow an actor's performance. He said that it wasn't that far removed from having to follow an actor's vocal performance. Just as you cast different animators for different kinds of scenes, like comedy or action, you had to cast animators who enjoyed this challenge of empathetic acting. That made sense to me.

To this day we have people in the Animation Branch who view motion capture as an evil threat to animation. I have never viewed any technology as "evil". New inventions are just new tools to employ to entertain an audience. This debate would come back in force two decades later, and again I'd be in the middle of it.

This task of "defining what constitutes an animation film" was not the only decades-long conflict of my tenure in the Academy. Soon after I joined I was immediately drawn into another problem that had plagued our branch for years. That was the effort of the live action members to have our Short Films removed from the Oscar telecast.

Their argument was that our Short Films were not truly "theatrical" anymore. The Academy had started as an organization that promoted films seen *in theaters*. There was no TV in 1929, and when TV came along in the 1950s, the Academy more fully embraced the theatrical definition to distinguish itself from the small screen competitor.

Short Films had once been a staple of the movie-going experience, but by the 1990s, they had largely ceased to be a companion to feature films. The live-action members felt that these films did not deserve to be included in the Oscar because "no one watches shorts anymore". Every few years the Board of Governors would consider a motion to remove the Shorts. I was told of a famous incident where it appeared the vote would go against our Branch, but then-Academy President Gregory Peck had ominously denounced the motion. "It sounds to me like we're just picking on the little guy", he said in that famous baritone voice. The vote narrowly lost.

As the twenty-first century rolled in the push to get rid of the Short Films was renewed. In our Branch meeting our Governors told us of a motion that was coming before the Board of Governors that would take the Shorts off the show. They felt it was critical for us animation members to contact as many of the other Governors as possible and campaign to keep the Shorts on the show. They mentioned that they felt they could reach most of the Governors, but the one Governor who was most opposed to our position was the one they could not get a meeting with. That was the legendary and powerful live action producer and studio head Howard Koch.

As luck would have it, I was working with Howard Koch's grandson. Billy Koch was a producer at Rhythm & Hues. Billy never made a "thing" about being related to an industry legend. He was just great at his job. I went to Billy's office and gently broached the subject. I said that we were facing a disaster in the Animation Branch and that his Grandfather was a key player in the drama. Was there any way I could possibly get a very brief meeting with Howard Koch where I could explain our reasons for keeping the Short Films on the show?

To my surprise, Billy was instantly supportive of the idea. He came to my desk fifteen minutes later and said we were having lunch with Howard Koch at Paramount Studios the next day! Yikes!

That night I called several of my friends in the branch and loaded myself up with facts and statistics about Short Films. I learned there were over fifty major film festivals around the world devoted to short films. These featured big audiences watching them *in theaters*. Short films were not just renowned for experimenting with new film techniques; they were often the entry medium for filmmakers who would go on to great careers, like Steven Spielberg and Robert Zemeckis. In the car on the way to Paramount the next day, I practiced my speech on Billy, reciting all the great selling points about Short Films.

We arrived at Paramount and were directed to the executive Dining Room. We only had to wait for a few moments before Howard Koch arrived and sat down. I was nervous. I didn't know what Billy had said to his Grandfather, or if he even knew why we were having lunch. We had just said hello when we were interrupted by a visitor. The equally legendary producer Robert Evans had spotted Howard and wanted to say hi. After a few pleasantries, Mr. Evans departed and Mr. Koch turned to me.

"Billy told me why you wanted to meet with me, so I'm going to tell you right off the bat. I'm against the Short Films staying on the telecast".

That was abrupt. I didn't know how to respond. I didn't even know if I had the right to argue with such an industry icon in his own dining room. I was trying to formulate a polite response, but before I could get a word out, Billy spoke up.

"Grandpa—do you have any idea how cool Shorts are!?" he said. Billy proceeded to vociferously defend my position. In fact, Billy went into a tirade and basically repeated, word for word, all the arguments I had said to him in the car on the way over. And he did it with a fearless tone that I never, ever could have mustered when speaking to the great Howard Koch. I barely said a word.

I could see that Howard was somewhat taken aback at his Grandson's speech. Oddly, he was not irritated. In fact, I got the sense that he had never heard many of the arguments we made about the value of Short Films. In the end, he thanked me for coming. As for the motion before the Board: "I'll think about it", he said.

A few weeks later we got the word that the motion had been defeated. The Short Films would stay on the Oscar telecast, for now. In a decisive vote, Howard Koch had voted in our favor. We had won this round, but the battle to defend Short Films was not over.

45
Animation in the Digital Age

My next assignment at Rhythm & Hues was to be Animation Supervisor on the next major "talking animal movie", *Garfield*. *Garfield* was expected to be another hit, and the studio achieved a major coup when they got the reclusive and eccentric comic genius Bill Murray to agree to do the voice of the famous cat. This movie had a few new wrinkles in the command structure.

There would be two Animation Supervisors on the show. My old friend Chris Bailey would be the on-set consultant for the live action shoot, and I would be at R&H directly supervising the animation. It was to be a long shoot, so they needed us to start the animation right away as soon as the first live action shots were approved. That's why we needed overlapping Supervisors.

An interesting conflict happened right off the bat when Chris and I were listed on the call sheet as "Animation Directors". The film's Producer got quite upset, claiming that a movie only had one director. I believe he even appealed his case to the Director's Guild of America (DGA), the powerful union. The live action Director, Peter Hewitt, did not disagree, and our titles were changed to Supervisors.

A curious side-note here: that year the DGA had invited a large group of Animation Directors to a meeting at the guild headquarters on Sunset Boulevard.

DOI: 10.1201/9781003558231-45

I was invited by virtue of having directed *FernGully*, but the group also included most of the Disney, PIXAR, and Dreamworks directors. The DGA pitched us on joining the guild, and it was an attractive idea considering the very lucrative revenue-sharing benefits a guild director automatically received in his contract.

The idea only lasted long enough for the studios to get wind of it. The major animation studios made it very clear that they would never, ever allow a DGA director to direct an animated feature. The DGA contract was too rich, and the studios felt that an animation director (or co-director) could be any talented artist elevated from the story or animation departments and do just fine. That was how all the current animation directors had been chosen, and the studios would continue to do that.

Even though Chris was our on-set guy on *Garfield*, I visited the set often, and the one aspect of the picture that surprised and impressed me was the performance of the real animal co-star, Garfield's lovable little dog buddy, ODIE. Odie was being performed by another of Boone Narr's trained dogs, but unlike *Cats and Dogs*, where there had been four or five similar-looking beagles playing the lead part, this movie had just two dogs doing the Odie performance. More incredibly, one of the two dogs did 95% of the acting scenes! The little guy was so brilliant that he could nail almost any trick or acting bit in one or two takes. That was such a valuable resource that they kept him on the set almost all the time. When you watch the movie, pay attention to this dog's performance.

The ASPCA (American Society for the Prevention of Cruelty to Animals) polices every movie set, and they are very strict in protecting animal actors from danger or overwork. Because our Odie dog was so essential to the production, and had to be on the set for long hours, he had a luxurious "break room". He had his own large sound-proof cage with custom snacks, and as soon as his scene was over he was whisked into his hideaway where he could rest, eat, and sleep in peace and comfort. The union rules for his trainers were equally as strict, so he often had different trainers working tag-team shifts to account for the long hours.

The second trained dog was Odie's actual sister. She looked exactly like him but had none of the talent. They used her sparingly, particularly in shots where there was any chance at all of an accident or injury, like standing on a curb as a car drove by, or falling off a chair. Basically, a stand-in stunt dog!

I had a very large crew of animators on the show, so I divided them into four units, each with a supervising animator. For me, working on this picture felt like a "mileage marker" for my career in animation. Not only had the industry gone completely over to CG-animation, but most of my animators had never animated a scene in 2D. Some couldn't even draw.

It had been twenty-eight years since I had arrived in my van from Chicago to apply to an industry where drawing was the entry ticket. When I submitted my reel of hand-drawn animated commercials to the Disney Review Board in 1977, I had only a few dozen competitors. Now there were hundreds, even thousands of artists working at studios around the globe with the screen credit of "animator". That was the testament to the difference in the skill sets required to do the job.

You no longer had to have that rare talent to draw a dimensional character over and over with believable precision, or to draw it in motion doing a performance.

Now an animator was essentially a puppeteer. The computer provided you with a character model that always looked like the character, no matter how you manipulated it. Not only that, but forty different animators could use the same exact model to create a single performance. If 2D animators were generators of the imagery, CG animators were manipulators.

What had been lost was that ability to use the freedom of pure illusion. You could not make the ears migrate across the head, ala Mickey Mouse, or make the nose float off the end of the nose, like *Family Dog*. The animator did not have pure freedom to create any image he thought would give the impression of motion. You were constrained by the work of an artist who came before you in the animation production pipeline: the rigger.

The task of rigging has been around as long as there have been CG models, but it is a skill very few moviegoers understand, or even know exists. A CG model that is not rigged is basically a motionless sculpture. It is the job of the rigger to create a system of controls that the animator can manipulate to move the model.

The oldest and most basic tool is the skeleton. The skeleton is exactly what the name implies. It is a jointed armature-like structure that sits within the model. The animator has controls to move all the "bones", making them pivot around the joints. This structure in a puppet looks just like a stick figure, but in a digital model, which has no actual physical reality, it is usually represented by images of lines connected by circular pivot points.

The real art of rigging in attaching the outer skin of the character to the inner skeleton so the surface skin will move when the underlying skeleton moves. In the first CG models, which were just hollow vector shapes, the vectors surface simply distorted. As rigging got more sophisticated, CG models had actual (but invisible, imaginary) muscles attached over the skeleton. These muscles moved, and they, in turn drove the surface skin they were attached to.

As you can imagine, these attachments, and the design of the degree of movement they generated, got very complicated. Just the face on an R&H cat model could have fifty-five controls! As an animator, you were constrained by the number and design of the controls the rigger provided you.

For this reason, the "Art of Animation" was moving away from the spontaneous flow of imagery to the very calculated mechanics of motion-creation. The people who wanted to do this—who could do it—had to have a significant technical savvy.

Although Garfield was one of the world's most famous cartoon characters, he had never appeared before as a photo-real furred cat, so our interpretation of his movement was original. I really received very little specific direction on his acting from the live action director, so I just followed my own instincts on directing the animators.

The toughest task for me on the show was pleasing our Visual Effects Supervisor, Dan Deleeuw. Dan would go on to do some of the biggest movies in the *Marvel* universe, but *Garfield* was one of his early projects, and his eye for detail was extremely precise. I always focused on the artistry of the performance, but Dan focused on the details, like toe splay or tail overlap. We would get the performance of the character approved after one or two takes but be required to do seven or eight more versions to satisfy minute actions that I was sure no audience member would ever notice.

That ease and ability to do retakes was a mixed blessing of the computer age. In the days of hand-drawing, it was so much work to redraw a shot that you worked very hard to get it right the first time, and if there were changes, you tried to complete them precisely on the second pass. On *Tron*, with CG in its infancy, it was very laborious to do corrections and extremely time-consuming of CG resources to refilm shots. We rarely did more than two takes of any shot. By the 2010's, technology had advanced to the degree that you pressed a button and could recompute a scene. It was not uncommon to see a *hundred versions* of some Visual Effect shots!

That's why the older hand-drawn cartoons have charming mistakes that were either missed or deemed too expensive to fix. In Disney's *Bambi*, there was a shot where the deer simply disappeared because the camera operator forgot to include the correct cel. In another scene, a baby raccoon pops from one side of the frame to the other because the operator put the cel on *upside down*! You can't see these now; they were fixed when Disney did the digital restorations for the DVD release.

In the computer age, the ability to spot a mistake is a vanishing joy. Each scene is examined to death. I'm not sure that's as much fun to watch.

46

The Marriage of Animation and Visual Effects

The highly technical nature of CG animation changed the culture of the animation industry. In the old 2D age, the animators were clearly the kings, the "essential workers". They were the elite, and their personalities and habits dictated the vibe of the studio.

In the digital age, the modelers, riggers, lighters, effects artists, etc., had equally complex and essential tasks within the production. Even the animators themselves had less and less connection to the crazy artists of the Termite Terrace days and more of a similarity to the rest of the crew who, like themselves, labored in front of computer monitors and used software to do their work.

The complexity of the productions increased. The budgets increased, and the risks involved in bidding to do a job for a set price could break a studio. As the ubiquity of technology made it possible to open more and more competing studios, the pressure to do more for less increased.

As I mentioned earlier, John Hughes would hold his employee meetings on Friday after work and review the company's financial status. As *Garfield* wound down, the numbers started to look scary. To get work, R&H had to out-bid other CG studios. A typical tactic in those days was to intentionally "low ball" the bid, then, once the job was awarded, slowly add-on overages and additional costs.

DOI: 10.1201/9781003558231-46

John Hughes would not use that tactic. A few of the major studios who had been burned by these low ball bids began to realize that they were better off going with an R&H bid because it was honest and accurate. R&H would stick to their numbers. Unfortunately, that made our profit margins low.

There was no big job in the pipeline to keep the studio employed once *Garfield* was finished. There was a huge film franchise gearing up in Hollywood, the series of films based on the book *The Chronicles of Narnia: The Lion, the Witch, and the Wardrobe*, but for some mysterious reason R&H had not been invited to bid on them.

Narnia was a Disney project. I really felt we should have a shot at doing the animation. I pressured our President of Production, Lee Berger, to get us a meeting. We were finally invited to the Disney lot to meet with the director, Andrew Adamson, and the producers. Just Lee Berger, our VP Richard Hollander, and me went to the meeting.

Although I did not know Andrew Adamson personally, he came from the animation world. We had many mutual friends, including his co-director on his Oscar-winning film *Shrek*. That co-director was Vicky Jensen who had worked for me for years at Kroyer Films and was a key designer on *FernGully*. I suspected that Andrew might have heard of me in a positive way. I gave him a very hard sell about how great our animation team was at R&H. At the end of the meeting, they agreed to let R&H join the few studios that would compete for the job. That competition involved doing a fully-produced animation test.

All of the studios were provided the same CG model of a character. It was a beaver. I felt we immediately had an advantage because beavers have fur, and the R&H fur software was still the best in the business.

We were then provided a soundtrack, a few lines of dialogue voiced by the actor Ray Winstone. We were asked to animate the beaver saying that dialogue. The test offered no other specifics.

I listened to the soundtrack, looked at the model, and thought about the many ways we could interpret the acting. Then I did something that seemed so ridiculously obvious that I was aghast that I was the only one who did it. I asked the Director if I could show him storyboards of what I was planning. Andrew agreed.

Two days later I showed up at his production office with a detailed storyboard of the proposed sequence. He reviewed it and had a lot of comments and suggestions for changes. You might think that I was worried that my original "take" was far from satisfactory to him. In fact, I was elated. This meant that he was a director who had definite ideas about what he wanted.

That made sense, because unlike the live action directors of the talking animals I had recently done, Andrew Adamson was a director of animated movies. In animated movies you do not have the luxury of shooting multiple takes and choosing versions. You get to make one take, so you better decide on exactly what you want before you make it.

Something you learn in the world of animation is that there are almost infinite ways to portray the exact same idea. If you told ten animators to do a general action, like having a character unpack a suitcase, you could get ten completely different versions of the scene. More remarkably, every one of those versions could be well-done and very entertaining. Every director soon learned that if you had definite ideas about how to play a scene, you had better be very specific with your animator or you could get something very different.

On *FernGully* I had a shot where two characters shake hands. For some bizarre reason, the animator had them shake with their LEFT hands! It was technically correct, but looked odd. That's why I started to record my handouts on VHS tape, so I could define every detail of what I wanted!

I took careful notes of Andrew's comments and returned the very next day with the re-drawn storyboard. That's one of the great powers of storyboarding. It might take the studio weeks or months to actually produce the scenes, but you can draw them in a few hours. Andrew looked at the board, liked the changes I had made, and added a few more comments. I pressed him a bit for any more details about exactly how he might like the acting to play out. I went home and did one more version of the storyboard, this time adding a lot more drawings that suggested facial expressions, hand gestures, and specific camera staging. I practically animated the shots.

It may seem obvious, but the two ways to make a Director happy are (1) find out exactly what it is he wants, and (2) *give it to him!*

Using my storyboard as the guide, we finalized the beaver model with fur, built the sets in the computer, and animated the performance with the same gestures, scene cuts, and camera staging that Andrew had suggested. I suppose the other studios had a bit of that malady I call "the seduction of technology" because they assumed that by loading their tests with amazing CG effects, they would win the job. They prioritized form over content. In the end, Andrew liked our test for simple reason it was exactly *what he had in mind.*

As a result, Rhythm & Hues was awarded the biggest contract it had ever had in its history. In fact our budget for the first *Narnia* film exceeded the total revenue the company had earned the previous year. R&H would enjoy several years of financial security!

I had done the *Narnia* test while I was working full-time finishing *Garfield.* We were just about done with the work when the studio asked us to do one more sequence. They wanted us to animate a sequence that would go over the closing credits. It would have Garfield dancing to the James Brown hit "I got you". I thought this was a terrible idea. Having the famously sedentary, grumpy, and sarcastic Garfield dancing like an extroverted rock star was completely out of character. Such a request was, sadly, not unusual.

To animators, it is a wonderful, almost magical thing when a character becomes so real that you know exactly how it will act in any situation. Studio executives and live-action filmmakers often don't see it that way. They just see a cartoon. The worst example of this is the first *Space Jam* movie, where Bugs Bunny is portrayed as a helpless victim. That is not the Bugs we know from the Warner Bros. short films. That Bugs never gets screwed. Bugs is the screwer, never the screwee.

We did the Garfield song and wrapped the film. I had not had a break for a year, and it would be months before the *Narnia* characters were built and ready to animate, so I took several months off. Sue and I were on vacation in Florida when I got some unexpected news. The R&H contract on *Narnia* was going to be cut in half. The Disney studio had second thoughts about awarding such a large contract to a single company. They decided to split the work. We all suspected that the real reason was that a competing studio had lowered their bid so much that the producers could not resist giving them a major chunk of the work.

The good news was that R&H retained all the key character-acting sequences, which included my beaver and the real star of the film, the lion Aslan. The bad news for me personally was that R&H had already committed to hiring a second Animation Supervisor to split the work with me, and since he was already heavily into the rigging work on the characters they decided he would stay on the film. I was very disappointed, because I sensed that *Narnia* was going to be an exceptional film.

That said, the other Supervisor was my friend Richie Baneham, and I had to admit that he was better than me at the increasingly complex technological machinations of modern CG animation. I was, at heart, an "old school" animator who focused on performance and dealt with technology as a necessity. Richie was a great performance guy, but also had a total grasp of new tools and was a technological innovator. He would not only do a wonderful job on *Narnia* but years later become the Oscar-winning Animation Supervisor of all the *Avatar* films.

I returned from my badly-timed vacation to wonder what was next for me at R&H. Luckily, our commercial division was still going strong, and I resumed directing the animation on some very fun and innovative commercials. I even started to direct live action if the spot called for it.

I did a commercial for an insurance company of a mouse finding its way through a maze. We shot that live action, with a real maze and real mice. We would photograph the real mice and add some CG expressions to make them act. The live shoot was quite easy because Boone Narr's animal handlers had pre-trained the little mice to act on cue! To get the mouse to move, they would blow on his butt with a straw. I never would have thought of that!

The next spot I directed had the opposite experience. This commercial would feature a dozen glass fish bowls, each containing one brilliantly colored tropical fish. Our "hero" fish would decide that he could get a better experience jumping from one bowl to the next. That jump would be done using a CG fish, but someone decided that it would be more economical if the rest of the characters were real fish. To do that we had to rent a real soundstage with lights, camera, and a full production crew.

We assembled the dozen glass bowls on a table, carefully lit the shot, and started to shoot. What could go wrong? The answer: things you could never imagine. For one thing, every time the camera rolled, it seemed as if the sound made the fish run for cover. Instead of floating contentedly in the middle of the bowl, they would dart to the side of the bowl. The curvature of the glass made them basically invisible to the camera. We could never get more than three or four of the fish visible at the same time. We finally decided we would have to magically combine the bowls in post-production.

The most difficult shot to achieve was a fish simply swimming one way, stopping and reversing direction. You would think fish did that all the time—*but not exactly!* What made it even more frustrating was that we were shooting real 35mm film stock at high speed: 120 frames per second! That was because fish move so fast that unless you shoot them at high speed, you can't really see them. The result was that we were burning through dozens feet of expensive film stock on every wasted shot.

I had what I thought was a brilliant solution. Why not just sew a tiny, thin filament wire through the fish's dorsal (top) fin and literally drag it along the path we wanted it to take? That idea was quickly squashed by the representative from the ASPCA. That's right; we had a rep from the American Society for the Prevention of Cruelty to Animals on set!

I am the world's biggest animal lover, and I have always been absolute in my support for the safety and care of animals on film sets. It sickened me to read about the old days when horses would be crippled by trip wires in action films. There was the famous story of a nature film that sacrificed twenty raccoons to get the fake shot of a raccoon protecting her young from a mountain lion. In contrast, I loved the way we pampered our little dog Odie in the *Garfield* movie.

As it happened, there was a writer's strike going on in Hollywood at the time we were shooting this commercial, and almost all film production had been shut down. Normally the ASPCA rep would be on a set that had larger animals doing risky things, but we were literally the only game in town that day. Hence we had a full-time fish protector.

I argued that the fish couldn't feel a tiny thread in its dorsal fin. We weren't even using fish hooks! Unfortunately the idea was rejected. The bizarre irony of this situation is that once the shooting day was over and the production was wrapped, we could legally fry these fish for dinner (we didn't!).

We finally came up with another solution. We put clear plastic barriers inside the tank to make the fish swim in a straight line. That's big-time filmmaking.

One of my oddest experiences was being "loaned out" by R&H to a small start-up game company to consult on animation in their video game. The R&H admin folks were interested in the new motion capture technology and wanted me to experience that. I spent a few weeks in a studio in the valley working with actors and animators, creating "motion modules" for a first-person shooter game.

Those modules were, in principle, just like the ones I had done years earlier on *Pitfall Harry*, but now the motion was created by real people dressed in skintight suits with reflective marker balls. An array of cameras, called "a volume", photographed the motion from all angles, and the motion of those reflective balls was processed in the computer to synchronize with the joints of CG models. Classic mo- cap.

The obvious advantages were that you could capture, and therefore create, human-like motion must faster than animating it by traditional frame-by-frame methods. At that time, the technology still required some clean-up in post but worked fine. The disadvantage was that the motion did, indeed look just like real motion—because it was! It was fun to direct real actors, especially the martial artists we used for fight scenes. In the end, it felt like compromised motion. It did not have the exaggerated, stylized motion that made animation so captivating.

You could push those parameters by having your actor do exaggerated actions, or by customizing the rig of the CG character to automatically exaggerated the captured motion. Motion capture has expanded by leaps and bounds and is widely used today.

Although R&H had a thriving commercial division and an industry-leading feature film animation/visual effects division, the company was facing stiffer and stiffer competition. Part of that came from the proliferation of new CG production companies made possible by the availability of "off the shelf" software. In the ten-plus years since R&H was founded and prospered by using its own in-house proprietary software, software companies like MAYA and HOUDINI were making and selling software that could be used in film production. A company no longer needed to create their own software. They just bought it. Plug and play!

This caused dozens of small "boutique companies" to pop up. Run on shoe-string budgets, and offering little or no benefits to their employees, these studios underbid jobs and nipped at the heels of the bigger shops.

Why would a worker choose to work longer hours with less benefits? A company like R&H could not hire everyone, and there were more and more young artists anxious to enter the business. The video game mindset held by so many young people translated well to the manipulations of animation or visual effects software. You didn't need a college degree. You just needed some technical proficiency. If you started to doubt the wisdom of working eighty-hour weeks with no benefits, there were always younger, hungrier computer geeks ready to replace you.

That was why the visual effects industry has never been able to unionize. There are too many people willing to work "for anything" to strike and demand better conditions.

The biggest threat to a company like Rhythm & Hues was a new trend completely out of its control: foreign competition. As I mentioned earlier, there have always been foreign companies competing with U.S. companies, and the main advantage was cheaper labor. In the old animation model, the U.S. retained the more skilled, creative jobs and the "grunt work" went overseas.

That was not the case in the digital age. The computer leveled the playing field in terms of skill and talent, as did the ubiquitous software. Other countries saw the chance to land thousands of new high-paying jobs, financed by Hollywood, and they did three things to tilt the market their way.

First, Canada, the United Kingdom, France, Australia, and others started to offer production funds to support production. They subsidized the VFX studios.

Second, these countries offered tax breaks and tax incentives to American companies that would fund work in their countries. If you spent $100,000.00 you might get $18,000.00 kicked back as a tax credit.

Third, all these foreign countries provided free, universal health care to their workers. Because R&H wanted its workers to have health care and retirement benefits, and America was the only first-world country without universal health care, an R&H bid against a foreign company was automatically at a 6% disadvantage.

John Hughes came up with an interesting idea. How about partnering with a European Visual Effects Studio? This would not just open the chance of tapping into the European market but also use lower-priced European labor in co-productions. To investigate this plan, he decided to send me and our VP Richard Hollander to Germany.

Richard and I had a fascinating time visiting our German counterparts. The German VFX companies were smaller than R&H, and many had interesting locations. One was a stone's throw from the old Berlin Wall. Another was inside Berlin's historic Babelsberg Studio lot, one of the world's oldest filmmaking locations. One of the studios was funded by an extremely wealthy German entrepreneur who was, we were told, of "royal blood". It was a meeting at his studio that a surprising opportunity presented itself.

Unlike PIXAR, Disney, and other CG studios, R&H had never developed and produced its own short films. I had pitched a few ideas to John Hughes, and told him that many staff members were willing to work for free after hours on an original short film, but John was set against making people work "for free"—and he couldn't afford to fund an in-house production. Nevertheless, I developed a project that eventually expanded into a full screenplay. It was called *Armour Star*, and it was a CG-animated feature film about the adventures of "the fastest armadillo in Texas".

In the course of the meeting with the German millionaire, that project came up, and he instantly sparked to it. Whether it was that *FernGully*-like attraction to a new venture or a fascination with American cowboy culture, our "Prince" wanted to not just partner with R&H, but fund the movie!

This was the kind of out-of-the-blue miracle that only happens in Hollywood movies. Richard and I returned to Los Angeles with the news that seemed too good to be true.

It was. It ended in the most tragic and unbelievable way.

Less than two weeks after we returned, we got the news that the Prince had been killed in an avalanche while skiing in the German Alps. His plans, our movie deal, and even his VFX studio dissolved. Something about that tragedy caused John and our group to forget about expanding to Europe.

Meanwhile, many of our competing American VFX studios were being bought by huge conglomerates. Now, those companies could cut their bids because the larger parent corporation could absorb any losses.

John, Pauline, and Keith refused to sell out to a bigger company, and they also refused to cut benefits or wages. They turned to another solution. If you could not beat a foreign studio, become a foreign studio.

47

R&H India

In the late 1990s, R&H hired a brilliant computer scientist named Prashant Buyala. Prash was from Mumbai, India, and in addition to helping with technical issues in Los Angeles, he opened the door to an entirely different opportunity for the company.

At the time, all the workers on a computer graphics film spent their day "setting up" their files. Animators would create motion, lighters would set lights, effect artists would program water, etc.—but all of those things could only be viewed in their final form *after* the scenes were rendered. In other words, the computers "crunched the numbers" all night so you could see the final results in the morning.

As with any process, things could go wrong, so engineers had to monitor the numbers all night long to make sure the process didn't stall or crash. They worked the night shift, 9 PM to 6 AM.

Prash made the rather obvious observation that since India is exactly on the other side of the world from Los Angeles, that same time period in India is 9:30 AM to 6:30 PM, a normal day shift (weirdly, India's time zone is 30 minutes staggered from ours). If R&H used Indian engineers to monitor the render queue, not only would those people be working a comfortable daylight shift; they would do

DOI: 10.1201/9781003558231-47

it for about 1/3 the salary. Since Indian workers were emerging as very competent computer workers it was a grand idea. R&H India was born!

The other thing that made this possible was the vast improvement being made in high-speed data transmission. By purchasing dedicated lines the L.A. office could have almost instantaneous data transmission with Mumbai. An Indian worker could view files almost as fast as an American worker within the building.

The system worked so well that other jobs started to be transferred to the Mumbai office. Remember that job called "tracking", the labor-intensive process of converting a 2D film sequence into a 3D workspace? All of those jobs went to India. I remember the day I walked into our L.A. soundstage, once lined with fifty workstations, to find it vacant. More surprising was the sight of fifty computer monitors stacked in the dumpster outside. They had become so instantly outdated that they could not be resold or repurposed.

A natural reaction to this change would be the accusation that R&H was sacrificing American jobs for profit. The truth was quite different, and bore a striking similarity to the results of a similar situation that happened decades earlier, the period I previously referred to as "runaway production". When 2D animation studios sent their "grunt work" overseas, they made animation production more economically profitable, thus increasing production and adding higher-paying skills jobs here in America.

The same thing happened to R&H. The company had to cut costs somehow to simply compete with subsidized competitors, so the Indian operation allowed R&H to not just win bids, but add more skilled American workers.

The Mumbai office proved a success in another surprising way. It turned out that Indian workers were not just suited to the "grunt" work. They soon proved their capability at handling increasingly more complex and demanding tasks. It was becoming widely recognized that Indian workers had a talent for mathematics, which translated comfortably to computer skills. Within a year, R&H was assigning Indian workers to do modeling, layout, and lighting tasks. The last skilled job category to be considered was animation.

As I have mentioned before, Americans seem to be blessed with a sense of entertainment that plays well on the world stage. The American audience doesn't typically respond strongly to foreign films with a foreign sense of humor, but the opposite is true. The one thing America exports that it does well is entrainment.

The first tasks R&H assigned to the animators in Mumbai were simple motion assignments. They could do effects animation pretty well, and also character animation that had basic movements like background walks or falls from buildings. When it came to acting, they struggled.

The R&H management had the idea to send me to India to give the Mumbai animators a crash course in character performance acting. I had always wanted to see India, which seemed very exotic, so I didn't resist what was in any case an assignment I was not expected to refuse.

India is almost exactly on the other side of the world from L.A., so it's a long journey, about eighteen hours of flying time. R&H always allowed their workers to break up the trip into two segments, so I had a non-stop flight to London, where I spent the night in a hotel and continued on to Mumbai the next day.

My first impression of India came before I even left the airplane. The poor quality of the runway made the plane bounce as we landed. We bounced quite a bit more as we taxied along, and I could see grass growing in the cracks of the pavement. This was 2008 and the airport was in poor shape. The old terminal looked like it could have used paint job.

If you were a first-time visitor to India, R&H put you up in a nice hotel for the first two nights to ease you into the culture. I stayed in the Westin, which was as sleek and modern as any hotel I had ever been in. But when my driver picked me up the next morning it didn't take long to see the contrast in living conditions. The Westin was surrounded by a concrete wall, and there were lean-to tents crammed with people along the outside of the wall. If you have never been to Mumbai, the overwhelming feeling you have is the sheer mass of humanity. People are everywhere. I was particularly amazed by fact that the narrow grassy strips that divided the main roads were always crowded with sleeping workers.

I had seen traffic in Bangkok, Seoul, and Manilla, but the Mumbai street scene is like nothing else. It is the ultimate demonstration of fluid dynamics and collision detection, where cars, trucks, buses, motorbikes, rickshaws, bicycles, cows, dogs, people, and the occasional elephant all move around and through each other with studied indifference. Drivers honk their horns constantly, not out of anger or frustration, but to simply signal that they are there. There was no such thing as "defensive driving". You could not possibly keep track of those around you. The rule was simple: don't hit anyone—and they, following the same rule, will hopefully not hit you.

The R&H office was in a beautiful new high-rise office building. It was in complete contrast to the tents and shacks in the empty lot right beside it. Prashant and his wife Vani had done a remarkable job building the facility. They told me that in Mumbai every task required to create a studio, from building permits to construction to air conditioning contracts, were only achieved through intense negotiation; a.k.a. bribery.

The office itself was beautiful, and from what I learned from the workers and from other outside observers it was considered quite exceptional for Mumbai. R&H treated their Indian workers like they treated their American workers. Everyone had a spacious, comfortable workspace. The bathrooms were nice. There were break rooms with tea and snacks. The company even provided a free luncheon every day. Although these "comforts" seemed excessive to some employers, they were a strong reason that R&H maintained their staff with a loyalty that was unmatched in the ruthless Mumbai market.

What I loved was the atmosphere Vani had created. This was not your typical modern computer company. Like R&H L.A., she had allowed workers to decorate their own cubicles. Some had thatched roofs, others had brick-like walls with local paintings. Every door in the building was unique. Vani had scoured the old street markets for cast-off doors and windows. She could buy a hand-painted door from an Indian palace for a few dollars—one-third the price of a bland hollow core door from Home Depot.

I had planned a "crash course" in character animation for the animation crew. They didn't need any technical instruction. Every one of them was proficient with the R&H animation software. What they needed was the mental adjustment of learning to analyze and emulate character performance in a way similar to the sensitivity of the American animator.

I started with a lecture of the famous twelve principles of animation. I gave them their first assignment exercise, a bit of animation that utilized most of the principles. The studio had allowed them two hours each morning for my lectures, but because I knew they would have to put in a regular eight-hour workday, I told them I expected them to have the assignment done the day after tomorrow.

I came in the next morning to find that every animator had completed the assignment. They had stayed up half the night doing the work. That was my introduction to the Indian work ethic. These kids were manic.

I had always felt that the one advantage we Americans had was a unique sensibility for entertainment that appealed to the world. Watching these Indian animators make their creative choices, I sensed that they indeed lacked the inherent cultural perspective that I believed made American humor work so well. However, they were clever enough to begin to imitate that sensitivity to a reasonable degree. My prediction, which I believe has been proven right, was that Indian animators would not be very successful as storytellers, but would do just fine executing specific direction from a good director.

After my two week session, I felt I had gotten them started on the right track. Indeed, R&H started shipping more animation to the Mumbai office. The cost savings was keeping the L.A. office afloat.

While in Mumbai I stayed at a rented guesthouse on the North end of the city in a rural area called Madh Island. Vani thought I would enjoy being near the fishing villages, and she was right. Each morning I would walk past a pond filled with bathing water buffalo to the end of the road where I would hail a "tuk-tuk" (three-wheeled motorized rickshaw) to ride into town. On the walk I would pass a compound with a huge, run-down house that seemed to be crawling with kids. Kids were everywhere; on the porch, in the yard, hanging out of the windows. Oddly, there seemed to be no adults. One evening I decided to investigate. I walked up to the front porch and said hello. None of the children spoke English, so I was escorted inside and taken to a small office. There I met a middle-aged woman in a sarong who introduced herself as the founder/manager of the place. It was an orphanage!

I have lost her name, but she had found the place to care for kids who had been left parentless by the AIDS epidemic. She had about seventy kids, ranging in age from five to seventeen. I was so moved by her generosity that I reached in my pocket and handed her all the cash I had, which happened to be my entire two-weeks' per diem. I figured I'd just eat at the studio.

I asked her what she needed the most, and she said that her biggest wish was to provide real bathrooms for the girls. I asked her how much that would cost, and she estimated several thousand dollars.

When I got back to L.A., it was December and time for Sue and I to throw our yearly Christmas party. This year I did something I never did before or since. I made it a fundraiser. We put a jar on the table asking for donations for the orphanage. We raised over 3,000 dollars. I wired the money to Vani in Mumbai, and she hired contractors to do the job. I've never been back to see the orphanage, but I hear it was a nice improvement.

The next year, R&H opened another office in the Indian city of Hyderabad, and once again they sent me over to train the animators. On the way, I made a stop in Bangkok, Thailand, at the request of a former R&H colleague, Juck Somsaman. Juck had returned to his home country to start a CG-animation studio. Bangkok had a chapter of SIGGRAPH, the international CG society, and they asked me to give a talk about computer animation.

I had set aside a few days to see a bit of Bangkok, and my timing was fortuitous. Juck's small animation company had just completed work on their very first animated feature film, and they were having their wrap party the next day. They invited me to come along. It was going to be a rather unique party: they had rented tour buses and were taking the entire staff out of the city to a ranch—to ride elephants!

If elephant riding seemed unusual, the detour we took on the way to the ranch proved to be even more memorable. The movie they had made was called *Khan Kluay*, and was based on the true story of an elephant that was ridden by the King of Thailand in the battle that saved the country from invaders. Remarkably, the ancient temple where the King prayed still existed. Even more remarkably, our entire group, the entire staff of the animation company, would now visit that temple and ask the Monks to bless the film.

It was an impressive scene. A hundred animators sat quietly in the great hall of the temple as six Monks in white robes knelt and prayed around a stack of film cans. They weren't praying over a print of the film. I was told the cans contained *the original negative* of the film! In other words, all the work done by every artist was in those cans. If anything had happened to them—no movie.

I had never seen anything like it. Hard to imagine the executives at Warner Brothers or Paramount taking their film to the church or temple for a blessing. But maybe they should. *Khan Kluay* was a huge hit.

I then flew to the new R&H office in Hyderabad, a city on the middle of India. The training went fine, but it was a tougher visit for me. I had very bad jet lag, and to make matters worse, my rented flat was next to a mosque, so I was awakened at the crack of dawn each day by prayers from the loud speaker outside my window.

The deepest impression I had of India was the ever-present crush of humanity. You were never alone. Every street, every shop, every alley was full of people. And it was like that twenty-four hours a day! Since many, many Indians worked at call centers catering to the US market, they worked on US time, meaning their workday was 9 PM to 6 AM. So if I went out of my flat at 2 AM in the morning, the streets were full of people on their lunch hour.

When I returned home to Burbank, I got out of my car one night and looked up and down the street. I could see for blocks in both directions, and it was absolutely quiet, with not a single human in sight. I realized that this was a moment of solitude I could never have in India. I still think of that on quiet nights.

48

That Party

As I mentioned earlier, Sue and I threw a yearly Christmas Party that became not just well-known, but dare I say without sounding too puffed up—legendary?

It started when we moved into our new dream house in Burbank, the one I bought with the *FernGully* director's advance. We had always hosted small parties, but before Burbank we had never lived in a place with enough room to throw a big bash. The first Christmas after we moved in we decided to have a Christmas party, not just to celebrate the season, but to have everyone see our new digs.

We were never into "open" parties, or industry-promoting parties, so we just sent personal invitations to our close friends. Having worked in Hollywood for fifteen years at that time we had formed a lot of close relationships. Our "gang" showed up and we had a wonderful time. The Burbank house was by no means a mansion. In fact, it was just 1,500 square feet, but we had a huge patio and back-yard, and that's really where the party took place. Luckily, California had a warm December weekend so we were good outdoors.

The next year it rained in the middle of the party. Everyone jammed—and I do mean jammed—into the house or under the relatively small covered portion of the back patio. I remember the wall of humanity standing inches inside the sheet

DOI: 10.1201/9781003558231-48

of water pouring off the patio roof. As sometimes happens, adversity seems to create bonding, and weirdly, that party became jovial and everyone remembers it fondly.

After that we learned our lesson and began renting tents. The outdoor facilities expanded, and as the years went by we had three huge tents, a bar, a piano, a dining area, and, one year, a full-size sleigh and artificial reindeer for posed pictures. For a few years I hired a caroling group, but since everyone just wanted to talk to each other no one was listening. Another tradition that everyone loved was our idea to fly our lovely nieces out from Wisconsin to be the bartenders. Every year they got marriage proposals. Jokey proposals.

But the outstanding and notable feature of the vaunted Kroyer Christmas Party was the guest list. The spirit of the party never changed. We always invited only personal friends. But as the years went by, those young struggling animator/roommates of ours ascended in the business to become the most famous lead animators and Oscar-winning directors in the Hollywood animation industry. Suddenly, everyone wanted to come to our party.

We did add new people as we made new friends, but we kept the party selective. Certain Academy Presidents and Governors who I formed friendships with were newcomers, and they really got a kick out of mingling with the animation community, a world they were not familiar with. Once you were invited, you were always invited, so some of our friends from our early days in the business that didn't climb the ladder of success were very happy to still be equally welcomed with the stars. Many, many people said (and still say) that our party was the one time of the year where they got to connect with all their old animation friends. Even when people moved away, they would fly in from New York, or Seattle, or San Francisco to attend the Kroyer Christmas Party.

We made a special effort to include our older friends, animation legends like Bob and Cima Balser, Carl Bell, and Alice Davis. No animation celebration could be complete without June Foray, the unofficial Queen of Animation. June was the most legendary female voice in animation history (Rocky the Flying Squirrel and dozens of Jay Ward characters). She had been our Branch Governor for years and was the fiercest defender of animators' rights. When she got too frail to drive herself, we always hired a car service to bring her to and from the party.

The Cartoonists' Union traditionally had its Christmas party a week or two before our party. As Union supporters Sue and I had always attended, but it got awkward when half the people would approach us and stay, "Hey, isn't your party coming up?", looking for an invitation. We stopped going to the Union party.

There was one year when we allowed a bit of Hollywood politics to intrude on what had become a "family get-together". It involved none other than the direct descendant of Walt Disney himself, his nephew Roy Disney, Jr. Roy was the one who forbade Eisner and Katzenberg from shutting down the animation division when they took over the studio. "Disney is animation", Roy had said. There were many wonderful stories about Roy, and I can't resist telling my favorite.

There was a tavern across the street from the Disney Studio called the PagoPago. It was the legendary watering hole for the Disney animators in the glory days of hard drinking. When Eisner took over the studio, he made many changes, but two of the most devastating: he kicked the animators out of the animation building, moving them to warehouse in Glendale, and he tore down the Pago-Pago to build a daycare center for the execs' kids.

There was a Disney animator named Dave Spafford who loved the old traditions. He happened to be driving past the Pago-Pago as the wrecking ball was knocking it down. The tavern's sign was still standing, a sixteen-foot tall classic neon sign. Dave approached the construction foreman and asked what was happening to the sign.

"We're trashing it", the foreman said. Dave asked if he could have it.

The foreman rubbed his chin for a minute. "You can have it for twenty bucks" the guy answered. "But you have to move it yourself". Dave forked over the money and, amazingly, found a contractor that not only helped him take down the sign, but move it to his house and set it in cement in his backyard. He converted his garage into the new PagoPago bar!

A few months later, Dave got a phone call from the Disney legal department. "You have stolen our sign", the lawyer told him. "The foreman had no right to give it to you. Return it or we will bring charges".

Dave was stunned. What to do? Hire another construction crew? Hire his own lawyer and fight Disney legal? "I'll call Roy", he thought.

When Roy Disney heard Dave's story he laughed. "Dave", Roy said, "Enjoy the sign. It's yours". Dave never heard another word from Disney legal.

One year Roy was in a tense struggle with some major investors in a battle for control of Disney Studios. In addition to that, Dreamworks and other studios were using that uncertainty to entice animators away from Disney. Roy wanted to connect personally with the leaders of the animation community to let them know he was 100% behind saving and preserving the Disney animation traditions.

I had known Roy for years, but I had never considered inviting him to the Christmas party because I didn't feel I was on close enough personal terms with him. I was quite surprised when a mutual friend told me that Roy had heard about the famous Kroyer Christmas Party and would love to attend. I extended an invitation and sure enough, Roy and his wife Patty showed up.

It was the one and only time in the history of my party that I secretly hired security guards. I just didn't want to the chance that someone with a grudge, or some other complaint, would embarrass Roy. As it turned out there were no problems at all. He and Patty loved the party. Roy was a genuinely great guy, and he connected very personally with the crowd that night. He was ultimately successful in saving Disney "his way".

Years later, when Roy passed away, the animators payed him a unique and touching tribute. Roy had been an avid yachtsman, and loved his boat that he named "Pyewacket". When it came time for Disney to update their opening theatrical logo, they gave the task to Disney designer/director Mike Gabriel. You've seen that logo appear before many Disney films. The camera flies back through the flags and ends up looking at Snow White's Castle. If you watch carefully as the camera pans past the background, you will see, in the distance, a boat floating serenely on the river. That boat is an exact CG-model of the Pywacket. "We snuck that in there", Mike Gabriel said, "because we wanted a bit of Roy to always be watching over Disney animation".

I think it is the coolest secret "Easter egg" in the history of animation.

49

How about a
Career Change?

By the end of the first decade of the twenty-first century R&H was feeling the pressure of competing with subsidized foreign competition. When I started at the studio, the forty-hour week was not just standard; it was mandatory. By 2009, things had changed. The sixty-hour week was not uncommon. Unlike some CG studios that required their workers to agree to eighty-hour weeks with no extra pay, at least R&H paid overtime. But the vicissitudes of the VFX industry were getting more brutal. Bids were driven lower and lower, and once awarded, a studio could demand change after change while refusing to pay for them. That was the competitive environment.

It made news in the trade papers when a studio producer proudly proclaimed that "he was not doing his job if he did not bankrupt at least one visual effects house on every film".

Although "special effects" had been a hallmark of filmmaking since Melies' groundbreaking silent film *A Trip to the Moon* in 1902, the more recently-christened "visual effects" industry was inextricably tied to the digital medium and could trace its origin to the first *Star Wars* movie. Although that movie had few true digital effects, it was the harbinger of the genre of sci-fi mega-epics that dominate cinema to this day.

DOI: 10.1201/9781003558231-49

What made those films possible were the large visual effects companies that were almost completely focused on computer graphics imagery. Los Angeles could be called the birthplace of visual effects, and the biggest companies were based there, including Digital Domain, Illusion Arts, Asylum, CafeFX, Metrolight, Robert Abel & Associates, Boss Films, and, of course, Rhythm & Hues.

As I have described earlier, by 2010, all of these companies were being driven out of business by foreign companies that were benefitting from tax breaks, government subsidies, and the advantage of universal health care. The strain on R&H was not the "canary in the coal mine"; it was the opposite. R&H would end up being "the last man standing".

Amidst these tough times in the industry, I was having a personal "come to Jesus" moment. I had been at R&H for twelve years. The only people older than me on the payroll were the owners. At the age of sixty did I really want to deal with these new conditions?

It was right at this moment that a phone call came from out of the blue. It was from a man named Bob Bassett, and he was the Dean of the Dodge College of Film and Media Arts at Chapman University in Orange, California. I had never heard of Dean Basset, but I did have a vague recollection of there being a film school in Orange County. It was the school where Gil Bettman, the director of a rock video I had once storyboarded, taught directing.

Bob Bassett told me that Chapman wanted to start an Animation/Visual Effects program in the film school. They had determined that the ideal person would be one with experience in both traditional and digital animation, deep knowledge of visual effects, and strong industry connections. According to Bob, when he read that wish list to his professors, one of them said: "You just described Bill Kroyer".

I was flattered by Bob's offer, but leaving the business for a full-time teaching position was not something I felt I was ready to do. Because my wife Sue had been teaching animation at Cal Arts for several years, I had been invited to speak at her school. In fact, I had lectured at USC, UCLA, Loyola, and other schools and I felt that the academic environment was not for me. I declined Bob's invitation to visit.

When Sue heard that I had dismissed Bob's offer she was furious. "You are going to call him back and agree to a meeting", she said. Since I have always lived by the rule "happy wife, happy life" I did just that.

I traveled to Orange the following week for a luncheon with Bob Bassett. Although I had lived in Southern California for 35 years I could only remember passing through the City of Orange once before. As I drove slowly through the charming downtown on Glassell Street I understood why Tom Hanks had used it for a Mid-western main street in his film *That Thing You Do*. It was a throwback to the old days. It had charming restaurants, antique stores, and boutique shops that seemed out of the fifties, including a vintage vinyl record store.

Chapman University, I was to learn, was expanding rapidly and buying up real state beyond its original campus, and sure enough, five blocks from the "main campus" of the university stood my destination, the spanking new Marion Knott Studios, home of the Dodge College of Film and Media Arts.

Bob Bassett had founded the film school in 1996. It was the newest of Chapman's eleven colleges. He started with three classrooms, a moviola, and a few cameras the students could borrow. Recognizing the necessity of funding, Bob set out to schmooze the wealthy elite of Orange County, and had meager success until he met one of the county's true pioneers, Marion Knott. Marion had literally come to the county in a pioneer wagon with her family. Her father started a berry farm, and young Marion sold baskets of their newly harvested boysenberries from a roadside stand. That enterprise eventually grew into the county's biggest attraction, the Knott's Berry Farm theme park.

Ms. Knott liked Bob's enthusiasm and gave him a small grant to help the film school. One day she stopped in for a surprise visit and found Bob dressed in filthy clothes painting the walls of the classrooms. When she asked him why he was doing this himself instead of using her donation to hire painters, Bob responded that by painting walls himself he could buy more film equipment for the students. Impressed by that dedication, Marion increased her donations—by millions. That's why the studio was named after her.

The school was called "Dodge College" because a local real state magnate, Larry Dodge, had pledged a huge amount to start actual construction. Ironically, Larry's fortunes turned and his original pledge was never fully funded, but Bob kept the name as a gesture of gratitude for getting the ball rolling with the rest of his funders.

I met Bob in the front lobby of the studio and he gave me a quick tour of the facility. It was impressive. There were state-of-the-art mixing stages, recording booths, a fully-equipped Foley stage for doing sound effects, and a huge equipment room with every piece of gear needed to make a motion picture. The school even owned its own equipment trucks for doing location shoots. What was slightly odd for me was the condition of the soundstages. Not only were they real soundstage—they were new! After spending my career on the decades-old stages at Fox, Warner Bros., and MGM it was very odd to see a stage that was clean and nice.

In addition to the beautiful facility, I had a visceral reaction to the environment. There were students everywhere, using all this gear as if they really knew what they were doing. This was not the academic environment I had encountered when I lectured at other schools. This felt like a *working movie studio.*

At lunch, Bob told me the story about how my name had been suggested by his current professors. As a live-action guy he had naturally focused the school on live-action moviemaking. Now, he was aware that by 2010, 85% of the world's box office dollars were being spent on movies that were either digitally animated or contained digital effects. He needed those skills taught in his film school.

I assumed he was interested in me teaching, but what he said next really floored me. He was prepared to start a new "area of study" in the school that taught animation and visual effects and make me the director of the program.

I would have the authority to design the entire four-year curriculum and hire the entire faculty. Although he knew he could not offer me "industry money", he set my salary at a very acceptable number. That number would be augmented by full health coverage and the University's very generous retirement plan.

I said what I think most people would say. "I'll have to talk this over with my wife".

Sue had always predicted that a move to education was in our future. She had been teaching as an adjunct Professor at Cal Arts for several years and loved it. She had recently started to teach a few classes at Loyola Marymount University. She thought I should take the Chapman gig. I called Bob Bassett and said I was in.

As it turned out, my timing was fortuitous. I informed my friends at R&H that I would be leaving at the end of my yearly contract. There was a ripple of disbelief in the studio. I had been a decade-long fixture at my desk in the corner of that office, and many said it would be disconcerting not to see me there. I was honored to be considered an integral part of the company, and I felt, and still feel, that John, Pauline, and the rest of the R&H family were much more meaningful to me than I could have been to them.

So off I went to Orange to be an academician. Things at R&H got rougher. Although the company's work continued to excel, garnering the Academy Award for Best Visual Effects for their incredible work on *The Life of Pi*, two years after my departure, R&H declared bankruptcy. John Hughes had been keeping the doors open by "robbing Peter to pay Paul". He would run into debt finishing a project, then would use the cash advances on future productions to cover the costs. We had seen these situations before on his balance sheets during those Friday company meetings, but for years, he always seemed to come through with the money. But after the very expensive cost overruns of *The Life of Pi*, all three of the projected future projects went into "turn-around". That meant that the studios put a halt to those projects because of creative issues. When they turned off the cash spigot, R&H went broke.

The company would eventually be sold to outside investors and resume business under the R&H banner, but the magnificent company that had been run in such a unique way by its dedicated and generous founders was now a piece of history.

50
Teaching in the Digital Age

In some way, it was appropriate that my next turn in the animation industry would be teaching youngsters because the animation business was about to explode and evolve in a way never before seen in the history of the business. Theatrical movies were going to vastly expand their payrolls, and the television series business was going to have a seismic growth spurt do to a new and unexpected form of distribution—internet *streaming*.

When I applied for that Disney internship back in 1977, I was competing with about seventeen people who had the ability to animate on paper with Disney-level quality. By 2011, there were seventeen *programs* in colleges in just Southern California offering animation courses and pumping out hundreds of graduates.

I hadn't had any formal experience in academia, but as one of the earliest pioneers in the medium of computer animation I had usually, by default, been the older and more experienced artist in any team. With decades of directing, much of my time was spent teaching young animators how to do the job. I felt pretty confident that I could create a plan for a good animation/visual effects program.

I had one foundational belief that to this day has not changed. Technology does not create art. Artists create art. I wanted to create a system that would provide the students with solid fundamental training in universal principles of

DOI: 10.1201/9781003558231-50

animation, story, and design, principles they could and must apply no matter how technology evolved. In my plan, the first two years had classes that drilled into these principles. Every student, no matter what they expected to specialize in, took these classes. I did this for two reasons.

First, I knew that no matter whether the student chose animation, design, or visual effects, an understanding of the entire production pipeline would help them understand how every step of the process affected the other steps. Second, being teenagers when they entered the program, I knew that few of them really understood all the different job titles in the business. By making them cover the gamut, to be "generalists" and not "specialists", I hoped to introduce them to all the career paths available—some of which they may not have to know about at all.

In the third year, they would choose an "area of emphasis" and take specialized, advanced courses in one specific discipline.

Dodge College, like most film schools, required each student to make their own short film as a graduation requirement. This was supposed to be the culmination of their education, utilizing everything they had learned in their four-year curriculum. It was also supposed to be their "calling card" to the world of real employment, their sample reel.

I was quite surprised to learn that before I took over the program, very few of the seniors actually finished their Senior films. One of the first things I did was to change that policy. No finished film, no degree—no excuses.

Having been an Animation Director in the industry for the previous twenty-three years, I had gotten used to a certain relationship with those working under me. If I asked an artist to do something, I expected it to be done the way I wanted it, when I wanted it. If an artist failed to deliver, I'd ask for the explanation, and consider the situation, but if the lack of performance continue the solution was simple. The artist was let go.

Now I was faced with students that would be late with assignments, do sloppy work on their assignments, or simply not do the assignments. At first I reacted like a boss. I told them that we were running this program like a studio, to better prepare them for the real world. They—or their parents—were paying a lot of money for them to attend the school and slacking off was not an option.

In defense of my approach, it should be mentioned that my generation had teachers who were pretty tough. Cal Arts had a design teacher named Bill Moore who struck fear in everyone. He would walk slowly down the bulletin board, looking at the students' assignments pinned to the board. If he didn't like a drawing, he would silently pluck it off the board, drop it on the floor, and step on it as he proceeded. Sometimes he would crush his cigarette on a drawing before dropping it. His critiques could be vicious, laced with profanity—things that would not be tolerated for a minute in today's environment.

And yet, every student who took his class said that Bill Moore was the greatest teacher they ever had, and the one who influenced their careers the most.

His students became the directors and art directors of most of the Disney and PIXAR mega-hit animated features. Quite a legacy.

It didn't take me too long to recognize that the generation of students I was teaching did not respond well to tough love. That wasn't how they were raised. My primary goal was results, and I adjusted my teaching style to one that was more effective than intimidation. I became a coach. I analyzed students on an individual basis. Some needed extra guidance. Some needed motivation. Some even needed a kick in the pants that bordered on intimidation. Most responded to positive reinforcement far more than negative criticism. At the end of my first year, every Senior finished their film on time for graduation. That record continued until I retired.

51

The Science of Keeping Up

Teaching at Chapman University did not mean that I was isolated in the ivory tower of Academia. If anything, as an Academy Governor I was more involved than ever in the changing industry.

For a bit of perspective, the 2010s were a bit like 1927, when major changes were happening in the film industry. Back then, sound recording was transforming movies. Pictures would be shot in color. Cameras, recording equipment even projectors were being manufactured with no common standards. It was confusing and expensive for studios to keep up with the changes. To deal with this Wild West confusion, one of the first actions of the newly formed Academy of Motion Pictures Arts & Sciences (AMPAS) was to form a special technology committee. The name of this committee changed over the years, but its purpose remained the same. It created standards that all studios and manufacturers could follow. You may have heard of some of these standards, like "Academy leader" or "Academy aperture".

Remarkably, in 1976 some people thought that all the major innovations that could be made to the filmmaking process had been done. It was similar to the government closing the patent office because they believed that all new

DOI: 10.1201/9781003558231-51

inventions had already been invented. The Academy suspended the operation of the Technology Committee.

Jump to 2003. It was becoming apparent even to cinema luddites that the digital age was going to transform Hollywood like nothing had since sound. The Academy announced it would reform the committee under a new name: The Science & Technology Council. They asked all of the Academy's branches to nominate members for the new Council.

I was surprised and flattered when the Executive Committee of my branch nominated me. True, I did have a profile as a technology innovator, starting with TRON and continuing with my work at Rhythm & Hues. My reservation was that I was not really a scientist or technologist. I was an animation director, i.e., a *user* of technology. But everyone felt I had the strongest handle on what kind of issues the Council would be addressing.

I became one of the founding members of the reborn Council. For the first few months, I felt my initial hesitation was correct. Sitting around the conference table with industry geniuses like Richard Edlund, John Erland, and Ray Feeney, I sometimes could barely understand what they were talking about. What I did understand I knew to be both fascinating and critically important.

One of the first products of the Council was the report titled "The Digital Dilemma". It explained that the current methods of saving film imagery were fatally flawed. All the methods for preserving imagery through digital media were unreliable. Data was inevitably damaged after a few years. Additionally, since the machines and storage mediums being used to create, store, and restore imagery were constantly changing, there was no guarantee that one could even find a device to restore certain formats in the future.

Ninety percent of the films made during the silent era have been lost. They were made on nitrate film, an unstable film stock that deteriorated and burned easily. The warning of the new report was that we were now living in an age of "digital nitrate". There was, and still is, a danger that all the movies we create and enjoy using digital means will be unviewable in one hundred years.

Another innovation that was aggressively studied by the Council was LED lighting. For the entire history of the film industry, film sets have been lit by tungsten lights, generating light by heat. LED lights don't work that way. Because of that, all the principles of how light reacted to emulsion in film had to be rethought. The science of color.

My fellow members of the Council were people who created these new technologies. I was one who applied them to the filmmaking process. A timely opportunity to do just that came from an unlikely source: my sister-in-law Karen in Racine Wisconsin. At a high school reunion she met a visiting New York City-based producer named Howard Grossman. When she told him about me, he contacted me to help on an innovative idea for a show called *Taxi Dog.*

Howard had optioned the graphic novel about a dog named Maxi who accompanies his cabdriver/owner around the city and meets, and helps, the people who get into the cab. Howard asked me to conceive a plan to do the show on a manageable budget, and we conceived an interesting test.

We decided to make Maxi a puppet, and hired the Henson Studio to create him. To do the myriad locations necessary for such a show, we conceived the idea of doing every show on a soundstage but creating all the locations in the computer.

To do this, we used the then-cutting-edge technology of motion-synced camera rigs. We would build a house, or a shop, or even the exterior of a NY street in the computer, and the cameras we used to shoot the characters would have their motion synchronized to the CG environments. We shoot our live actors and any real props in front of green screens on the stage and composite the two source images together in real time. We would not have to combine them in post production. We would have a finished shot after each take.

We didn't know the term at that time, but we were unwitting pioneers in a process that came to be known as "virtual production". A new addition to this process is the super hi-resolution "video walls" that replaced the environments in the computer. By displaying those CG environments on the wall, and filming the actors in front of the wall with synchronized cameras, the filmmakers are compositing the shots "on the fly". That's the newest trend in production.

I worked with Howard on *Taxi Dog* on an off for several years. We produced the pilot using all those innovations, one of the first projects to do so. In the end, he could not get the series financed, but it remains one of the most fun projects I have worked on. And most visionary.

It was exactly these kinds of innovations that I felt were important to share with the professionals at the Academy. The Sci-Tech Council's mission was to educate the Academy's members about the changes happening due to science and technology. I proposed the idea of producing a series of public programs to do that.

I headed the subcommittee that followed the theme of how distinct filmmaking crafts were being affected by tech. I thought it would be a good idea to start with the craft I knew best. The first program was titled 'Animation in the Digital Age".

I had a line-up of the best animators and directors in the industry taking about how computers were affecting everything about animation, including the act of creating animation, the nature of storytelling, the shift in the talent base due to new skills, the globalization of the workforce, and the explosion at the box office due to the universal appeal of CG characters.

Since these public programs were meant to be archived as a "preserved moment" in film history, I had the idea to do a side-by-side demonstration of how a traditional 2D animator compared to a CG animator in the production of a scene. I took my documentary film crew to DREAMWORKS ANIMATION to film Kathy Zielinski working on their latest CG feature film. Kathy walked through every step of her process, highlighting what was the same, and different, of animating on a computer. In a memorable moment, she pretended to claw at the computer screen to express her frustration at not being able to physical touch the images she was creating.

For the 2D animation demo, we went to the Disney Archives in Glendale. The irony was not lost on me. There were no traditional Disney animation desks left in the actual Disney Animation Building in Burbank! They had all been dumped or donated to schools.

The studio had thought to save one desk as a relic of its history. We "dressed" that desk to look at how it would have looked during a production. We added a shelf called a "scene stacker" beside it. That shelf was filled with scene folders of the shots of the animator would be working on. We put a bulletin board on the wall above it and pinned model sheets and storyboards. We restored the exposure sheets and pencil sharpener. I got my friend Randy Cartwright, a veteran Disney animator, to explain his process.

We edited the two films together and the result was a clear and dramatic demonstration of the evolution of the animation process. When we showed it to some animator friends, they loved it, and had an observation that hit home. None of them could recall ever seeing a traditional 2D animator explain how he worked.

I once belonged to a "gourmet club". We had four couples who would dine together once a month. The host couple chose the menu and assigned dishes for the other couples to make. You could pick any cuisine, so we typically had French, Chinese, German, or Italian menus. One month, our friend Tom Sito, animation's resident historian, gave us a menu consisting of recipes he had assembled from books about ancient Rome. It was interesting. The Romans did not have potatoes, so they used beets as their starchy course.

Sito had a fascinating historical note. Many of the recipes included an ingredient called "liquamen". Apparently, it was so common, so ubiquitous and well-known, that no one had ever bothered to write down exactly what it was or how it was made. Sito said that historians guessed that it was close to soy sauce, so we should use that in our recipe.

I thought of this when we watched the film of Randy explaining how a Disney artist used his desk and surrounding tools. Animators had been following this process for eighty years, but apparently, no one had thought to record it for posterity. Now we had that on film.

The first public program was a smashing success. We filled every seat in the Academy's main theater, and we were told there were over a hundred people on the sidewalk outside pleading to sit in the aisles.

My next program was called "Acting in the Digital Age". It focused on the new sensation of motion-captured performances. We had the cast of *Avatar* as well as Andy Serkis, the actor who portrayed Gollum in *The Lord of Rings*. It was wonderful to capture the impressions of these veteran actors and they discussed the challenges and similarities of acting in a mo-cap suit. For some, it was distracting to act without a costume or a set. Others said it hearkened back to their days in live theater, acting on a bare stage with a folding chair, having to imagine everything in their heads.

Program #3 was "Editing in the digital age". New digital tools were quickly expanding the role of the editor. The editor could now create a wide variety of special effects without having to ask a specialist to do them. The explosion of digital Visual Effects was making the job more complex. Long gone were the days of an editor simply splicing film clips together. Now, staring at several huge computer monitors, the editor manipulated rows and rows of digital effects, from storyboards to previs tests to post-viz images.

At that time, 3D, or stereoscopic filmmaking, was emerging as a potential game-changer, so editors had to deal with new terms like screen planes and convergence. Editors were learning to manipulate the effects of how deep and severe the "illusion of depth" changed from scene to scene. They were beginning to create "depth scripts" to guide the cinematographer in capturing the shot. This was exactly the kind of innovative invention we felt the Sci-Tech Public Program should be teaching.

I had a special treat producing the program called "Production Design in the Digital Age". To compare the differences and similarities of the old and the new, I engaged two giants of the industry. For the "old" I had the legendary Robert Boyle, who had designed Hitchcock's greatest films. For the "new" I had my close friend Ralph Eggleston, who was literally creating this new design process through his work on the biggest PIXAR films, starting with *Toy Story*. The two men sat side by side on the stage and compared their work process. Bob Boyle would arrive at the studio lot each day and make the rounds of all the shops; blueprints, painters, carpenters, plasterers, etc.. Ralph would do the exact same rounds, but under one roof, visiting the PIXAR departments that did modeling, lighting, crowds, etc.

I suppose it was creating these programs that raised my profile within the Academy as a guy who was in touch with the changing times.

By 2009, I had been a member of the Academy of Motion Pictures Arts & Sciences (AMPAS) for twenty-three years. My branch, Short Films and Feature Animation, had three Governors who represented us on the Academy's Board of Governors. For many, many years, those three Governors were "old school" veterans who got reelected term after term. They were legendary voice-over talent, June Foray, independent Animation Director Bill Littlejohn, and former Disney assistant animator Carl Bell. The Academy had been a rather staid organization without a lot of turmoil or controversy, so the re-election of those three, who were not subject to term limits, may have been the member's inclination to preserve the status quo.

As the industry started to feel the effects of the "second Golden Age" and the advent of new technologies, the newer, younger members of the branch felt it was time to get some new faces on the Board. A Governor's term lasted three years, so each year one of the three incumbents would be up for reelection. Like many of my fellow members, I had habitually thrown my name on the ballot for Governor every year, and every year watched one of the three incumbents retain their seat.

In 2009, Carl Bell decided to step down, and low and behold, I found myself elected to take his seat on the Board. Carl, like many of the old-timers, had not been one to shake things up. When I asked him how I should behave as a Governor, his advice was: "Sit back and enjoy the ride".

That was not to be.

52

Everything Changes

When I give my lecture about the making of *Tron*, I like to point out that when I started at the Disney studio in 1977, the desk I sat at, the tools I used, and the process I learned had not changed at all since the 1920s. An animator from *Snow White* could have dropped out of a time machine, sat down at my animation desk, and gone to work on a scene without one minute of training.

In 2010, Disney didn't even have animation desks. They had workstations. And that was just the metaphoric tip of the iceberg of the seismic changes happening in animation.

As I refined the new curriculum for my animation program at Chapman, the most influential force in the animation industry was string of mega-hit feature films being produced at PIXAR. Watching the success of *Monsters, Inc.*, *Finding Nemo*, and *The Incredibles*, it was no wonder that the desire of every animation student was to master the skill of CG-character animation. I held firm to my belief that there was a real advantage to having some experience animating in 2D, on punched paper, as a learning experience, even though that methodology had vanished from the industry. That idea became an increasingly hard sell with my students. Sure enough—a few years after I left, they discontinued teaching animation on paper.

DOI: 10.1201/9781003558231-52

The rest of my curriculum seemed solid, and the idea of having everyone learn the basics of the entire pipeline before they chose a specialization worked well. For the first three years of our program, our classes were held in the regular classrooms in the film school. We used the same computer labs as the live-action students, and our drawing and animation classes were in a large, empty space called the design lab. In 2003, Dean Bassett gave me some great news. There was an old, empty wire factory across the street from the film school that the University had just purchased. Bob planned to renovate that building and dedicate it to our animation/visual effects program. We would have our own home.

Bob showed me the blueprints for the new building and my excitement hit the brakes. The layout had very traditional hallways and classrooms. It was nothing like the buildings that were being created for creative interaction. Microsoft, Facebook, Google and other companies were all moving into new headquarters that had designed spaces that promoted collaboration. I told Bob that we should ask the architects to take another pass. As it happened, Disney had recently renovated a warehouse in Glendale to house their new TV Animation division. John Lasseter had used his PIXAR architects to design it. It had exactly the vibe I was looking for. I got permission to have our Chapman architects take a tour.

The Disney building had a wide-open lobby with plenty of chairs and couches for relaxing and mingling. It had food service in the lobby. It had various textures for the floors and walls that suggested an organic flow. Being Southern California, where the weather is always nice, it had an outdoor patio with tables and chairs. Our architects took all this in. Their response to me: "We get it".

They came back with a completely redesigned plan that incorporated all those innovative features. In 2014, we cut the ribbon and moved into our new state-of-the-art facility, the Digital Media Arts Center, or "DMAC" for short.

It was astounding to me that the film school's main building, the Marion Knott Studio, had no lounge space. The DMAC became an instant hit with the students. More than that, by moving all of our classes into one building, it became our program's "home" and was instrumental in promoting a feeling of unity and esprit within our program. Years after I retired, almost none of the students or new faculty remembered me as the founder of the program, but I like to think that the DMAC stands as permanent evidence of my positive impact on DodgeCollege.

In my entire career, the strange and unique bond that existed among animators was one of the most magical aspects of the business. I wanted my students to feel that special bond. Unlike the live-action students, we didn't just record the real world. We created our own worlds. That had always been the distinguishing feature of the artform, and I based our identity on that idea.

We did things differently. We had the best Senior Thesis Show, with student hosts, awards, and amazing graphics. Our post-show party always had surprises, like rear-projected posters or immersive 3D screens. We had a "photo-cake", a huge sheet cake that had edible frosting with images of all the student films. I jokingly promoted our program is the only one in America where you got to eat a piece of your own project.

When Glen Keane, the famous Disney animator, came for a visit, we moved aside all the furniture in the lobby and made a giant seventy-seat long table for a "Viking feast". With Glen sitting at the head of the table, I rigged him with a lavalier microphone so he could tell his stories and everyone could hear them over the speaker system.

When one of my star students, Sam Wickert, created a true 360 Virtual Reality film that took place in a barn, with an interactive VR game in the CG barn, we decorated the lobby with hay bales and farm equipment to premiere the project.

Because I was an Academy Governor, I had the ability to bring student guests to all the Academy's programs. Meeting and mingling with the industry's greatest talents gave my students a more personal experience of the professionalism they should aspire to. My Academy connection played no part in one monumental achievement. Three of my Animation/Visual Effects students became the first Chapman film school students to be nominated for Student Academy Awards. One of them, Daniel Drummond, took the Gold Medal for his film *Chiaroscuro*.

My status as Governor did, I believe, give my students another one-of-a-kind experience. I decided to take my Chapman students to Europe on a "Travel Course". This was a legitimate for-credit course that I could construct if it was a legitimate learning experience. What could be more educational than visiting the world's oldest and largest animation festival—Annecy—while also visiting some of France's most famous animation schools? That was an easy course to get approved, and I quickly registered the maximum twenty students I could chaperone.

At the time, there was a new important player in animation that I thought would be worth learning more about. The company was ILLUMINATION, and the founder and head producer was Chris Meledandri. I had known Chris since his days at FOX STUDIOS, but his switch to Illumination at Universal Studios had resulted in spectacular success with a film called *Despicable Me* and its sequels. There were three fascinating details about that franchise.

First, the original film had included the Minion characters as background comic relief for the main characters, but they soon emerged as the starring appeal of the films. Chris had recognized this and shifted focus to the Minions in the sequels, and now they were hugely popular in both the films and merchandising.

Second, Chris created the stories in a unique way. We traditionalists in animation have always felt that the best way to create a story is have the story crew under one roof, working together, collaborating, and bouncing good ideas off each other. Chris did it totally the opposite. He sent story ideas to storyboard artists all around the globe and simply asked them to board the sequence in a funny way. I knew some of these artists, and they confirmed that they had no idea what the movie's plot line was, or what any of their fellow artists were doing. In fact, they weren't even given explicit instructions on their own sequence. If the task was to show the Minions robbing a bank, they weren't told if the Minions succeeded, failed, were caught, goofed up, etc. Just make it funny!

Chris and his Director and editors gather all that work and put the sequences together to make a move.

Third, Chris did all the animation outside the United States, in Paris, using all EU talent. Not only did it give the films a fresh artistic feeling—the budgets were far smaller than a PIXAR or DISNEY film.

I thought to would be great for my students to visit that studio and meet those European artists. One problem—Illumination/Paris never gave tours. But again, I suspect it was my Governor status that tipped the scale when I asked Chris if we could visit his studio. He agreed and arranged the tour.

Illumination was in an industrial building, and the artists worked in close quarters. We didn't get to walk through the entire place, but instead, went to a conference room where the Directors, Art Directors, and animators came in in shifts and showed us their stuff. As we passed through the hallways, I noticed that artists giving us curious looks. One of them asked me, "Who are you people?" When I told him we were American animation students, he was stunned. "We never have visitors!" He said.

That tour was part of the odd juxtaposition of having my teaching career run concurrently with my three terms as an Academy Governor. I was experiencing the animation industry from opposite ends of the spectrum. I was training novices with no experience while representing the most experienced, accomplished and distinguished artists in the world.

Having started my career in a basement in Chicago doing cut-out films about a food co-op, I now would meet at the conference table in the Academy's Wilshire Boulevard headquarters surrounded by Hollywood's elite power players. Steven Spielberg, Tom Hanks, Annette Bening, Michael Moore, and Hollywood's greatest Directors, Cinematographers, Editors, and other cinematic giants were my fellow Board members. It was daunting to feel I had an equal voice at the table, but as it turned out, an old issue kept popping up that made my voice an essential one. Short films continued to be questioned as whether it deserved an equal seat at the table.

You might recall my experience years before getting Howard Koch Sr. to support the short films. The issue would not die. There was always pressure to make the Oscar telecast shorter, and cutting the Oscar presentation for Shorts was always the first suggestion. I became quite vocal in reminding the Board why I believed Shorts Films were special. Not only were shorts historically the first form of films, not only do they provide the launching pad for many future feature film directors, and not only are they a crucible for experimentation. They are also the most personal form of filmmaking because they are not bound to the commercially-dictated length of theatrical films that must have box office success. By that measure, I argued they could be considered the "soul of the Academy" because they are films made purely for artistic reasons.

As you might guess, these arguments were nice, but ultimately not persuasive. The key issue with the Board was the accusation that no one was watching short films *in theaters*. Yes, there was an explosion of short films being viewed online, but the Academy still defined itself as a theatrically-based entity. We countered this argument with the fact that there were scores of film festivals around the world showing shorts on the big screen to theatrical audiences. And, in a lucky, timely coincidence, there was a company that was having great success showing short films in theaters.

That company was SHORTS INTERNATIONAL, and it was run by a visionary producer named Carter Pilcher. Carter was an American guy who had transplanted to London. He was building a company with a streaming channel to show short films all over the world. His other venture was licensing the Oscar-nominated shorts and getting them into theaters, worldwide, as a program in the weeks before the Oscar telecast.

Needless to say this helped our cause two-fold. It not only proved that people wanted to watch shorts in theaters (the program increased its box office take every year) but it helped promote the Oscar telecast. I was happy to support Carter in his efforts, all the while carefully preserving my professional neutrality as a Governor and not favoring any film or artist.

It was thanks to Carter that I had a memorable encounter with two of my favorite artists. Sue and I were in London and Carter invited us to take the train with him to Bristol, England to give an award to Nick Park, whose Oscar-winning short films were big hits on Carter's channel. We happily agreed, and a few hours later, we were guests at Aardman Animation.

Aardman was the world's premiere stop-motion animation company. Stopmotion is a very different kind of animation than hand-drawn or CG animation. In "stop-mo" you build real sets (in miniature) with real character models that have internal armatures that allow the animator to bend and move the model. Although some CG techniques have modernized these films, stop motion is still created the way it has been done for 90 years. Under regular studio lights, with a real camera, the stop-mo animator moves the model a tiny bit, each frame, and takes a picture. It can take eight hours to do one second of animation. Not for everybody.

Nick Park was the genius who created two of the most popular, successful, and beloved animated characters of all time, *Wallace & Gromit*. If you have never seen *Grand Day Out* or *The Wrong Trousers*, you are in for a treat. To me, the character of Gromit, Wallace's canine sidekick, is one of the most significant achievements in character animation. In the age of CG, when precise articulation and complex rigging is deemed necessary for acting, Gromit's extreme simplicity seems incomprehensible. He has no cheeks, no mouth (he never speaks), and no eyebrows. He has one brow and two ping-pong shaped eyeballs, but with these spare features gives a performance of phenomenal range and sophistication. He is the Charlie Chaplin of animation.

I always felt the appeal of Gromit, and heard a wonderful story from Nick about the character. When Nick first achieved some fame he was invited to speak at New York University. He brought with him the original, actual 10-inch tall clay model of Gromit that he had used in the film. When the cab dropped him off at the NYU Visitor Center near Washington Square, he was so nervous that he left the model in the back seat of the cab. He didn't realize it until he got to the classroom. He panicked. He had no idea how to find the cab that had dropped him off.

It was then that he got a call from the Visitor Center. He was informed that the cab driver had noticed the model and had returned it to the front desk. The driver, a recent immigrant who barely spoke English, told the receptionist that there was something about the character that "just seemed like someone would miss him." In animation, we call that "appeal".

That's why it was a thrill for us to visit the Aardman model shop and see the genuine model of Gromit and all of the Aardman characters. It was literally holding stardom in your hands. We visited the multiple stages where the next movie was being shot. In a stop-mo studio, there can be twenty "stages" shooting at once because each stage is actually a tabletop-sized miniature movie set with little ten-inch tall characters. The lights and camera are full size.

I never had the patience to sit for hours under the hot lights and move a character 1/8th of an inch per frame, but my original Disney Rat's Nest roommate, Henry Selick, chose this style of animation and became one of the greatest. You have seen his brilliant directing in *The Nightmare before Christmas*, *Coraline*, and *Wendell & Wild*.

As we finished our visit with Nick Park, he told us something shocking, Richard Williams, the legendary animator, was working at Aardman. But not *with* Aardman. Richard had given up big studio filmmaking after the debacle of *The Thief and the Cobbler*. He was working alone on his own film, so Aardman had supplied Dick with his own rent-free studio.

We walked to the back of the lot and climbed a staircase to a small doorway over a storage shed. Inside, sure enough, we found Dick Williams hunched over the only piece of furniture in the room—an animation desk.

Dick was as jovial as we remembered him. I had first met him way back on my European adventure in 1977, when his London office was ground-zero for the world animation community. Sue had worked for him as an animator at the Hollywood branch of his company. We had all celebrated when he won his Oscar for *Who Framed Roger Rabbit*. Here he was, happily doing what he always loved: animating with a pencil!

In fact, this film, called *Prologue*, would be only pencil. His plan was to do every drawing himself, and not colorize it., Just leave it in pencil. Because of that, he was going through a lot of pencils. In a funny reminder of an old Disney method, he would use the pencil until it got too short to hold, then use a "pencil extender". Next to his desk, he had a small box full of discarded, tiny, 2B Pencil stubs.

Just like Cordell Barker and many others, here was the ultimate testament to the pure animator; the lone, dedicated artist who could sit at a desk alone and make a film that could entertain a theater full of fans. And this was Dick Williams, acknowledged as one of the greatest draftsmen ever, an animator whose unique style put him on the same level as Disney himself, an Oscar winner, and author of another essential animation guide: *The Animator's Survival Kit*.

In a moment of unabashed admiration, I asked Dick if I could have one of his 2B pencil stubs. I carried that little stub around for years. My wife took a photo of it and Photo-shopped a word above it: "Meant". It reminded us not just of Dick, but that fortuitous coincidence years ago when standing in line for a pencil brought us together. The picture she gave me for our anniversary said it all: "Meant 2B".

53

Fringe Benefits

Despite the success of SHORTS INTERNATIONAL and the other valid arguments about the value of short films, in the end, my tactic for successfully defending them was practical and political. I was truly honored to be on the Board, and I was fully conscious of the immensely talented people in all of the seventeen branches. It was not a chore, but a pleasure, to find reasons to socialize with the Governors of the "minor" branches. While Actors, Directors, Producers, and Executives never had to worry about their awards coming under attack, that wasn't necessarily the case with the Costume Designers, Hair Stylists, Production Designers, and other branches. Those personal relationships I cultivated produced alliances that allowed our branch to never lose a vote on the subject.

Under California law for non-profit corporations, the Board of Governors has ultimate power over all aspects of the Academy's business, so being one of those fifty-four members came with incredible privileges. Not only did we get main-floor seats to the Oscar show, we were allowed to attend the rehearsals. Most Governors did this as an enjoyable lark, but I actually felt a duty to be on hand to watch how they handled our awards. The Academy had a history of treating animation like kids' stuff. Many of our members felt slighted with the nature of past presentations, so I was on the alert for that.

DOI: 10.1201/9781003558231-53

Sure enough, I was in the theater the day before the show for the dress rehearsal. Presenting the Oscar for Best Achievement in Short Film was the ensemble cast of a major live action comedy film. The joke in the dialogue said that "there are two things in the world where length is not necessarily a measure of enjoyment: short films and penises".

Disrespectful? I'm no prude, but I thought the joke was pretty crude. I went back stage and met with the Academy CEO. I said that it would not sit well with my Branch members to have their award associated with the very first use of the word "penis" in Oscar history. Whether it was my argument or not that did it, the joke was cut.

I started to attend the Oscars the year I was nominated, 1989. It was at the Shrine Auditorium that year. At the Shrine, everyone entered through the same doorways so the stars mingled with the crowd. You would literally rub shoulders with movie legends.

When the Academy moved the show to the Dolby Theater in Hollywood, the famous Red Carpet "pre-show" was born. A nationally televised event, the Oscar Red Carpet was a guantlet that the stars walked through, with screaming paparazzi on one side and bleachers filled with cheering fans on the other side. There were red stanchion ropes that separated the movie stars from the regular Academy Member-attendees, but the Members still got to walk alongside the stars and experience the mayhem. I have talked to people who have been to Super Bowls, Fashion Week, and the World Series; they said nothing compared to the electricity and energy of the Red Carpet.

To me, this was one of the great perks of being an Academy Governor. I got to be on the celebrity side of the ropes. It was fun to talk to the stars. Once I entered the fray with Sacha Baron Cohen right behind me. He was dressed in a mid-Eastern garb to promote his new comedy film *The Dictator*. He was carrying a funeral urn that supposedly contained the cremated ashes of his father the King.

When I got inside the theater an Academy security official came to my seat. He said that Sacha was to occupy the seat right in front of me, and they wanted to put a Security guard in my seat in case he did something wild. I was reluctant to move—it was a terrific fifth row seat—but I agreed to do it.

A few minutes later the same official told me I didn't have to move. Sacha had dumped that urn of "ashes" (it was pancake mix) on Ryan Seacrest on the Red Carpet! Sacha was escorted out of the Oscars!

The animators who were nominated for Oscars were rarely well-known celebrities. I felt that one of my duties on the Red Carpet was to greet these folks. No one in the crowd was going to cheer for them, and none of the paparazzi or TV interviewers was going to recognize them, so I wanted them to feel appreciated.

Sadly, the Academy chose to reconfigure the Red Carpet in 2022. They got rid of the cheering fans and moved the Members' entry away from the movie stars, making them walk behind the bleachers. I felt it was a sad demotion of the Members' status—at the even that could not happen without them!

One event that has thankfully remained unaltered is the Nominees' Luncheon. The luncheon is perhaps the most enjoyable event of Oscar week. There are no press or crowds; just the nominees, their guests, and the Governors. As a Governor, I would be seated at a table as the "host" of that table. One never knew who would be at your table.

One year, I had Harvey Weinstein directly across from me. This was before his scandals broke open. There was a constant parade of people, including actresses, chatting with him. When I sat next to Katie Couric, she had a similar non-stop assault of visitors. Although she was literally right beside me she never turned her head my way once because of the continual parade of people kneeling by her chair. Later, when guests were mingling after lunch, she came up to me and said, "Weren't you sitting next to me?"

The luncheon would be another chance for me to make sure my humble animation nominees were not overwhelmed, which they usually were. One year, we had a Belgium film nominated as Best Short, and the young Producer and two co-directors were very starry-eyed. They had no desire to meet or talk to any of the movie stars. They desperately wanted to meet a fellow nominee: Kobe Bryant. Kobe had been nominated for his short, *Dear Basketball*, animated by Glen Keane. I went to Kobe's table and told him that some fellow animation folk wanted to meet him. Kobe went right over and spent ten minutes chatting with the guys and having photos taken. Those Belgians did not win the Oscar, but in their opinion, they were the real winners because of the minutes they shared with their hero.

I was blessed to have some unusual perks as a Governor. In 2015, the Chinese government invited the President of the Academy, Sid Ganis, to visit China on a goodwill tour to promote better understanding between the two nations' filmmaking industries. Someone thought it would be a nice idea to screen a program of Oscar-nominated films. They also mentioned that since the Chinese had pirated almost every feature film produced by Hollywood, the only films the Chinese would probably not have seen were short films. Sid decided to play a program of animated shorts, and since I was Governor of the Branch, invited me and Sue to go on the trip.

Sue and I had been to China in 1982. At that time China was still in the dark ages and it had been a rough visit. Sue was reluctant to return, but I convinced her it would be quite different. I could not have been more right. The China we visited in 2015 seemed to have advanced a hundred years. Our hotels were first-world spectacular.

The Chinese government treated us as if we were heads of state. We had police escorts and limousines everywhere we went. We were even driven into the Forbidden City! Almost every night was an official reception with Chinese film stars, or a state dinner. We had the rare privilege of a luncheon in the Great Hall of the People in Beijing—with solid gold tableware.

As it happened, giving and receiving toasts is an important custom to the Chinese, and since Sid was not drinking alcohol on the trip, it fell to me to give and receive many of these toasts. One night I had to honor a list of dignitaries, forcing me to down ten glasses of the liquor they call Moutai. Miraculously, I stayed coherent long enough to gracefully depart in my limo. Once back in my hotel, I will admit I had a rocky trip to the bathroom, where I mercifully disgorged enough of my stomach contents to prevent me from dying from alcohol poisoning.

A few times on the trip I was asked to give short lectures on the state of the American animation industry. I kept these very positive, and told what I thought were some very funny anecdotes about legendary animators. At one school these stories seemed to really connect with the students. When the school's Professor interpreted my words into Chinese the students laughed heartily. As we walked out I mentioned to my Chinese guide that the kids' seemed to "get it." There was an awkward pause. He said to me: "Every time you told a joke, their Professor would say to them, 'He is telling you an amusing anecdote. Please laugh.'"

When our group reached Shanghai on the last few days of the trip, Sue and I made a special request to visit the legendary Shanghai Animation Studio. In 1982, we had been the very first Western animators to visit there. It was the only Chinese animation studio to survive World War 2 and the Cultural Revolution. Back in '82, it had been a unique experience. It may have been behind the "Chinese curtain" for half a century, but it felt just like an animation studio!

The animators could not have been more culturally isolated from us, but it seemed as if the "peculiar art of animation" trumped those differences. We connected with them instantly. Like us, they worked in old warehouses, drawing all day, and filling their walls and cubicles with hilarious caricatures of each other. The films they were doing were beautiful. To us, it was one of the most meaningful experiences of our lives: to feel a true kinship with fellow animators that transcended distance or politics.

It took a special request, but our Sid Ganis group got permission to visit. In the intervening decades, the place had changed. Only one person remained from our '82 visit, and he was now an administrator. The studio, once the source of incredibly varied, individualistic short films, had been turned into an animation subcontracting company that did pretty standard TV fare. The one positive (I guess) was that the building was clean and modern.

We ended our trip at the famous Jing Jiang Club in Shanghai. Joining us for a farewell dinner were not just our Chinese hosts, but the famous film director Danny Boyle, who happened to be in town.

Before we left, Sid gave the Chinese officials an amazing gift. It was a 35mm copy of the only live footage of the notorious "Rape of Nanking", the horrible atrocity committed in 1937 by Japanese invaders that the Japanese government still denies. This footage had been smuggled out of China and kept safe in the film archive of our Academy for all these years. It was quite an emotional presentation.

A few years later, thanks to the Academy, I had another unique experience. Prince Charles decided to hold a reception for every British citizen who had ever won an Oscar. As a courtesy, he invited all of us Governors. Only about ten Governors attended, but it was an event that left deep impressions on me.

The reception was held at the Palace of the Court of St. James in London. We all arrived on time and were escorted through rooms lined with lances and shields to the ballroom. I was standing in a room that was filled with what I would describe as "Show Business Royalty". Judi Dench, Ben Kingsley, Michael Caine, Emma Thompson, Colin Firth; everywhere you looked was a superstar. And yet—they were not behaving like Hollywood superstars. All of them had arrived on time. All of them were following the directions of the Palace stewards. This was unlike any atmosphere I had experienced. To these Brits, they were not royalty. They were *subjects*, with the real royalty coming through the door.

When Charles and Camilla arrived, the crowd was arranged in groups of three couples to wait for the Prince to make his rounds. When he came to us, Sue and I were pleased and astounded to find Charles so personable. For those few minutes, he focused totally on us and made us feel like we were the only guests at the reception. When he learned we were animators, he expressed great admiration for the artform. We were surprised to learn that he personally knew, and had visited, many of the British animators that were our friends.

I had another satisfying moment at the reception. I was chatting with Vanessa Redgrave. When she found out I was in animation, she remarked that her husband, Tony Richardson, loved the medium. "Of course", I responded, "he worked with Richard Williams to produce one of the greatest animated title sequences ever for *The Charge of the Light Brigade*".

"Ah yes", Vanessa responded ruefully. "Richard Williams. I'm so sorry he passed away".

"I have great news for you", I said. In a moment that felt right out of a movie, I literally reached out my hand, grabbed his sleeve, and yanked Richard Williams into the shot. Vanessa and Richard looked at each other and immediately embraced. A magical moment.

54

Meeting Legends

One of the best decisions The Academy ever made was creating the event called THE GOVERNOR'S AWARDS. It would be a special dinner honoring people that the Board of Governors decided deserved special recognition. In some cases, it might be stars who never won an Oscar and were "overlooked". In other cases, it might be people in the business for whom there was no Oscar category.

This would be a gala dinner, in exactly the same format as the original Oscars. Most significantly, there would be no press. It would be a chance to mingle and celebrate with no fear of a publicity mis-step.

To me, the Governor's Awards were the culmination of the Hollywood dream come true. The long-haired untrained Chicago neophyte who had come to L.A. in his beat-up camper van was now bumping shoulders with the biggest stars in the world.

This event was made to mingle. There were open bars, and plenty of time before and during the meal service to wander the room and meet people. Because there was no press, and because everyone in the room deserved to be there for some reason of another, even the biggest stars were casual and open to having a conversation.

DOI: 10.1201/9781003558231-54

One of the rather odd interactions was with Tommy Lee Jones. When I told him that my wife had a dog rescue non-profit foundation, he went into a long description of his relationship his dogs. They lived on his ranch. He loved them. He used them to hunt wild hogs. To prevent the hogs from biting their ears, he had all his dogs' ears surgically removed. I decided to not repeat that conversation to my wife.

Movie stars were not the only attendees. One year, Angelina Jolie brought Louie Zamperini, the World War II real-life hero and subject of her movie *Unbroken*. Louie was in his nineties, but that infectious smile and buoyant energy, the energy that had made him "unbreakable", were still apparent. I was talking to a man who had stood on the field at the 1936 Olympics and faced Adolph Hitler, and who had survived the most vicious Japanese prisoner-of-war camps. What an honor to shake his hand.

Although the Governors' Awards gave Oscars to very famous actors, for me, the two most memorable recipients were men that many movie fans may never have heard of.

Dick Smith was a make-up artist who invented many of the techniques used in movies. Not just that; he was, apparently, a completely kind and wonderful man who freely shared every "secret" he had about make-up. He helped almost every significant make-up artist start their career. When Dick got his Oscar, the dinner was packed with the all great celebrities of make-up, and I have never heard more genuine, heartfelt tributes given to any Hollywood figure than those for Dick Smith on that night. There was not a dry eye in the house. A rare moment of undisguised emotion from hardened industry professionals.

The other recipient that wowed me was Hal Needham. Hal was a career stuntman. Despite being the only people on a movie set who habitually literally risk their lives for the shot, there is no Oscar category for stunt work. Hal had done hundreds of movies, broken every bone in his body doing them, and had elevated his career by becoming a director of such smash hits as *Smokey and the Bandit*.

Smokey, if you recall, was a movie about "hicks and rednecks", exactly the people that Hal grew up with and that Hollywood either ignored or insulted. It was so unusual a film, and treated its subject of the rural South with such genuine familiarity that Billy Bob Thornton told Needham that "*Smokey and the Bandit* isn't a comedy. It's a documentary".

Who could not be moved by Hal Needham's acceptance speech? He told of being raised in a shack with a dirt floor. He didn't own a pair of shoes until he was ten. One of his first jobs was a parachute *tester*! He only wished his mother could have lived long enough to see him wearing a tux, holding an Oscar. When I shook his hand that night, all I could think of was this: if there is one person who *really* exemplifies the rags-to-riches story that is the Hollywood dream, this is it.

If you were curious, the Governors' Awards, as of 2024, had honored fifty- five people. How many do you think were from the animation industry?

One.

The Academy honored Japanese animation director Hayao Miyazaki at the 6th awards. Very few Governors knew anything about Miyazaki, but Governor John Lasseter, who at the time was a very popular and influential member of the Board, made a passionate, and ultimately successful, nomination speech. John reminded the Board members that Miyazaki's films, like *Princess Mononoke*, *Spirited Away*, and *Howl's Moving Castle* were not just international award-winners, but some of the highest grossing theatrical films in Japan's history.

The members of the Academy might not have recognized the name Hayao Miyazaki, but I am proud to say that my animation students at Chapman University knew everything about him. Although not embraced by American audiences, my students had studied every one of his films—without my urging.

That was why, when I published an announcement that I was offering a "Travel Course" as a for-credit two-week tour of Japanese schools and studios, the one question every student asked first was: Are we going to Studio Ghibli? Studio Ghibli was Miyazaki's studio.

There was one problem. Studio Ghibli never gave studio tours. Everyone knew that Miyazaki-san was incredibly private. No visitors!

I proceeded to plan the trip anyway. There was a shopping area I knew called "Japan Town" on Sawtelle Boulevard in West Los Angeles. They had a travel agency run by Japanese for Japanese-Americans to arrange tours of Japan. I suspected (correctly, as it turned out) that they would be the perfect tour-planners. They helped get terrific air fares, train trip packages, and unique local hotels that the American tour companies wouldn't know of.

The itinerary was shaping up nicely. I had done that European Travel Course two years before, but I had been to Paris and Annecy before and knew my way around. I had never been to Japan. I thought it would be a good idea to take a Japanese-speaking student with us. As luck would have it, I knew a graduate student in the film school who was Japanese. Although he was not an animation major, we had become friends because he loved animation. His name was Masa Suzuki.

I called Masa into my office and floated the idea. Would he like to come on the trip as a paid "Teaching Assistant"? Masa immediately agreed. He told me that he would even reduce the cost, because he wouldn't require a return ticket. He would stay in Japan to visit family after the tour. Another bonus: his girlfriend was tour guide in Tokyo. She would be happy to arrange our meals and museum visits. This was terrific news! Done deal!

As he was leaving my office, he stopped and said, "Do you want to visit Studio Ghibli?" Of course, I replied, but I knew it was impossible.

"My Godfather is Toshio Suzuki", He said. "Do you want me to ask?"

I know the term "jaw-dropping" is an overused expression, but in this case my jaw did literally drop. Toshio Suzuki was the co-founder of Studio Ghibli and the Producer of all of Miyazaki's films.

"That would be great", I stammered.

Masa disappeared. He was back in twenty minutes. "OK, I called him. You're all set!' Suddenly, my Japan Travel Course became the hottest ticket around.

Six weeks later Sue and I landed in Tokyo with twenty lucky students in tow. We had terrific time, visiting museums, animation schools, and cultural sights. At one University, the professors showed us a collection of rare World War II Japanese propaganda cartoons. We were familiar with the American counterparts. Disney had made many such cartoons, the most famous being "Der Fuhrer's Face" that featured a horrendously rude caricature of a Japanese soldier.

It was interesting to see how the Japanese artists had caricatured Americans. Brutes! Beasts! I suppose that made sense. War is hell.

After the war, with photography equipment in short supply, the Japanese relied heavily on animation to fill their cinemas with product. It was far easier to find pencils and paint brushes than cameras, lights and sound stages. Japanese animated films took on every subject. Because of that, the Japanese produced more animated films than any culture, and the public did not consider animation to be "kids' stuff". It was cinema.

One of the biggest hits at the time we were visiting Japan was an animated film called *Your Name*, a very sophisticated sci-fi romance about a boy and a girl who, because of an extraterrestrial event, unwittingly swap bodies every night. The locations in the animated film were real Tokyo locations, and my students got a kick out of photographing themselves posing in the exact places pictured in the film.

The day finally arrived for our visit to Studio Ghibli. True to his word, Masa came through, and Toshio Suzuki himself welcomed us at the door and hosted a reception and Q&A. He confirmed, as we had been previously told, that although Hayao Miyazaki was in the building, we would not be seeing him. He never entertained visitors when he was working.

I had been thinking about this visit since the day Masa arranged it, and had prepared what I thought was a tasteful way to thank our hosts. I framed two very beautiful pastel paintings from *FernGully*. These had been painted by our Art Director Ralph Eggleston. I gave one to Suzuki-san and asked him to give the other to Miyazaki-san. He thanked me and took them away.

A half hour later, we were being walked through the studio when Suzuki-san diverted us toward another hallway. "Miyazaki has invited you to his office", he said. Seconds later, we walked into a large room with windows, and at the far end, standing in front of a weathered animation desk, was the man himself. Miyazaki-san was wearing an old apron absolutely covered with pencil and pastel stains. He greeted us, smiling.

I stood right beside him as our translator fielded questions from the students. I couldn't help but look at the artwork his desk. These were some of the first drawings of his "comeback film", the picture he had returned to make after his retirement. I was looking at the beginning of *The Boy and the Heron*—the film that would win the Oscar years later.

I think my students were as starstruck as I was. The questions being asked were hardly profound. Too bad, because this, I thought, was the chance to get wisdom from one of the all-time greats. Someone asked if he had a favorite of his own films.

"I can have no favorite", he said. "They are all my children".

Miyazaki has been compared to Walt Disney for his unique artistic vision and profound influence on the history of cinema. I had never met Walt, but here I was standing at the shoulder of a true legend. I could not help but feel the weight of the moment. I had started my career drawing with a pencil at a desk just like this one. Although the industry had been reshaped by the amazing technology of the computer, and all the vast logistical, financial, and cultural changes that came with it, this one man did not care at all about those things. He was untouched. He just sat and drew "as he pleased".

We thanked Miyazaki-san for giving us this memorable visit. When we left his office, we went down a stairway to the exit. Imagine my surprise to see the pictures hung on the wall. They were gifts to Miyazaki from PIXAR's John Lasseter.

They were framed pastel paintings by Ralph Eggleston.

55

Winding Down

In March of 2020, the COVID pandemic caused a shutdown of our classes at Chapman University. Like everyone else in America, we did our best to soldier on. We did have an advantage over most people. Our artists spent all their working hours in the digital world, so adjusting to ZOOM meetings and online lectures and presentations happened relatively easily.

In the previous five years, the industry had seen a major shift in production. The explosion of streaming series had created a huge new market for TV-animation. The quickest and most cost-effective medium for creating these shows was a 2D process, i.e., drawings instead of CG models. Drawings were quicker to create, and using new computer programs, very fast to animate and composite with CG-painted backgrounds. The high-end PIXAR-style 3D-CG pipeline was being supplanted by this new methodology.

It was easy to see where the new jobs were. The majority of my students no longer wanted to specialize in PIXAR-style animation, but TV animation. We adjusted our curriculum to the new paradigm. What became clear was that this method of animation production was quick to produce full-color cartoon episodes, but the actual animated movement was limited. Characters tended to pop

DOI: 10.1201/9781003558231-55

from pose to pose, and most of the personality of the characters came from held expressions and voiceover dialogue.

Sure enough, this style of filmmaking began to dominate the Senior Thesis Films in not just our school, but every school teaching animation. It was rare to see an "animated film" that had animated movement that was so fully-articulated and nuanced that it resembled what we had once defined as "classical animation".

In an ironic twist on Chuck Jones' famous saying, with this form of animation it was no longer possible to turn the sound off and tell what the story was.

In the Fall of 2020, Sue and I were both at home, teaching online courses. For the first time, I was beginning to feel a bit out of touch with my students' sensibilities. I had just turned seventy years-old, and we started to mention an idea we had never mentioned before: retirement. But it was another crisis that would dominate our lives for the next two years.

Ralph Eggleston was our close friend, but our relationship with him was much deeper. Ralph had been brought up in an extremely rigid, conservative environment in the deep South. When he finally "escaped" to Southern California as a student at Cal Arts, he found his tribe of fun-loving, free-thinking, super-creative animators.

Ralph's first job out of Cal Arts was animating on Brad Bird's animated short film *Family Dog*. Sue was on that crew and instantly clicked with him. When we started Kroyer Films, Ralph was one of our first employees. He was still in his teens. It was soon obvious that he could do anything, from animation to character design to production paintings. He became our key creative guy, culminating in his landmark work on our feature film, *FernGully, The Last Rainforest*. I suppose that since Sue and I were old enough to be his parents, and we had such a deep and complete connection to his quirky sense of humor and creative genius, he may have thought of us in that special way. Whatever it was, we bonded and stayed as close as family from then on.

After *FernGully*, when I had trouble getting a second feature financed, Ralph had a chance to do something very special. John Lasseter had just gotten the greenlight to attempt the very first CG-animated feature, the film that would become *Toy Story*. John had the golden eye for talent and understood Ralph's capabilities. He brought Ralph to PIXAR, and Ralph would spend the next twenty-eight years being the lead designer and innovator on some of the greatest animated films ever made, such as *Toy Story, Finding Nemo, The Incredibles* series, and *Inside Out*.

Ralph's impact on the PIXAR films, and the progress of CG in general, has been largely under-appreciated. Not when it came to awards and honors; he got plenty of those. I'm talking about the recognition and understanding of the inspired, brilliant innovation he brought to the medium. Few people have excelled at both the right-brain talent of a great artist and the left-brain comprehension of an engineer. There was Leonardo Da Vinci, and then there was Ralph.

Regarding the first talent, there is no argument. The thousands of gorgeous drawings and paintings he created, the images that guided all those PIXAR films, are undeniably spectacular. I mentioned in the FORWARD to this book that animation is an art form that utilizes all the creative disciplines. When you consider Ralph's creation of the coral reef in *Finding Nemo* you see this demonstrated in the most dramatic way. Sculpted shapes and brilliant colors and textures that might have been seen before in art are augmented with cinematic staging, lighting, and movement of light (refraction) that had never been possible before the medium of computer graphics. The same is true for that film's sequence featuring jellyfish. Astounding beauty.

What most people, including many in the industry, do not fully grasp is the huge challenge of getting those flat, 2D images into the 3D-calculated world of the computer.

From the beginning, Ralph understood the problem to a degree few could match. In a computer-generated scene, there is no actual camera, no actual light source, no actual color spectrum. All those are artificially mimicked through technology. It would take pages to describe the complexities and pitfalls of solving such problems. The PIXAR films will forever stand as testament to how successfully Ralph did that. I hope someday a fellow engineer/artist will write a book explaining those accomplishments.

Ralph was the most gifted artist I ever knew, and like most gifted people, he was also the most dedicated and hard-working. He seemed to know everything about every animated film ever made, and could talk for hours about the complexities of the greatest films in cinema history. An example of what he saw that you and I might never notice: in his favorite film *The Little Foxes* he would point out that the characters only tell the truth when they are seen in a reflection, like a mirror or a window. Would you notice that?

In the Fall of 2019 Ralph called us with terrible news. He had been diagnosed with pancreatic cancer. Sue and Ralph had chatted almost every day since he moved up North, but now our involvement kicked into high gear. Ralph had remained a single guy and lived alone, and although he had many good friends, he sometimes felt reluctant to impose on them. Sue would not listen those reservations. We began to make frequent trips to the Bay Area to help him with anything he needed, from house upkeep to 24/7 care after his chemo sessions.

Faced with the most dire prognosis, Ralph fought the illness with incredible courage and his trademark intensity. He researched every detail of the disease and possible treatments. PIXAR was very supportive, connecting him with the doctor that had personally treated Steve Jobs. Unlike Jobs, Ralph followed the experts' advice. Originally given three months to live, he endured many rounds of treatment that included experimental procedures. After three years of survival, placing him in the top 4% of survivors of the disease, we all hoped he had miraculously escaped the fate we all feared.

In 2022, the disease struck back with a vengeance. We were staying with him at his house, providing what emotional support we could, when his pain became too much to manage at home. I sat with him for four agonizing hours in the Marin Hospital ER, waiting for him to be admitted. When they finally took him in, none of us knew that he would spend most of his remaining time in the hospital.

It was during this last phase of Ralph's treatment that the community, the brotherhood, the tribe, and the family that we all we thought of as the animation industry demonstrated the depth of feeling and unity that seemed to be an ingrained feature of the artists that shared this unique vocation.

Although he had been in close touch with many friends during his illness, when word got out that Ralph was in this critical phase, the outpouring of concern was overwhelming. Sue and I were deluged with phone calls asking if it was possible to see Ralph. His friends in Los Angeles were ready to drop everything and fly or drive to the Bay Area on an hour's notice if they could visit. Everyone from PIXAR CEO's to mailroom workers asked for a visit. The list became so huge that we had to enlist his friend Heather Selick, an animation producer, to create and manage a database to prioritize and schedule as many people as his hospital schedule would allow.

Sitting in Ralph's room, listening to his conversations with the greatest directors, designers, animators, and craftspeople in the history of the business, it was sad to consider the loss of someone who had such immense talent, intelligence, creativity, and experience. His visitors were all members of his, and my, generation. Although most of them still worked in the business, it would not be long until they too would be passing the torch to the next generation.

How would that play out? Our generation of animation artists had been a generation of transition. We had personally known the artists who had created the industry, legends like Chuck Jones, Friz Freling, Grim Natwick, and Disney's Nine Old Men. We entered the business at its low point, but had been the key players as animation roared back to become the world's most successful theatrical film medium. We revered those pioneers. We hung on their every word, listened to their advice, and studied their work. Would that same attention be given to our generation?

I knew one thing; no one was going to match Ralph's intensity or dedication. He worked harder that anyone, and his depth of research and unmatched productivity were keys to the success of the movies he worked on. He could not contain his genuine passion for his work. So he was taken aback when he was told by some department managers that they were receiving complaints about him from the younger artists.

"Your passion intimidates them".

Could this be true? I had sensed some of this attitude in my current students. I recently had students who broke down in tears if I simply explained why their project had common flaws and mistakes. True, the brutality of Professor Bill Moore crushing his cigarette on your bad drawing would not be seen again, but would it be possible to create great work without passion, without intensity, without blunt honesty?

This remains to be seen. My guess was that the generation of artists who shared their careers with Ralph would be different from the one that would follow. Ralph passed away in August 2022. On a personal level, it was a deep, deep loss. To me, philosophically, it marked the passing of an epic age in animation. Personally, It coincided with my own withdrawal from the arena. Whatever was to happen next with the art and industry of animation, I'd experience it mostly from the outside.

56

Wrapping it Up

When I finished this book I was still an active member of the Academy of Motion Picture Arts & Sciences, with no plan to retire from that esteemed group. I still serve on my Branch Executive Committee, and am still involved in Oscar voting and Oscar rule-making. I was a member of that original subcommittee back in 2000 that created the rules for the Best Animated Feature Oscar. We defined animation as frame-by-frame filmmaking. Our intention, one that I strongly supported at that time, was to preserve the unique skillset of the animator, who did not "cheat" by using motion capture or puppetry. It was an extension of one of the original definitions of animation: movement that is designed.

As the years have gone by, my opinion has shifted. I am still passionate about the definition that the magical art of the animator—the act of connecting hand-made individual images into movements that convey *the illusion of life*—is still the soul of the artform. But now we are seeing people impart movement to inanimate objects using techniques other than frame-by-frame that also create the illusion of life. Motion capture has the disadvantage of being too literal and predictable but still makes things move. We had ruled that mo-cap was not an acceptable technique to create animated movement, but then "technically"

DOI: 10.1201/9781003558231-56

approved mo-cap projects (like *Beowulf*) because they contained frame-by-frame animated movement on parts of the character. We were splitting hairs.

Animation by computer has stretched the definition of frame-by-frame. Animators may still set key frames, but scripted in-betweens, or the use of curve-editors, have done away with individual articulation of images. The day is approaching when behavioral programs, some driven by artificial intelligence, will dictate the movement of these created characters without an "animator" ever touching them. These films that have non-real characters, I.e., inanimate objects, will never be accepted by the Academy as live-action films. Should they be "orphans" during awards season?

At Chapman University, my successors are doing a great job with the animation program, but one change struck me as particularly generational in nature. During my tenure, we had competitive awards for Best Animation, Best Visual Effects, etc.. The year after I left, the students voted to do away with the awards. Projects became more "group-oriented" with less emphasis on what we once described in film as the "auteur theory", where an individual vision dominated the film.

The animation industry still gives its own competitive awards. They are called The Annie Awards, or "Annies". I started attending those as soon as I arrived in Hollywood in 1975. At that time, they were just a big dinner party that gave "lifetime achievement awards" to the aging legends. As the years went by and those legends got fewer and fewer in number they switched to an actual competitive award, like the Oscars. They do, however, continue to give a life achievement award, named for none other than our friend, the late June Foray. Sue and I were given that award a few years ago for making "a significant impact on the art and industry of animation". We were the first couple to be so honored with the June Foray Award. It was a nice capper on a fun career.

The animated feature film continues to be a powerful player at the box office. Films like *Inside Out 2* and *Spiderman: Across the Spider-Verse* perform very much like their VFX competitors. With most animation studios now run by business executives as opposed to "showmen", one might expect the future of these films to have the formulas of being loud and action-packed and often sequels. Would the odd and individual peculiarities of the single vision-film, like Brad Bird's *Ratatouille* or Pete Docter's *Up*, ever be made again?

Every actor - and every animator - will tell you that it's impossible to predict the reception any film will have while you are creating it. You do your best, and hope for the best. I consider it rare good fortune that some of the projects I worked on have had remarkable popularity. I mentioned earlier that the original TRON stays fresh in the public's eye thanks to sequels, theme park attractions, and a fan base. Some of our animated titles ended up attached to perennial favorites like *National Lampoon's Christmas Vacation* and *Honey I Shrunk the Kids*.

FernGully stayed in legal limbo for decades because of the FAI bankruptcy, and it wasn't until after I retired that a company called THE SHOUT FACTORY acquired the rights and asked me to supervise a brand new 30th Anniversary hi-resolution digital master from the original negative. It was wonderful to see our film so brilliantly restored and preserved for - I hope - generations to come.

The industry has had its ups and downs since its creation in the early 1900's, and in this decade it is having a rough patch. After the boom in hiring caused by the increased production for streaming series, that bubble has burst. Those streaming shows were not as profitable as the studios expected, so they have been cut back. With fewer shows being produced and a dramatic increase in off-shore production there have been great job losses in the American animation community.

There is uncertainty about the potential impact Artificial Intelligence on production. Animation could be quite vulnerable to the implementation of A.I. Already there have been films made using A.I. that have a crew with one-tenth the workers of a traditional animated film.

And my generation? Many of my contemporaries are finding it tough to keep working in a industry that seems to value youth over experience.

That said, animation still has that unique quirk of being a medium where an individual artist can make a movie by themselves in their bedroom.

That thought takes me back to the moment I mentioned at the start of this book, the evening I sat between Cordell Barker and John Lasseter at the Academy Awards. How could I have imagined that those two Oscar nominees would experience the most diametrically opposite experiences possible?

Cordell would just animate. He would return to his room in Winnipeg, avoid politics and industry, and with funding from the Canadian Film Board peacefully and privately animate his own films. It took him fourteen years to complete his next animated short film, called *Strange Invaders*, but it too would garner an Oscar nomination.

And John Lasseter? He would shake the world.

John left Disney (more specifically was "released"!) and progressively elevated the artistry of computer animation through his series of PIXAR short films. Those films were the proving ground for what became the most revolutionary, transformative film since *Snow White and the Seven Dwarves*: the first *Toy Story*. Not only would it usher in the age of CG features; it would establish PIXAR as the most successful studio in history. Under John's leadership the studio had thirteen straight hit films. The secret: let the creative people run the show without executive interference.

Credit must be given to PIXAR's other key figures in that decision. The technical leader, Ed Catmull, and the financial leader, Steve Jobs, both had the unheard-of wisdom and discipline to not insert themselves into the creative process.

When the reputation and success of Disney Feature Animation faltered, Disney CEO Bob Iger had the solution: acquire PIXAR and bring John Lasseter back to save the division. A big problem at Disney were the multitudes of "creative executives" who were not really animation people. In a very famous move, when Lasseter and Catmull took over, the first thing they did was to get rid of those people.

When John and I were serving as Academy Governors, we would carpool together from Burbank to meetings at the Academy. I had the very rare privilege of having this extremely busy and brilliant guy to myself for an hour each way. John, who had moved to Sonoma years before and owned and operated his own vineyard, had a rather charming view of what he was doing at Disney.

In the late 1800s, vintners from France has brought cuttings from their best vines to Napa and Sonoma to populate the fields with the world's best vintages. Decades later, when a blight wiped out the vines of many of those famous French wineries, the vintners were able to go to California and bring those cuttings back to restore their vines.

John saw that as his new role at Disney. He felt that he and the PIXAR artists had kept true to the original Disney animation traditions and now he had a chance to restore them to the place where they had been invented.

As the world knows, he was wildly successful. So successful that when the Disney parks hit a slump, Iger drafted John to consult on their redevelopment. John Lasseter was doing three full-time, incredibly demanding jobs: running PIXAR, running Disney Animation, and running the parks, all at once. Could anyone do that without straining under the pressure—or making enemies?

When I interviewed John for my 2020 book *The Director's Perspective*, I wrote in the introduction that one of the most amazing things about him was that in the thirty years I had known him, he had hardly changed at all. He was still the same guy we knew as a cub animator. That is why I was so shocked when the hammer fell on him. He was forced out of Disney.

It is well known that John voluntarily took time off from his Herculean tasks in response to accusations that he had behaved "inappropriately". What behavior? Made at the height of the "woke" and "#me too" movements, these rumors about his "behavior" did not resemble the guy we knew.

Of course, there were areas of conflict between him and management that had nothing to do with the accusations of misconduct. It was well-known that John was a dedicated protector of Disney animation and opposed suggestions to "farm out" animation to overseas studios—something the studio began to do soon after he was gone. He was known to disagree with other executives on which future projects to develop.

But the sad result of his "release" was the damage to John's legacy. His name was no longer mentioned at PIXAR, the studio he built. People continued to question his character. Despite these conditions, in a bold move, the Skydance Studio decided to hire John as their Head of Animation. I heard from several insiders that to protect themselves from future embarrassment or financial exposure, Skydance conducted an extensive examination of John's history at Disney and PIXAR, interviewing hundreds of people.

To this day, no one has ever made a personal accusation against him, and it does not seem logical that Skydance would have hired him if they had found any basis for such a claim.

I confess that I have not spoken to him since his ordeal. I have learned that I'm not the only one of his older colleagues to be in the dark. I can only guess how he must have felt when the world he built came down around him, when the industry he had done so much for rejected him, and how that experience might have affected the cheerful, curious, brilliant young guy who, so many years ago, sat behind me and watched me work on this new thing called "computer animation" on *TRON*.

I do know that in the midst of these travails, John and his wife Nancy still found time to care for my dear friend Ralph Eggleston in his last months. Quietly, privately, John and Nancy would call, or come to Ralph's house, or bring dinner. Sue and I were so touched to see those gestures of love and loyalty.

So there you have it. Chuck Jones, Eric Larson, Richard Williams, Hayoa Miyazaki, Cordell Barker, Ralph Eggleston, John Lasseter, Mr. In-Between was lucky enough to be in the midst of these remarkable people in this remarkable industry. Disney and PIXAR go on, as do the other big studios, but there are still those lone animators around the world making small, personal innovative, entertaining films. There are still worldwide festivals screening and honoring these films, and the internet makes it possible for everyone to see them. It doesn't take an industry, or a studio, or even a film crew to make an animated movie.

It just takes an animator.

When that individual animator makes the character move, whether it's by drawing or CG programming or some yet-to-be-invented process, they will hopefully have that same transcendent experience that I had with my little snake. When it moves, and by moving seems to have a thought, or a feeling—the animator will have created life!

Thank you, God.

Index

Printed in the United States
by Baker & Taylor Publisher Services